Iolo Goch : Poems

Welsh Classics Vol. 5
Series Editor Lynn Hughes

IOLO GOCH : POEMS

DAFYDD JOHNSTON

1993

First Impression—August 1993

© Dafydd Johnston

British Library Cataloguing-in-Publication Data.
A catalogue record for this book is available from the British Library.

ISBN 0 86383 707 7

This volume has been published with the support of the Welsh Arts Council.

Printed in Wales
at the Gomer Press, Llandysul, Dyfed

To
my mother,
and in memory of
my father

ACKNOWLEDGEMENTS

These translations are based on my edition of the poems, *Gwaith Iolo Goch* (U.W.P., 1988), and I am grateful to the University of Wales Press for permission to reproduce the original Welsh texts. This book is published with the financial support of the Welsh Arts Council, which I gratefully acknowledge. I am deeply indebted to Professor J. E. Caerwyn Williams, who directed my original research in this field, and whose dedication to scholarship has been a constant inspiration to me and many others. Professor D. J. Bowen and Dr Gruffydd Aled Williams have given me much valuable guidance and support at all stages of this work, and I wish to thank them for their generosity. I have benefitted greatly from the encouragement and constructive criticism of the series editor, Mr Lynn Hughes, and this book has been produced most efficiently by the Gomer Press. As ever, I owe a special debt of gratitude to my wife for her good-humoured tolerance of my attachment to an old friend.

DAFYDD JOHNSTON

CONTENTS

INTRODUCTION

The Poet

Iolo Goch is the only Welsh poet of the fourteenth century whose career can be dated with any degree of certainty. The evidence of his surviving poems shows him to have been active throughout the second half of the century. His earliest dateable poem is an *awdl* in praise of Dafydd ap Bleddyn, bishop of St Asaph, who died in 1345. This is followed by his *cywydd* addressed to King Edward III, sometime after 1347. Moving to the end of his career, at least two of his poems can be dated to the last decade of the century. He addressed another bishop of St Asaph, Ieuan Trefor, on the occasion of his journey to Scotland in 1397, and his poem to Sir Roger Mortimer belongs to the period of Roger's campaign in Ireland, 1394-98. On the basis of these firm dates it is reasonable to assume that Iolo was born about 1325, and was into his seventies, a very old man by medieval standards, when he died at the end of the century.

Iolo was a native of the Vale of Clwyd, and is known to have been the son of Ithel Goch ap Cynwrig ab Iorwerth ap Cynwrig Ddewis Herod ap Cowryd. The epithet *coch* ('red') seems to have run in the family, but Iolo's reference to himself as a 'red fox' (26.34) indicates that he was indeed red-haired. The fact that one of his forefathers bore the title *Herod* ('Herald') is interesting in view of the knowledge of heraldry which Iolo displays in his poetry. Some valuable information about Iolo's family background can be derived from the survey of the lordship of Denbigh made in 1334. His father Ithel Goch is there said to be joint holder with his cousin of one sixth of his hereditary *gafael* in the township of Lleweni, the remainder being forfeit by escheat. However, as a result of the policy of resettlement after the Edwardian conquest, this hereditary land was given to settlers forming an English colony on the fertile land around Denbigh castle, and Ithel received in exchange land in the township of Llechryd, on higher ground to the north-west of Denbigh. The evidence of a journey homewards described in poem no 13 suggests that Iolo lived in Llechryd all his life. His father is known to have held other lands in the area by rent, and seems to have been a moderately prosperous freeholder, but the loss of most of the patrimony and the forcible exchange of the rest for inferior land must have caused long-lasting resentment in the family.

It should not be assumed, however, that the relationship between the natives and the English settlers was one of constant hostility. Many of the English families were gradually absorbed into the Welsh society by a process of intermarriage, and this area remained one of the strongest bastions of traditional Welsh culture into the Renaissance period. A striking example is the

Salesbury family, one of those given lands in Lleweni, who were prominent patrons of the Welsh poets by the late fifteenth century. Positive evidence of interaction with the English is provided by the large number of new English loan-words in Iolo's work, as distinct from older borrowings of French origin. Some of these loan-words belong to obvious areas of English influence, such as land cultivation (e.g. *balc*, 20.22 and 129, and *tir bwrdd*, 10.63) and architecture (e.g. *cwpl* and *plad*, 10.28 and 37). Others are more difficult to account for, such as *wnder* from English *wonder* (34.70), and suggest that Iolo's knowledge of English was very extensive. It seems that his readiness to use loan-words in his poetry is evidence not of weakness, but rather of confidence in the strength of Welsh to absorb foreign elements, and delight in the rich linguistic resources available to him.

We are given a tantalizing glimpse of Iolo's boyhood in poem no 12, where he reminds Ithel ap Robert that they sang psalms together under the same teacher. This indicates that he was educated as a chorister, probably at the nearby cathedral of St Asaph. His ecclesiastical education has left its mark in the handful of Latin and Greek words and learned references in his work. Since next to nothing is known of the musical accompaniment to the performance of medieval Welsh poetry, it is difficult to gauge the influence of Iolo's musical education on the practice of his art as a poet, but it may well have been considerable.

High ranking churchmen enjoyed the same luxurious life as wealthy secular noblemen, and were equally willing to welcome the poets at their courts, as can be seen in Iolo's exuberant account of his reception as an honoured guest at the court of Bishop Ieuan Trefor. Iolo in his turn was ready to put his art to use in defence of the worldly pleasures of his ecclesiastical patrons, as he did in his two poems asserting the right of priests to keep concubines, nos 34 and 35. The fact that his earliest and latest dateable poems are addressed to bishops of St Asaph shows that he had a firm basis of patronage from the church in his native region throughout his life. This was probably due both to his church education and to ties of kinship, since Iolo was third cousin to one of his principal patrons, Ithel ap Robert, archdeacon of the diocese 1375-82. Kinship may also have secured for Iolo a place of honour at the court of Ithel's nephew, Rhys ap Robert, near Abergele.

However, the poets of late medieval Wales did not confine their activities to any particular region. After the demise of the independent princes they could no longer be maintained at one single court, and were forced to undertake extensive circuits around the country from one noble house to another. This practice was known as *clera*, that is the way of life of the *clêr*, who were itinerant minstrels. The best evidence which we have for these circuits is a poem by Iolo Goch, no 14, which describes a journey down through the March and across to south-west Wales, visiting numerous noble patrons and the monastries of Whitland and Strata Florida, and calling on Owain Glyndŵr at Sycharth on the way home to Ithel ap Robert's court. None of Iolo's other poems to those patrons in the south have survived, but the eye-witness account of the funeral of Sir Rhys ap Gruffudd at Carmarthen in 1356 shows that he was active in that region quite early in his career.

He would have visited his patrons in the north-west on a separate circuit, and they are rather better represented in his surviving work. Foremost among them was the Penmynydd family of Anglesey, ancestors of the Tudor dynasty. Poem no 5 in particular is a striking evocation of the abundant patronage available to Iolo from the four sons of Tudur Fychan. Two poems have survived to patrons on the Llŷn peninsula, most notably his famous description of Cricieth castle, and the mock-satirical poetry associated with Ithel Ddu (nos 23, 36 and 37) shows that Iolo had close connections with the bardic fraternity of that area. It seems likely that Iolo regarded the whole of the old kingdom of Gwynedd, both below and above the river Conway, as his province, consciously following the old court-poets of Gwynedd.

Dafydd ap Gwilym was probably some ten years older than Iolo Goch. Iolo's elegy on his death acknowledges Dafydd's pioneering contribution to the development of the *cywydd*, and salutes him as the teacher of all other poets. It is very likely that Iolo would have come into contact with Dafydd, perhaps when visiting south Wales early in his career, but there is no suggestion of friendship between the two poets in his elegy, which expresses respect for a great master rather than personal grief at his death. The elegy which Iolo composed to the Merionethshire poet Llywelyn Goch ap Meurig Hen about 1390 is a much more personal expression of grief at the loss of a lifelong friend, looking back to the time when the two companions were pioneers of a new type of poetry in Gwynedd, perhaps carrying Dafydd ap Gwilym's influence to the north around the middle of the century.

Only thirty nine poems have survived by Iolo Goch, although many more are falsely attributed to him in the manuscripts. This must be a very small proportion of his total output, being less than one poem for every year of his career. Only one contemporary manuscript, the Red Book of Hergest, contains poems by Iolo. Had more such collections survived we would no doubt have a much clearer picture of his work and his contribution to the development of Welsh poetry in this crucial period. But even this small corpus shows a remarkable variety of subject matter and tone, which is unsurpassed even by poets with much larger bodies of work. About half of his surviving work consists of eulogies and elegies, the product of his principal function as a praise poet.

The two other most important topics of medieval Welsh poetry were religion and love, both of which are quite well represented in Iolo's work. His religious poetry is especially valuable as an expression of the popular beliefs and cults of the time, in particular the emphasis on devotion to the saints, and above all to the Virgin Mary. The Day of Judgement is constantly present as an imminent event, a source of both terror and comfort. Two of Iolo's three love poems are in the light, humorous style popularized by Dafydd ap Gwilym, dealing with the hindrances encountered by the would-be lover (nos 25 and 26), but he also has an impressively detailed and evocative description of a girl in the traditional eulogistic manner of the *gogynfeirdd* (no 24). A fourth group within Iolo's work is formed by his satirical poems, which range from jesting parody to deadly serious lampoon (see note on poem 34). The humorous account of the discomforts of a sea voyage (no 33) is an interesting combination of satire and eulogy, conferring praise by contrast, and is typical of the thematic variety to be found in Iolo's work as a whole. Some of his other poems also defy neat classification, in particular that to the ploughman, which is a unique combination of praise and religious poetry, closer to the medieval sermon than to any recognized genre of Welsh poetry.

Iolo's praise poetry varies in tone from serious political comment and advice to light-hearted banter. Good examples of the more light-hearted eulogies are the witty poems requesting and giving thanks for the gift of a horse and of a knife, which reflect the way of life of the minstrel dependent on his patrons' generosity. But Iolo's most important work is the body of weighty praise poems which he addressed to some of the leading noble-men of Wales. The significance of these poems cannot be properly appreciated without some understanding of the complexities of fourteenth-century Welsh society.

The Historical Background

One of the most important developments in the period between the Edwardian Conquest and Glyndŵr's rebellion was the rise of the *uchelwyr* class to a position of power within native Welsh society. The term *uchelwyr* is not easily translated. The corresponding social class in medieval England is known as 'gentry', but that term does not really convey the high status of the *uchelwyr* as a native aristocracy which took great pride in noble lineage. Wales was ultimately ruled by English overlords, but the day-to-day administration of local government was generally entrusted to the *uchelwyr*, most of whom were very ready to co-operate with the new regime in order to attain power within their localities. Several of Iolo's secular patrons held influential offices, such as Sir Hywel of the Axe, who was constable of Cricieth Castle for many years, and his nephew

Ieuan, sheriff of Caernarfon. Such men can be seen as mere self-seeking opportunists, and no doubt many of them were just that. There is evidence that Rhys ap Robert was particularly unscrupulous in exploiting the local Welsh population when he served as sheriff of Flintshire. But on the other hand, Welsh officials could act as a buffer protecting their people from harsh treatment by their conquerors. That was the ideal cherished by the poets, and memorably expressed by Iolo in his elegy to Tudur Fychan of Anglesey. The claim that no one ever lost his patrimony whilst Tudur was alive is especially poignant in view of the loss by forfeit of the greater part of Iolo's father's land.

However ambiguous the political allegiance of the *uchelwyr* may have been, they remained faithful to Welsh cultural traditions, and the abundant patronage which they extended to the poets filled the gap left by the disappearance of the independent princes. The central element in the relationship between patron and poet was the nobleman's house. It was customary for the wealthy landed gentry of the later Middle Ages to build themselves fine houses as imposing symbols of their social status, which served as focal points for the surrounding communities. The poet's work would be performed in their halls as entertainment at feasts, and the hospitality extended to him there was representative of the nobleman's generosity and care for his people. This paternalistic ideal was held by all the Welsh praise poets. It was a profoundly conservative social philosophy, setting great store by aristocratic lineage as the means of inheritance of noble virtues, just authority, and land. The ideal is seen in its most positive form in Iolo's description of Owain Glyndŵr's house and estate at Sycharth. It is ironic that such a classic vision of social stability should have been composed in praise of one who subsequently shattered the stability of Welsh society, but in fact the image which Iolo presents is entirely consonant with what we know of Owain's life before 1400.

Some of the discontent which ultimately led up to the rebellion of 1400 is apparent in another of Iolo's poems to Owain, no 8. The elaborate recital of Owain's genealogy here has more than a merely eulogistic purpose. It is intended to substantiate Owain's claims to the lands of his ancestors, the royal lines of Powys and Deheubarth. But it is typical of Iolo's conservative social ideal that the injustice is presented as a failure of the law, to be rectified by recourse to righteous judgement. There is none of the incitement to rebellion which with the benefit of hindsight one might expect. Indeed, the view of the future at the end of the poem is one of peaceful family life at Sycharth. It seems to me that the crucial event which changed the conformist Owain of Iolo's poetry into the leader of a rebellion against English rule in Wales was the usurpation of Richard II's throne by Henry Bolingbroke in

1399. Owain was thereby released from his allegiance to the ultimate authority of the Crown over England and Wales alike.

Several references in Iolo's work testify to his interest in the English royal line and his acceptance of its authority in Wales. Early in his career he addressed a poem to King Edward III commending his success in subduing his rebellious subjects in England, Scotland, and France. Almost fifty years later he addressed Edward's great-grandson, Roger Mortimer, stressing his strong claim to the throne through his descent from the royal line of both England and Gwynedd, and urging him to suppress the rebellion in his territory in Ireland. The Crown was clearly synonymous in Iolo's mind with the maintaining of law and order. Most striking of all is the claim that Sir Hywel will be dear to Lionheart's descendant (2.69), that is the young King Richard II, a reference which shows knowledge of the history of the English royal line, probably from popular ballads about Richard the Lionheart's heroic deeds. Once again, the loyal servant of the Crown is portrayed in the following peroration as a guardian of the established order in his role as keeper of the castle.

Iolo's concern for the maintenance of law and order is expressed from a very different viewpoint in his praise of the ploughman. At first sight this is an unusual choice of subject, in stark contrast to all Iolo's other praise poems which are addressed to powerful noblemen. But in fact when viewed in its historical context this poem can be seen to be perfectly consistent with the rest of Iolo's work. The second half of the fourteenth century was a time of considerable unrest among the labouring class. Due largely to the devastation of the Black Death labour was scarce, and labourers took the opportunity to press for better treatment from their masters. This agitation culminated in England in the Peasants' Revolt of 1381, which spread as far as the border areas of Wales. The emphasis which Iolo places upon the ideal ploughman's humble acceptance of his lot is most probably a response to the threat which this agitation posed to the interests of the land-owning class, upon whom he depended for patronage. The ploughman's virtues are presented in entirely negative terms, avoiding any kind of social disturbance. Like many contemporary preachers, Iolo claims that the diligence of the humble plough-man will be rewarded in heaven. The learned references and the emphasis on the payment of tithes suggest that this poem was intended for an ecclesiastical audience, and it should be borne in mind that the Church held substantial lands. It is very likely that this is another of the poems which sprang from Iolo's close association with the churchmen of the diocese of St Asaph.

Another surprising element in Iolo's praise of the ploughman is the contrast with the destruction wrought by the warrior class, represented by the traditional hero Arthur. At first sight it is difficult to square this with Iolo's obvious appreciation of martial prowess in his other poems. This apparent inconsistency can be explained by reference to medieval social theory. Iolo's view of the ploughman is based on the traditional division of society into three mutually supporting castes or 'estates', labourers, warriors, and clergy. It was the duty of the labourers to provide food, the warriors to protect from attack, and the clergy to care for souls through prayer. The point of the contrast between ploughman and warrior here is that whereas the ideal ploughman diligently fulfills his duty towards the rest of society, the warrior caste often abuse their strength by disruptive aggression. If we assume that this poem was intended for an ecclesiastical audience then it is quite natural that the duties of the third estate should be taken for granted.

Iolo's praise of his patrons' martial prowess can therefore be viewed as an expression of the warrior's duty to maintain order within society and to defend it from external attack. Such an interpretation applies very well to the long poem of advice to Sir Roger Mortimer. The young heir to the throne is first of all advised to gain practice in handling weapons in tournaments. This is more than just a matter of personal accomplishment befitting a nobleman. The point of Iolo's advice becomes clear in the final section of the poem, where Roger is urged to suppress the rebellion in his territory in Ireland by military action. The nobleman needs to be an accomplished soldier in order to deal with any threat to the peace of his domain. The same ideal can be seen on a smaller scale in the elegy to Tudur Fychan, whose prowess on the tournament field made him a capable defender of Anglesey against attack by pirates. The young Owain Glyndŵr is praised for his feats of arms in defence of the emergent British state against the threat posed by the Scots. It is interesting to note in passing that Iolo has no sympathy whatsoever for his fellow Celts in Ireland and Scotland, whom he regards with contempt as wild savages meriting the harshest treatment.

The ideal of military action in defence of the security of the realm was rather less obvious in the campaigns in France, where Sir Rhys ap Gruffudd and Sir Hywel of the Axe distinguished themselves on the field of battle. Indeed, the bloodthirsty account of Sir Hywel's feats at Poitiers seems to be a particularly blatant instance of the celebration of violence for its own sake. However, it should be noted that the Hundred Years War was held by the English to be a just war because Edward III had a legitimate claim to the French throne. In theory at least, Sir Hywel's feats could be regarded as being in defence of the king's rights which had been usurped by the French. But on the other hand, it should also be borne in mind that the nobility's obsession with warfare, whilst common throughout the Middle Ages, seems to have reached new heights during the reign of Edward III, promoted by the king himself and later by his eldest son the Black Prince. It is that obsession, rather than any theory about the social rôle of the warrior, which explains the emphasis on martial prowess in Iolo's praise poetry, reflecting the interests and tastes of his patrons. Iolo's treatment of this theme drew strength from the Welsh poetic tradition, which had been celebrating heroic deeds for over seven hundred years. One of the keys to the success of his poetry was the merging of this powerful tradition with contemporary fashion.

One of the most devastating events of the fourteenth century was the Black Death, which wiped out about a third of the population of Europe in the late 1340s and in recurring epidemics in the following decades. The amount of attention given to the Black Death in Welsh poetry is disappointingly small. The only fourteenth-century poet who dealt specifically with the subject was Gruffudd ap Maredudd of Anglesey, who addressed a short poem to God praying that Gwynedd be spared the devastation of the plague. The reason for the silence of the Welsh poets was the personal nature of their work, which only encompassed events of general significance in so far as they affected their individual patrons. It is in his elegy on the death of Ithel ap Robert in 1382 that Iolo Goch's reaction to the plague is expressed. The symptoms are represented in enough detail to show that Ithel died of the pneumonic plague, which caused death within three or four days. The sense of bewildered terror at this sudden death is vividly conveyed in the opening lines of the poem and sustained through the powerful rhetoric of the funeral scene. The plague is not mentioned elsewhere in Iolo's work, but I think it can be seen to have left its mark on his treatment of death. His elegies contain a strong awareness of life's transcience, of the ever-present horror of death, and of the stark contrast between life's finery and the desolation of the grave. All but one of his elegies end with Christian consolation. The exception is the bleak conclusion of the elegy to Tudur Fychan. It is in such a desolate vision that the fear of social collapse in the aftermath of the plague can be most clearly perceived.

Iolo Goch's poetry reveals many incidental details of life in the fourteenth century, on such diverse subjects as horses, musical instruments, agriculture, and funeral customs. But the real value of his work to the historian, and also the essence of its value as literature, lies in its vivid realization of the hopes and fears of the age, and in its sense of living response to events and social forces which is beyond the reach of the chronicler.

Metre and Style

The fourteenth century was a period of adaptation and innovation in the Welsh poetic tradition. The most fundamental innovation was the development of the new *cywydd deuair hirion* metre, generally known simply as the *cywydd*. As is often the case in literary history, a new metrical form emerged in response to a major social change, with the *uchelwyr* replacing the independent princes as patrons of the poets. The new metre then provided the basis for a number of other changes in the form and content of the poetry.

Of course the *awdl* continued to be used throughout the medieval period. Iolo has five *awdlau* (18, 19, 30, 31, 38) and one sequence of *englynion* (39) amongst his thirty nine surviving poems. It is no doubt significant that his earliest dateable composition is an *awdl* in praise of Bishop Dafydd ap Bleddyn. Nor was his use of the *awdl* confined to the beginning of his career, since that to Hywel Cyffin can be dated after 1380. Iolo used the *awdl* as a medium for eulogy, for invective, and for devotional poetry to Christ and Mary. Four of Iolo's five *awdlau* follow the traditional pattern of the Poets of the Princes, using only one metre and sustaining the same rhyme throughout. Only the *awdl* to Mary reflects the new practice of using more than one metre, a number of *englynion* of different types being followed by an extended passage on one rhyme. Iolo's *awdlau* contain passages of impressive sustained rhetoric, but considering his poetic output as a whole it is clear that most of his creative energy went into the development of the new *cywydd* metre.

Compared to the complex metres of the traditional *awdlau*, *the cywydd* was a simple metre, consisting of rhyming couplets of seven-syllable lines. The only element of complexity was that the pair of rhymes involved one stressed and one unstressed syllable, thus:

> Myned yr wyf dir Môn dráw,
> Mynych im ei ddymúnaw. (5.1-2)

The strengths of the new metre lay in its line-length and its rhyme-scheme. Seven syllables was a happy medium between the short and long lines of the *awdlau*, long enough to contain a full statement, as in both lines above, but not so long that it had to be filled out with a ponderously wordy style. The advantage of the couplet form was that the rhyme changed constantly, creating a much lighter effect than the extended mono-rhyme passages of the *awdlau*, and putting less strain on the verbal resources of the poet. The *cywydd* was a swift-moving, flexible metre which could be used for a variety of different styles, based on the couplet, the individual line, or the long sentence extended over a number of lines. One of its most striking stylistic devices was the *sangiad*, an interpolated phrase cutting across the main syntax of the sentence. The *sangiad* is occasionally a mere metrical filler, but is is usually much more than that, amplifying on the main statement by comment or imagery, and allowing the poet to vary the tempo of his composition, thus adding to the flexibility of the form.

The *cywydd* probably derived originally from a popular song-metre used by minstrels, but it seems that Dafydd ap Gwilym was responsible for its development into a refined medium suitable for bardic poetry. The most important step in the refinement of the *cywydd* was the addition of *cynghanedd* (literally 'harmony'), an elaborate system of ornamentation by alliteration and internal rhyme which had developed over the preceding centuries. There are four main types of *cynghanedd*, one of which must be present in each line of poetry. The simplest is *cynghanedd lusg*, in which the accented penultimate syllable of the line rhymes with an earlier syllable, as in this example:

> Cyrch hyd ym m*in* Const*in*obl   (1.65)

Cynghanedd groes and *cynghanedd draws* both involve consonantal correspondence between the two halves of the line. In *cynghanedd groes* the two halves correspond fully as far as the main accent, thus:

> *Ll*oeg*r* a *Ff*rainc, *ll*e gorau *ff*rwyth   (1.24)

In *cynghanedd draws* some consonants in the middle of the line play no part in the correspondence, producing a bridging effect, thus:

> *G*e*l*yn fuost i'r *G*a*l*ais   (1.37)

The fourth type, *cynghanedd sain*, involves both rhyme and consonantal correspondence. The line is divided into three parts, the first and second being linked by rhyme and the second and third by alliteration, as in this example:

> C*rest* gwedy *cwncwest canc*aer   (1.6)

In its essence *cynghanedd* is a means of highlighting the main accented syllables in the line, and it is thus a valuable support to the sense, allowing the poet to link key words by sound. It may seem at first sight to be a restrictive and repetitive system of ornamentation, but in fact the different combinations of accented and unaccented syllables which are possible within each of the four types allow the poet to create a rich variety of musical effects.

The ornamentation of the *cywydd* couplet was often taken to even greater lengths by linking the beginnings of the two lines by means of alliteration (a technique known as *cymeriad*), which sometimes formed full consonantal correspondence in the manner of *cynghanedd*, on top of the *cynghanedd* in each separate line. An example can be seen in the opening couplet of poem no 5 quoted above. Here is another in the final couplet of the same poem:

> *Trafn* Glorach, trefn goleuryw,
> *Tariaf* i *Fôn* tra fwyf fyw.   (5.87-88)

These three types of ornamentation, end-rhyme, *cymeriad*, and *cynghanedd*, made the *cywydd* couplet into a very complex interwoven pattern of sound. The mastery of these techniques required lengthy bardic training, and their use would have disguised the lowly origins of the new metre. However, the *cywydd* did not immediately achieve the same status as the *awdl*. It was used initially, in the second quarter of the fourteenth century, by Dafydd ap Gwilym and his imitators as a medium for poetry of a very personal kind, primarily love poetry. The more dignified *awdl* continued to be used for the most exalted of the poet's functions, praise of noble patrons. Dafydd ap Gwilym ventured to use the *cywydd* for informal and intimate eulogy of his friend and patron Ifor Hael, but it was Iolo Goch who was responsible for the crucial step of adapting the *cywydd* as a medium for traditional praise-poetry.

Of the *cywyddau* which have survived, the most significant in this respect is the one to King Edward III, composed probably in the late 1340s. The use of the *cywydd* in this case may have been facilitated by the fact that this was a political poem intended for a wide audience, rather than a direct address to a Welsh nobleman. The earliest surviving use of the *cywydd* for true praise poetry is Iolo's elegy to Sir Rhys ap Gruffudd in 1356, and it may be significant that Sir Rhys was one of the king's principal supporters in south Wales. By 1367 Iolo was able to use the *cywydd* for an elaborate elegy in traditional style to the head of one of the most conservative families of north Wales, Tudur Fychan of Anglesey, whose ancestors had served the princes of Gwynedd. From then on we have a number of *cywyddau* in praise of prominent noblemen, most significantly the three to Owain Glyndŵr, descendant of the princes of Powys, one of which (no 8) begins with the archaic term *arwyrain*, 'to exalt', often used by the great twelfth-century court-poet Cynddelw of Powys. What Iolo did in these poems was to transfer the language, imagery and ideals of the traditional praise poetry to the new metrical form. His great contribution to the development of Welsh poetry was to act as a bridge between the Poets of the Princes and the Poets of the Gentry. Iolo had an enormous influence on the poets of the following two centuries, who revered him as the ideal type of the praise poet, just as Dafydd ap Gwilym represented the ideal for love poets.

The fourteenth century was a time of crisis for the bardic order because the patronage of the gentry had to be actively won in competition with a lower class of entertainers known as *clêr* (see 37.51-54). The great advantage of the *cywydd* in such a situation was that it was very well-suited for entertainment. Its light and swift movement made it an effective medium for both narrative and description, as can be seen in many of Dafydd ap Gwilym's love poems. In addition to its innate qualities, the *cywydd* was characterized by a number of poetic devices which made it a lively and dramatic form. These include personification and conversations, the extended sequences of imagery known as *dyfalu*, and the creative use of themes and conventions from popular poetry, such as the serenade and the dream vision. The primary purpose of most of Iolo Goch's poetry was praise, but in adapting the *cywydd* he took over many of its entertaining characteristics, and thus ensured the popular appeal of his praise poetry.

One of the hallmarks of Iolo's work is the use of conversations. These are sometimes between human beings, as in the opening lines of the elegy to Llywelyn Goch, where the young lovers of Meirionnydd ask what has become of the popular love-poet. But the conversations also involve giving a human voice to a dumb creature, such as the old horse which gives advice to Iolo in no 13, or to an inanimate object, such as the very striking personification of the *cywydd* itself which laments Dafydd ap Gwilym in no 21. The most extended conversation in Iolo's work is that between the body and the soul in no 14, which is an example of the creative use of a conventional literary device in praise of a number of patrons. The device of the dream vision is very effectively used for the purpose of praise in the description of Cricieth castle in no 2, serving both to heighten the visual quality of the poem and to suggest that Cricieth is like an ideal romance castle. The technique of *dyfalu* is used creatively in no 33 to produce a strikingly original praise poem in which the extended metaphorical description of the ship's discomforts serves to convey by contrast the desirability of Rhys ap Robert's court.

There is a strong vein of humour in much of Iolo's poetry—a quality for which he is not often given credit. Some of his poems are overtly humorous, such as his mock-elegies to Ithel Ddu and Hersdin Hogl, or his complaint to his beard. But more typical of Iolo's blending of eulogy and entertainment is his use of humorous touches or conceits in his praise poetry. This is often humour at his own expense, as in his poem requesting a horse, where he says that he will be as unsteady as a goose's egg in the saddle of a frisky horse. A good example of his praise at its most exuberant is his poem to the sons of Tudur Fychan, no 5, with its string of conceits based on the theme of service to the brothers, subtly implying their noble qualities.

Iolo's inventive use of a wide variety of devices has the great virtue of making each of his poems an unique composition which would have been very effective in performance. However, the strong impact of his poetry is not dependent solely upon such devices. On a more fundamental level his work is characterized by a powerful visual sense which produces very vivid evocations of scenes and events. The depiction of Cricieth castle has already been mentioned. Two other outstanding poems of this type, which I would argue to be among the classics of medieval European literature, are his account of Ithel ap Robert's impressive funeral and his detailed description of Owain Glyndŵr's court at Sycharth. The latter poem is an excellent example of the use of the ordered, leisurely movement of the *cywydd* as an effective medium for description. It is highly entertaining on the superficial visual level as a portrait of a fine house, but its real power lies in the symbolic significance of the description as a reflection of the ideal social order. Such specific evocations of the noble household were an integral part of Iolo's eulogistic method, since a nobleman's social status depended to a large extent on the visible display of wealth and largesse.

Iolo's keen appreciation of the architectural features of Owain's court reflects his own concern for the design of his poetry. Generally speaking, ordered design is not one of the strengths of medieval Welsh poetry, which tends to circle around the same point without any linear progression. The *cywyddau* of Dapydd ap Gwilym, for instance, tend to be relatively short and to be constructed as a single thematic unit. Iolo's *cywyddau* are generally conceived on a larger scale, and he stands out from his contemporaries in his ability to arrange discrete sections as parts of a whole. A good example is his elegy to Ithel ap Robert, one of the longest of all medieval *cywyddau*. The whole poem is constructed according to a clear temporal scheme, beginning with Ithel's sudden death. His soul left his body immediately, so the reception of his soul into heaven is described first, followed by the interment of his body, the vivid description of the funeral cortège forming the centre-piece of the poem. As the grave is closed the mourners' despair reaches a climax, but the poem ends on a note of consolation by extending the perspective to the Day of Judgement.

Another poem to Ithel ap Robert which is constructed on a grand scale is the conversation between the body and the soul. It is not in fact apparent that this is in praise of Ithel at all until the end of the poem, when it becomes clear that the lengthy journey has been recited in order to stress the old poet's relief at reaching Ithel's house, where he can give up the life of the wandering minstrel. The point of that poem is missed unless it is seen as a whole. The same is true of the eulogy to Sir Roger Mortimer, the most complex of Iolo's long poems. The elaborate recital of Roger's heraldic titles and the estates which go with them is much more than just personal praise. The point is that one of his four countries is in a state of disorder due to the rebellion of the Irish, and it is Roger's duty to restore order there by military action. The fierce exhortation at the end of the poem links up with the advice to Roger at the beginning to gain experience in handling arms. The poem was conceived as a coherent whole in response to a specific political situation. Thus the consideration of construction brings us back to the question of historical context. It is because of his mastery of the wide range of techniques and devices available to him that Iolo was able to express so forcefully his experience of and response to life in fourteenth-century Wales.

Text and Translation

The Welsh text printed here is taken from the critical edition, *Gwaith Iolo Goch* (Cardiff, 1988), which contains detailed discussion of the various manuscript readings and editorial decisions. In addition to correcting some minor misprints, emendments to that text have been incorporated at the following points, all of which are explained in the notes to the poems: 1.57; 4.28; 13.36; 14.117-18; 16.41; 28.71; 29.4; 38.8, 13; 39.17.

The translations have no pretension to literary merit in their own right. They are intended merely as an aid to the understanding of the Welsh text, and aim above all at a literal rendering of the sense of the Welsh, as far as that is consonant with good English has been retained as far as possible. A line-for-line correspondence between text and translation has been attempted, but in some places the differences between Welsh and English word order have made this impossible. The *sangiadau* often sit in uncomfortable isolation in prose renderings without the binding element of *cynghanedd*, but in general the temptation to give them a syntactical connection with the main statements in the translation has been avoided, since they are an integral part of the stylistic character of the poetry.

A major problem facing the translator is the enormously rich linguistic resources of the medieval Welsh poet, who could supplement the vocabulary of his contemporary language by drawing on both archaisms from the poetic tradition stretching back to the Dark Ages and neologisms borrowed from French and English. Not only do my translations frequently resort to the use of the same word to translate two different ones in the Welsh, thus giving a false impression of Iolo's style, but also they generally lose the impact of archaisms and especially neologisms.

Attention has been drawn to the source of many of Iolo's borrowings in the notes to the poems. It is to be hoped that the brief sketch of the metrical characteristics of Iolo's poetry will encourage the reader to keep one eye on the Welsh text in order to appreciate some at least of the rich music which is entirely lost in prose translation. It is not possible to reproduce *cynghanedd* in translation without sacrificing the sense altogether, but for those who wish to gain some impression of the *cywydd* form in English I would recommend Tony Conran's very skilful renderings in his *Welsh Verse*.

Recommendations for Further Reading

A O H Jarman and Gwilym Rees Hughes (eds.), *A Guide to Welsh Literature* , vol 2 (Swansea, 1980).

Eurys Rowlands, 'Iolo Goch', in James Carney and David Greene (eds), *Celtic Studies in Memory of Angus Matheson* (London, 1968), 124-46.

D Johnston, 'Iolo Goch and the English: Welsh poetry and politics in the fourteenth century', *Cambridge Medieval Celtic Studies*, 12 (1986), 73-98.

Rachel Bromwich, *Dafydd ap Gwilym: A Selection of Poems* (Llandysul, 1982; revised ed. Harmondsworth, 1985).

Tony Conran, *Welsh Verse* (Bridgend, 1986).

PLACES MENTIONED IN THE POEMS OF IOLO GOCH

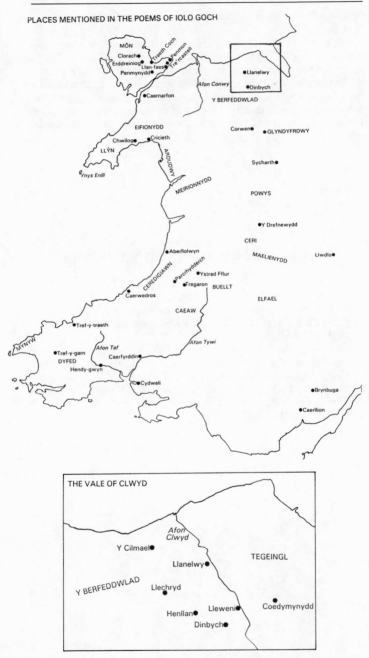

ABBREVIATIONS

APDG	Rachel Bromwich, *Aspects of the Poetry of Dafydd ap Gwilym* (Cardiff, 1986).
B	*Bulletin of the Board of Celtic Studies.*
Bartrum	P C Bartrum, *Welsh Genealogies A. D. 300-1400* (8 vols, Cardiff, 1974).
BD	Henry Lewis, *Brut Dingestow* (Caerdydd, 1942).
BT	J G Evans, *The Book of Taliesin* (facsimile ed., Llanbedrog, 1910).
CA	Ifor Williams, *Canu Aneirin* (Caerdydd, 1938).
CMCS	*Cambridge Medieval Celtic Studies.*
CO	Rachel Bromwich and D Simon Evans, *Culhwch ac Olwen* (Caerdydd, 1988).
DGG²	Ifor Williams and Thomas Roberts, *Cywyddau Dafydd ap Gwilym a'i Gyfoeswyr* (Caerdydd, 1935).
DGSP	Rachel Bromwich, *Dafydd ap Gwilym: A Selection of Poems* (Llandysul, 1982; revised ed. Harmondsworth, 1985).
EC	*Etudes Celtiques.*
EDD	Joseph Wright, *English Dialect Dictionary* (Oxford, 1898-1905).
EEW	T H Parry-Williams, *The English Element in Welsh* (London, 1923).
GDE	Thomas Roberts, *Gwaith Dafydd ab Edmwnd* (Bangor, 1914).
GDG	Thomas Parry, *Gwaith Dafydd ap Gwilym* (Caerdydd, 1952; second ed. 1963).
GDLl	W Leslie Richards, *Gwaith Dafydd Llwyd o Fathafarn* (Caerdydd, 1964).
GGGl	J Llewelyn Williams and Ifor Williams, *Gwaith Guto'r Glyn* (Caerdydd, 1939).
GIG	D R Johnston, *Gwaith Iolo Goch* (Caerdydd, 1988).
GMW	D Simon Evans, *A Grammar of Middle Welsh* (Dublin, 1964).
GPC	*Geiriadur Prifysgol Cymru: A Dictionary of the Welsh Language* (Caerdydd, 1950-).
GRB	Eurys Rowlands, *Gwaith Rhys Brydydd a Rhisiart ap Rhys* (Caerdydd, 1976).
GWL	A O H Jarman and Gwilym Rees Hughes (eds.), *A Guide to Welsh Literature*, vol 2 (Swansea, 1980).
HGC	Henry Lewis, *Hen Gerddi Crefyddol* (Caerdydd, 1931).
HW	J E Lloyd, *A History of Wales* (London, 1911).
IGE²	Henry Lewis *et al.*, *Cywyddau Iolo Goch ac Eraill* (Caerdydd, 1937).

Jenkins	Dafydd Jenkins, *Hywel Dda: The Law* (Llandysul, 1986).
LBS	S Baring-Gould and J Fisher, *Lives of the British Saints* (4 vols, London, 1907-13).
LGCD	E D Jones, *Lewys Glyn Cothi (Detholiad)* (Caerdydd, 1984).
LlA	J Morris Jones and John Rhys, *The Elucidarium and Other Tracts in Welsh from Llyvyr Agkyr Llandewivrevi* (Oxford, 1894).
LlC	*Llên Cymru*
LlDC	A O H Jarman, *Llyfr Du Caerfyrddin* (Caerdydd, 1982)
NLWJ	*National Library of Wales Journal.*
OBWV	Thomas Parry, *The Oxford Book of Welsh Verse* (Oxford, 1962)
OED	*Oxford English Dictionary.*
PT	Ifor Williams, *The Poems of Taliesin* (trans. J E Caerwyn Williams, Dublin, 1975).
PKM	Ifor Williams, *Pedeir Keinc y Mabinogi* (Caerdydd, 1930).
PWLMA	R A Griffiths, *The Principality of Wales in the Later Middle Ages*, I (Cardiff, 1972).
SC	*Studia Celtica.*
TDHS	*Transactions of the Denbighshire Historical Society.*
THSC	*Transactions of the Honourable Society of the Cymmrodorion.*
TMW	Ian Soulsby, *The Towns of Medieval Wales* (Chichester, 1983).
TYP	Rachel Bromwich, *Trioedd Ynys Prydein: The Welsh Triads* (Cardiff, 1961; second ed. 1978).
WCCR	Glanmor Williams, *The Welsh Church from Conquest to Reformation* (Cardiff, 1962).
WLW	Dafydd Jenkins and Morfydd E Owen (eds.), *The Welsh Law of Women* (Cardiff, 1980).
YB	J E Caerwyn Williams (ed.), *Ysgrifau Beirniadol* (Dinbych, 1965).

Poems

1 To King Edward III

Edward son of Edward, men's guardian,
son of Edward, Bedivere's nature;
you are Edward grandson of Edward,
4   Edward the Third, brown leopard;
you wore, and you reared war,
a crest after the conquest of a hundred castles;
it was at an auspicious hour—heroic lord,
8   golden surcoat, Windsor's eagle—
that you were born because of your goodness,
you will never fail in any feat;
you were endowed, thick-coated post,
12   with the heart and breast of the lion,
boar of honest commerce,
and head and sense and discretion
and a swarthy bright-eyed countenance
16   and a special talent and a fine face
and every angelic language, stout companion,
is yours, my lord;
and through splendour, fierce-fighting brother,
20   you are a good angel in the thick of battle.

    You had trouble, you had hardship
at the beginning of your life right fiercely
subduing the stubborn people
24   of England and France, place of finest fruit;
a shameful memory today
among the people of Scotland
what you did in every other battle, you weren't sluggish,
28   above York, ferocity of Hercules,
attacking the host where it was strongest,
capturing the king, hammerer of the Scots,
wounding some, capturing others,
32   dragging off all the earls, burning the rest,
battering with a catapult—image of a web—
the stones of pale-walled Berwick;
you starved—angry hindrance—
36   a very great army on the North Sea;
you were an enemy to Calais
by taking the town, splendid force;
gracious was your progress to Crécy,
40   you have fair grace from Christ;
you fed your army, cruel battle-line,
human crows, on the king of Bohemia;

I'r Brenin Edward y Trydydd

Edwart ab Edwart, gwart gwŷr,
Ab Edwart, anian Bedwyr;
Edwart ŵyr Edwart ydwyd,
4 Edwart Trydydd, llewpart llwyd;
Gwisgaist, a ririaist yr aer,
Crest gwedy cwncwest cancaer;
Ar awr dda, arwraidd iôr,
8 Aur gwnsallt, eryr Gwynsor,
Y'th aned o'th ddaioni,
Ni fetha twrn fyth i ti;
Cael a wnaethost, post peistew,
12 Calon a llawfron y llew,
Baedd y gyfnewid ddidwyll,
A phen a synnwyr a phwyll
A ffriw lygliw olygloyw
16 A phriod dawn a phryd hoyw
A phob iaith, cydymddaith cadr,
Engylaidd it, fy ngwaladr;
Ac o wychdawd, brawd brydaer,
20 Angel da yng ngwaelod aer.

Cefaist gost, cefaist gysteg
Yn nechrau d'oes yn wychr deg
Yn estwng pobl anystwyth
24 Lloegr a Ffrainc, lle gorau ffrwyth:
Cof cyfeddliw heddiw hyn,
Bob ail brwydr, gan bobl Brydyn,
A wnaethost, ni buost bŵl,
28 Ar ael Iorc, arial Ercwl,
Dyludo'r llu lle bu'r baich,
Daly'r brenin, duliwr Brynaich,
Dolurio rhai, daly ereill,
32 Llusgo'r ieirll oll, llosgi'r lleill,
Curo â blif, ddylif ddelw,
Cerrig Caer Ferwig furwelw;
Rhoist ar gythlwng, rhwystr gwythlawn,
36 Ar Fôr Udd aerfa fawr iawn;
Gelyn fuost i'r Galais
O gael y dref, golau drais;
Grasus dy hynt i'r Gresi,
40 Gras teg i gan Grist i ti;
Llithio dy fyddin, lin lem,
Frain byw, ar frenin Böem;

a danger to the gates of Paris
44 was the noise of battle where you struck a blow;
you will fly, you are so bold,
as far as heaven, you are a bird.

Now you will not be dispossessed,
48 no man will break the frontier of your land;
make a pact—your grandfather's custom,
good wisdom for your soul,
with your God, no bad practice,
52 take the cross in your strength:
there is a prophecy that if you go to Greece,
mighty bull, you will gain the Holy Land
and the grim black sad town of the Jews,
56 and touch the cross and Christ's temple,
and conquer from the crusade
Jerusalem as far as great Bethlehem.
Deal out punishment to the heathens,
60 tear your way through the land of Egypt;
march a while across Germany,
wolf's heart, follow the vanguard;
grand bull, you'll gain the land and the men,
64 break the stonework of Romans' houses;
press on as far as the edge of Constantinople,
beat people before the town of Babilon.

Before you die you will get to wear
68 the three fine well-adorned crowns
which they carried long ago on an easy journey
over three countries for the Lord God,
the splendour of the three gifts,
72 with your sword, line of fair sovereigns,
between the three worthy diadems,
king of great Cologne rich in wine,
to the bright land of heaven of He who rules,
76 thither will you come in the end.

Perygl fu i byrth Paris
44 Trwst y gad lle trewaist gis;
Ehedy, mor hy ydwyd,
Hyd y nef, ehedyn wyd.

Weithion ni'th ddigyfoethir,
48 Ni thyr dyn derfyn dy dir;
Gwna dithau, deddfau dy daid,
Doethineb da i'th enaid,
Cymod â'th Dduw, nid camoes,
52 Cymer yn dy gryfder groes:
Od ei Roeg mae darogan,
Darw glew, y ceffi Dir Glân
A'r Iddewdref arw ddudrist,
56 A theimlo'r grog a theml Grist,
A gorestwng o'r grwystaith
Gaersalem hyd Fethlem faith.
Dwg yn Anghred dogn anghraifft,
60 Dyro rwyg drwy dir yr Aifft;
Cerdda dalm dros yr Almaen,
Calon blaidd, calyn y blaen;
Tarw gwych, ceffi'r tir a'r gwŷr,
64 Tor faenwaith tai Rhufeinwyr;
Cyrch hyd ym min Constinobl,
Cer bron Caer Bablon cur bobl.

Cyn dy farw y cei arwain
68 Y tair coron cywair cain
A ddugon' gynt ar hynt rwydd
Ar deirgwlad er Duw Arglwydd,
Tirionrhwydd y tair anrheg,
72 Â'th gledd, hil teyrnedd teg,
Rhwng y tair teilwng talaith,
Frenin Cwlen fawrwin faith,
I wenwlad nef Ef a fedd,
76 Yno doi yn y diwedd.

2 To Sir Hywel of the Axe, Constable of Cricieth Castle

Did anyone ever see what I see
at night—do I not do well?—
when I, greatest pain that ever was,
4   am sleeping, ageing nature?
First of all I see, in truth,
a magnificent fort yonder by the shore,
and a marvellous fine castle,
8   and men at tables, and light,
and blue sea against a fair stone wall,
and foam about the base of a grim dark tower,
and lively music of pipes
12   and bag, and fine-looking men
enjoying dancing and song,
being entertained and praised;
maidens, no ugly ones,
16   weaving the pure bright silk;
proud men playing, in the castle hall,
at backgammon and chequers on a raised dais;
and a silvery-grey fierce-natured man,
20   Twrch Trwyd of battle, pouring vernage wine
into a golden gilded goblet
from his hand into mine like this;
and a beautiful long black standard
24   on a tower top, he was a good soldier,
and three fine white flowers
of the same shape, silver-coloured leaves.

Strange that there is no old sage
28   in Gwynedd, land of many feasts,
at all who might know
where it is that I desire to be.
'There is,' said one, 'you are refined,
32   you are dreaming wisely.
The fair wall which you see,
a good dwelling to come to,
and the bright fort high on a rock,
36   and the red stone on the edge of a croft,
this is Cricieth and its fine work,
an old edifice that is;
and the stout grey man with shattered spear
40   is Sir Hywel, lightning-throwing catapult,
and his wife, Sir, golden-belted,

I Syr Hywel y Fwyall,
Cwnstabl Castell Cricieth

A welai neb a welaf
Yn y nos—pand iawn a wnaf?—
Pan fwyf, mwyaf poen a fu,
4   Yn huno, anian henu?
Cynta' dim a wela'n wir,
Caer fawrdeg acw ar fordir,
A chastell gwych gorchestawl,
8   A gwŷr ar fyrddau, a gwawl,
A glasfor wrth fur glwysfaen,
A geirw am groth twr gwrm graen,
A cherdd chwibenygl a chod
12 Gorhoenus, a gwŷr hynod
Yn chwarae dawns a charawl,
Yn cymryd mynwyd a mawl;
Rhianedd, nid rhai anoyw,
16 Yn gwau y sidan glân gloyw;
Gwŷr beilch yn chwarae, gaer barth,
Tawlbwrdd a secr uwch talbarth;
A gŵr gwynllwyd, Twrch Trwyd trin,
20 Nawswyllt yn rhoi farneiswin
Mewn gorflwch aur goreuryn
O'i law yn fy llaw fellŷn;
Ac ystondardd hardd hirddu
24 Yn nhâl twr, da filwr fu,
A thri blodeuyn gwyn gwiw
O'r unllun, dail arianlliw.

    Eres nad oes henuriad
28 Ar lawr Gwynedd, wleddfawr wlad,
O gwbl a'r a allo gwybod
Petwn lle mynnwn fy mod.
'Oes,' heb yr un, 'syberw wyd,
32 Breuddwydio'n brudd ydd ydwyd.
Y wal deg a weli di,
Da dyddyn o doid iddi,
A'r gaer eglur ar greiglofft
36 A'r garreg rudd ar gwr grofft,
Hon yw Cruciaith a'i gwaith gwiw,
Hen adail honno ydiw;
A'r gŵr llwyd cadr paladrddellt
40 Yw Syr Hywel, mangnel mellt,
A'i wraig, Syr, wregys euraid,

Hywel, warlord in battle,
and her handmaidens, fair skin,
44   by the dozen they were weaving
the pure bright-coloured silk
in the sun's rays through fine glass.
Your vision, you did see
48   a standard—beautiful decoration;
this is Sir Hywel's pennoncel;
by Beuno, in his pennon
are three *fleurs-de-lis*, iris field,
52   in the sable, not uncourtly.'

        The spirit of Gruffudd's son, red spear,
is on towards his enemies,
honing a spear in their impure
56   blood, golden-footed lord,
battle hacker, fine red H,
eager to war, red shield,
the tusks of a savage boar,
60   old bone in our time of need.
When the bridle, harsh gift of a binding rope,
was put on the French king's head
he was a barber like Erbin's son
64   with spear and sword, harsh manner in battle:
with his hand and strength
he did shave heads and beards,
and he let, without delay,
68   blood over feet—grim for some.

        He will be dear to Lionheart's heir,
many his poets and the praises of his table.
He is warden, eighteen-pointed stag,
72   and steward of the rugged strong fort;
stout courser keeping the garrison,
long will this man keep the land;
keep the people in a fine stronghold,
76   keep the castle, he's better than a host,
keep two ridges, long field's keeper,
keep the two lands, keep the battle, keep the feat,
keep the sea-breaker with the seashore,
80   keep the sea-ebb, keep the houses, keep the land,
keep all the countries, keep the bright tower,
and keep the fort—health to the man!

Hywel, iôn rhyfel yn rhaid,
A'i llawforynion, ton teg,
44   Ydd oeddynt hwy bob ddeuddeg
Yn gwau sidan glân gloywliw
Wrth haul belydr drwy'r gwydr gwiw.
Tau olwg, ti a welud
48   Ystondardd—ys hardd o sud;
Pensel Syr Hywel yw hwn;
Myn Beuno, mae'n ei benwn
Tri fflŵr-dy-lis, oris erw,
52   Yn y sabl, nid ansyberw.'

    Anian mab Gruffudd, rudd rôn,
Ymlaen am ei elynion,
Yn minio gwayw mewn eu gwaed
56   Anniweirdrefn, iôn eurdraed,
Ysgythrwr cad, aets goethrudd,
Esgud i'r aer, ysgwyd rudd,
Ysgithredd baedd disgethrin,
60   Asgwrn hen yn angen in.
Pan rodded, trawsged rhwysgainc,
Y ffrwyn ym mhen brenin Ffrainc
Barbwr fu fal mab Erbin
64   Â gwayw a chledd, tromwedd trin:
Eillio â'i law a'i allu
Bennau a barfau y bu,
A gollwng, gynta' gallai,
68   Gwaed tros y traed—trist i rai.

    Annwyl fydd gan ŵyr Leinort,
Aml ei feirdd, a mawl i'w fort.
Gwarden yw, garw deunawosgl,
72   A maer ar y drawsgaer drosgl;
Cadr gwrser yn cadw'r garsiwn,
Cadw'r tir yn hir a wna hwn;
Cadw'r bobl mewn cadair bybyr,
76   Cadw'r castell, gwell yw na gwŷr,
Cadw dwy lins, ceidwad loensiamp,
Cadw'r ddwywlad, cadw'r gad, cadw'r gamp,
Cadw'r mordarw cyda'r mordir,
80   Cadw'r mordrai, cadw'r tai, cadw'r tir,
Cadw'r gwledydd oll, cadw'r gloywdwr,
A chadw'r gaer—iechyd i'r gŵr!

3 To Ieuan ab Einion of Chwilog

Who has the strength to surpass the nation?
Who is striving for the top of an old province?
A beloved ruler, great his fortune,
4   country's floor, holder of a hundred festivals,
weight of two islands—post of old gold,
you are the land's head—and their golden pinnacle;
Ieuan, it fell to your part,
8   son of Einion, to live as a ruler;
famous and good is your name,
seed of Gruffudd, as far as Offa's Dyke;
fine squire—is there a better man?—
12   and guardian greater than Cadell,
great sheriff over gold and mead,
his name rose over Gwynedd,
growth of a root and flourishing shoot,
16   power in the line of Collwyn and his seed,
vigorous bold man gifted with rank,
a dragon with his zeal through a hundred routs.

    Take up the banner of Eifionydd,
20   it will be a great enclosure within Wales;
if our land is gathering together,
Ardudwy went to your side;
trunk of Pasgen through our nation's roof,
24   strong and flourishing securing the province;
freely and finely you give gifts,
noble hawk of Urien Rheged,
peak of fair Gwynedd's nobility,
28   sprouting from Owain's line,
and you are her fine golden guardian,
and all her treasury, and you're her succour,
and her goodness in every stronghold,
32   and her exalted strength and her grace,
and their treasure where they make merry,
and their bridge to support them and their head;
bold and strong, you are a mirror,
36   godly and wise, you are humble,
maintainer, growing into a lord,
of Chwilog, finely gifted men,
a great fortress against men from the seas,
40   there was less expenditure in the castles,
Fulk's court by the side of the road,
sturdy lodging, across an old main road,

I Ieuan ab Einion o Chwilog

Pwy sy o rym pasio'r iaith?
Pwy'n dilid top hen dalaith?
Pennaeth, mawr ei hap, annwyl,
4 Parth gwlad, cynheiliad can hwyl,
Pwys dwy ynys, post henaur,
Pen gwlad wyd, a'u pinagl aur;
Ieuan, yn dy ran yr aeth,
8 Ab Einion, fyw yn bennaeth;
Hynod yw dy henw a da,
Had Gruffudd, hyd Gaer Offa;
Ysgwïer gwych—oes gŵr gwell?—
12 A cheidwad mwy na Chadell,
Siri mawr dros aur a medd,
Troes ei enw ef tros Wynedd,
Gwraidd dwf ac iraidd dyfiad,
16 Gallu'n hil Gollwyn a'i had,
Dyn irddewr mewn dawn urddas,
Dragwn a'i sêl drwy gan siâs.

Cymer faner Eifionydd,
20 Cae mawr o fewn Cymru fydd;
Os ein tir sy yn tyrru,
Ardudwy aeth ar dy du;
Coed Pasgen trwy nen ein iaith,
24 Cry' dilesg yn cau'r dalaith;
Rhwydd a gwych y rhoddi ged,
Rhywiogwalch Urien Rheged,
Brig bonedd bro Gwynedd gain,
28 Blodeuog o blaid Owain,
A'i cheidwad eurwych ydwyd,
A'i secr oll, a'i swcwr wyd,
A'i daioni 'mhob dinas,
32 A'i grym urddedig a'i gras,
A'u trysor lle'r wtresen',
A'u pont i'w cynnal a'u pen;
Dewr a chadarn, drych ydwyd,
36 Dwyfol a chall, difalch wyd,
Cynheiliad, ar dyfiad iôn,
Chwilog, eurddoniog ddynion,
Caer fawr rhag gwŷr o foroedd,
40 Cost llai yn y cestyll oedd,
Llys Ffwg yn llawes y ffordd,
Llety'n braff, lled hen briffordd,

       a prominent court below the land of Llŷn,
44 wine cellar, fresh Celliwig;
       there is goodness in the lives of men
       towards the family of this mother-hearth,
       full, fine, famous royal place,
48 lodging of poets where praise would stay;
       we look at the brightness of the mirror,
       your surface is like the stones of this house;
       maintainer of your father in your house,
52 we get that much in a hundred houses;
       you cast gold over your people,
       drawing all the blood from a tun of wine;
       you are a most excellent treasure,
56 you are a sceptre over lands.

       Plough a furrow in a golden footband,
       father of symbols—chain of burnished gold—
       of all the rulers of Gwynedd;
60 send a challenge amongst men of vigour;
       you are a fire to me from the mouth of Anglesey,
       and the men above are the sparks,
       a baron of a man in our land,
64 alive, and his wealth like Beli's.
       Throughout the region of Eifionydd's land
       as long as you live what you wish will be.
       Better to be very forceful, Rhodri's power,
68 than wretched, take your share;
       foundation of the nation surpassing everyone,
       the sign of goodness is in your face;
       official with the grace of Julius Caesar,
72 stand your ground, all men love you.

4 Elegy for Tudur Fychan of Penmynydd

       I heard yesterday in my right ear
       the hollow sound of a stray horn:
       by God, am I guiltless?
4 What is such a horn?
       The mourning horns of Môn's high king,
       empty-voiced poets are wounded;
       what commotion is this—I know a hundred groans—
8 what beating in my ear like a bell?
       The death-report of a fine patriarch,

Cwrt hynod is Llŷn frodir,
44 Cell y gwin, Celliwig ir;
Mae daioni 'myw dynion
At hil y fam-aelwyd hon,
Llawnwych frenhinlle hynod,
48 Llety'r glêr lle tariai glod;
Llewych y drych edrychwn,
Lliw dy frig fal cerrig hwn;
Cynheiliad eich tad i'ch tŷ,
52 Can hannedd y cawn hynny;
Trewaist aur tros dy werin,
Tynnu holl waed tunnell win;
Trysor mawr ei ragor wyd,
56 Tros wladoedd trosol ydwyd.

Tor di gŵys mewn troedog aur,
Tad arwyddion, tid ruddaur,
Teÿrnedd Gwynedd i gyd;
60 Tro'r fei trwy wŷr o fywyd;
Tân im wyt o enau Môn,
A'r gwŷr uchod yw'r gwreichion,
Barwn o ŵr i'n bro ni,
64 Byw, a'i olud fal Beli.
Trwy faenol tir Eifionydd
Tra fych a fynnych a fydd.
Gwell rhydraws, gallu Rhodri,
68 Na thruan, dos â'th ran di;
Sylfaen iaith sy o flaen neb,
Sein daioni sy'n d'wyneb;
Swyddog mewn gras Wl Casar,
72 Saf i'th garn, sy fyw a'th gâr.

Marwnad Tudur Fychan o Benmynydd

Clywais doe i'm clust deau
Canu corn cyfeiliorn cau:
Wi o Dduw, a wyf ddiorn?
4 Pa beth yw y gyfryw gorn?
Galargyrn mechdëyrn Môn,
Gogleisiwyd beirdd gwagleision;
Pa dwrw yw hwn, gwn gannoch,
8 Pa ymffust i'm clust fal cloch?
Marw gychwedl pencenedl coeth,

great wise Tudur of the steel-edged weapon—
I will not falsify his elegy—
12   Fychan, good knight of the tournament field;
most bitter to me—sister of blame—
is the concord of bell and trumpet;
what shouting—who knows?—
16   is this that we hear in our land?
Moaning and wailing from grief
for the most beloved man of all,
Tudur, scatterer of a thick throng,
20   helmeted father, mailcoated post,
column of prudence, I would not conceal who,
the heart of the sages of Dindaethwy.

Môn is ruined, by Egryn's hand,
24   man's best place is utterly ruined,
Wales is ruined after [its] guardian,
how fleeting are the lives of Ricart's tribe!
To the poor of the land of Môn
28   the furtive taking of Brynbyrddau's lion
will be a head wound to the brain,
his house has been completely uprooted;
taking fair Hywel was a harsh upset,
32   worse the taking of the prophetic poet's foster brother;
God of heaven, grim open conflict,
taking a pure open-hearted body,
descendant of holy Rhirid—golden tribe—
36   the Wolf, choice liquor without churlishness;
he ruled Gwynedd, unstinting hand,
bright Môn's head has been struck off, it's empty.
What if an evil grim fleet
40   comes by us to the Red Strand,
who will resist the Norsemen, we are sluggish,
with their keen-edged axes?
Who shall we get? Whose is Gwynedd?
44   Who will brandish spear or sword?
Who does not weep, penance of grief,
who loves you anymore above Conwy?
After the death of the great swift stag,
48   flourishing of the line of Brynffanugl's lord,
chieftain, ferocious tusked dragon,
and Môn's head against retreat or flight;
great land's shield, he was wealth,
52   a swain of battle is singing his praise;
darling of Môn, land of nobles,

Tudur arf awchddur wychddoeth—
Ni furniaf ddim o'i farwnad—
12 Fychan, farchog midlan mad;
Chwerw iawn yw gennyf, chwaer orn,
Gytgerdd rhwng cloch ac utgorn;
Pa weiddi—pwy a wyddiad?—
16 Yw hwn a glywwn i'n gwlad?
Ubain a llefain rhag llid
Am y gŵr mwya' a gerid,
Tudur, wasgarwr tewdorf,
20 Tad helmog, lurigog lorf,
Colofn pwyll, nis celwn pwy,
Calon doethion Dindaethwy.

Llygrwyd Môn, myn llaw Egryn,
24 Llygrwyd oll lle gorau dyn,
Llygrwyd Cymru gwedy gwart,
Llithriced hoedl llwyth Ricart!
Dyrnod pen hyd ymennydd
28 Ar dlodion gwlad Fôn fydd
Dwyn llew Brynbyrddau dan llaw,
Dadwreiddiwyd ei dŷ drwydddaw;
Dygn ymchwel dwyn Hywel hardd,
32 Ys gwaeth dwyn brawdfaeth brudfardd;
Duw nef, brwydr gyfaddef brudd,
Dwyn glangorff digalongudd,
Ŵyr Ririd lwyd, euraid lwyth,
36 Flaidd, difileindraidd flaendrwyth;
Llywiodd Wynedd, llaw ddinag,
Llas pen Môn wen, y mae'n wag.
Beth o daw heibiaw hebom
40 I'r Traeth Coch lynges droch drom,
Pwy a ludd gwerin, pŵl ŷm,
Llychlyn a'u bwyaill awchlym?
Pwy a gawn? Piau Gwynedd?
44 Pwy a ddyrchaif glaif neu gledd?
Pwy nid ŵyl, penyd alar,
Pwy mwy uwch Conwy a'ch câr?
Gwedy marw y rhygarw rhugl,
48 Ffyniant hil naf Brynffanugl,
Ffelaig, ysgithrddraig uthrddrud,
A phen Môn rhag ffo na mud;
Aesawr gwlad fawr, golud fu,
52 Yswain brwydr sy'n ei brydu;
Dillyn Môn, frehyrion fro,

he understood the art of piercing a shattered shield;
vigorous wise enduring friend,
56   home of lavishness, stag of Tre'rcastell.

Woe the South, mead must be given up,
it is quite bereft, woe the two parts of Gwynedd,
woe the roebucks, there are less in a clearing,
60   woe the stags that one who loved them has been taken,
woe to me without a dwelling place
seeing at the bottom of a grave
that there is a very cold covering today
64   of gravel and earth on his face;
it is most grievous that he's in Hirerw
with his cheeks concealed beneath oak;
he was not very familiar
68   with such a bed after wine;
a spirited stag has been dressed
in wood and thick harsh earth;
he was more used to wearing finely
72   in a joust, strong gentle lord,
a helmet always richly crested,
and a habergeon, swift straight hawk,
and a closely linked mailcoat
76   heavy and loose to enable him to fight,
a shield which was a heavy weight to him,
a squire's crowfeeding armburdening spear.

No weak one ever lost, vineyard of men,
80   his inheritance as long as Tudur lived;
no kinsman was indicted against his will,
scarcely was a poor man outlawed.
Speak not in Gwynedd,
84   harness no ox under a fine yoke,
talk not of what has happened,
plough not, it is useless,
laugh not about splendid fair ones,
88   sow no more in the land of Môn.

Dalltai bwyll dellt ebillio;
Gwyrennig câr pwyllig pell,
56   Cartre'r cost, carw Tre'rcastell.

   Gwae'r Deau, rhaid maddau medd,
Gweddw iawn yw, gwae ddwy Wynedd,
Gwae'r ieirch, mewn llenneirch mae'n llai,
60   Gwae'r ceirw ddwyn gŵr a'u carai,
Gwae finnau heb gyfannedd
Gweled bod mewn gwaelod bedd
Anhudded oer iawn heddiw
64   O ro a phridd ar ei ffriw;
Dihir ei fod yn Hirerw
Ynghudd ei ddeurudd dan dderw;
Nid oedd ef dra chynefin
68   Â'r rhyw wely gwedy gwin;
Pren a daearen dew arw
A wisgwyd am frowysgarw;
Gnodach iddo wisgo'n waisg
72   Yn ymwanfrwydr, iôn mwynfraisg,
Helm gribawg ruddfoawg fyth,
A habrsiwn, walch ewybrsyth,
A llurig rwymedig radd
76   Dromlaes i fedru ymladd,
Aesawr oedd fawr iddo'i faich,
Yswain wayw lithfrain lwythfraich.

   Ni chollai wan, gwinllan gwŷr,
80   Tref ei dad tra fu Dudur;
Ni thitid câr amharawd,
Odid od wtlëid tlawd.
Na ynganer yng Ngwynedd,
84   Na ddalier ych dan wych wedd,
Na sonier am a dderyw,
Na lafurier, ofer yw,
Na chwardder am wych heirddion,
88   Na hëer mwy yn nhir Môn.

5 Praise of Tudur Fychan's Sons

I am going to the land of Môn yonder,
often have I desired it,
to get to know the sons
4   of Tudur, chief jousters of Môn:
Gronwy, Rhys, lords of the island,
Ednyfed, Gwilym, keen spear;
Rhys, Ednyfed, gift-bestowing lord,
8   grim and keen his spear, Gwilym, Gronwy;
Ednyfed, Gronwy, Rhun's pride,
Rhys, Gwilym, splendour like that of Alun,
Gwilym, Gronwy, our lord,
12   Ednyfed, he gave a gift, mighty Rhys;
four great Nudds to me,
let Peter protect them, may it be at a good hour,
four sons—who insults them?—
16   children who will not let me be humbled,
solid as squares, four bright
evangelists by the sea of Môn,
prime oxen of Gwynedd, language of eulogy,
20   four yoked together in giving;
cubs of fierce Tudur Llwyd,
supporters of two hundred hearths,
giants of wine—it's easy to love the hawks—
24   magnificent stags, gentle hawks,
pillar shafts, chancellors,
columns of the edges of Môn,
fine magnanimous princes—
28   I am blessed—wine is their nourishment,
barons without fear,
proud plants of the front line,
descendants of Rhirid, eagles' flight,
32   the Wolf—not a man of churlish renown—
bulls of battle, bloody host,
augers of war, relentless in conflict,
children of Tudur, he was my eagle,
36   noble peacocks of a patriarch;
the host is armour on the sea-flood,
the foremost children are a golden litter.

I will go to Môn, I desire a gift,
40   sweet fair mountain land,
mother of Gwynedd, there I have
friends who are well-honoured in their locality;

Moliant i Feibion Tudur Fychan

Myned yr wyf dir Môn draw,
Mynych im ei ddymunaw,
I ymwybod â meibion
4   Tudur, ben-ymwanwyr Môn:
Gronwy, Rhys, ynys hynaif,
Ednyfed, Gwilym, lym laif;
Rhys, Ednyfed, roddged rwy,
8   Gwaywlym graen, Gwilym, Gronwy;
Ednyfed, Gronwy, rhwy Rhun,
Rhys, Gwilym, un rhwysg Alun;
Gwilym, Gronwy, ein gwaladr,
12 Ednyfed, rhoes ged, Rhys gadr;
Pedwar Nudd—Pedr i'w noddi,
Poed ar awr dda—mawr i mi,
Pedwarmaib—pwy a'u dirmyg?—
16 Plant ni ad arnaf ddim plyg,
Pedwar eglur, pedroglion,
Angelystor ger môr Môn,
Eithefigion, iaith fyged,
20 Gwynedd, pedwar cydwedd ced;
Cenawon Tudur llon Llwyd,
Cynheiliaid deucan haelwyd,
Cewri'r gwin—hawdd caru'r gweilch—
24 Ceirw addurn, carueiddweilch,
Cangau llyrf, cangellorion,
Colofnau ymylau Môn,
Gwehelyth gwiw ehelaeth—
28 Gwyn fy myd—gwin yw eu maeth,
Barwniaid heb erynaig,
Beilchion blanhigion blaen aig,
Hil Ririd, hwyl eryrod,
32 Flaidd—nid gŵr gwladaidd ei glod—
Teirw gryd, wyarllyd orllin,
Terydr aer, taer ar y drin,
Plant Tudur, fy eryr fu,
36 Peunod haelion penteulu;
Eirf yw'r llu ar fôr lliant,
Aur dorllwyth yw'r blaendrwyth blant.

    Môn yr af, dymunaf reg,
40 Mynydd-dir manwyeidd-deg,
Mam Wynedd, mae im yno
Geraint da eu braint i'w bro;

fine monastery with a lovely border,
44   it is a cloister to me by an inlet of the sea,
a snug enclosure to nurture poets
without refusing anyone who would be nurtured.

The first place I will go, a lion who gives,
48   fortress of Penmon, stag of Penmynydd,
the house, I saw the fine fair place before,
of Tudur Llwyd, good is the place;
there is there, with no limit to gifts,
52   a re-creation of the hearth of Rheged,
Gronwy of the shining spear, pleasant court,
very good renown, no unpleasant man;
I will carry for my golden hawk
56   a spear and a banner, proud baron,
and a shield, chieftain's body,
with him to protect his body,
to fair Môn, no need to fear any man
60   with Iolo following him.

To Erddreiniog, it ennobled the island,
I will go, I will feast, to Rhys;
I am treasurer—I will seize his silver
64   and his burnished gold, a hundred know him—
to Rhys and his receiver
and his true friend—oh what a man!
By a fine song I will claim
68   all the wealth of his country.

Tre'rcastell is not far off, chamber of gifts,
heavenly land, Ednyfed's dwelling;
I will be his cup-bearer there
72   and his steward always—he is my gold;
I will get, without any better visit,
as good as him in Tre'rcastell.

Backwards and forwards to the border
76   I will go to Rhys, true summons;
across Môn from Rhys's house then,
fearlessly, to Gronwy's house;
from Gronwy's house, the good of the island,
80   I must return to Rhys's house;
from Rhys's house, steel his shield,
to the house of fine Gwilym, there will be great profit;
Gwilym's court, a mansion full of herbs,

Claswriaeth deg glwys oror,
44 Clostr im yw ger clust o'r môr,
Buarth clyd i borthi clêr
Heb wrthod neb a borther.

Cyntaf lle'r af, llew a rydd,
48 Caer Pen Môn, carw Penmynydd,
Tŷ, gwelais gynt teg wiwle,
Tudur Llwyd, da ydyw'r lle;
Yno mae, heb gae ar ged,
52 Ail drigiant aelwyd Reged,
Gronwy loyw saffwy, lys hoff,
Gair da iawn, gŵr dianoff;
Arwain a wnaf i'm eurwalch
56 Gwayw a phenwn, barwn balch,
A darged, benadurgorff,
Gydag ef i gadw ei gorff,
I Fôn deg, nid rhaid ofn dyn
60 Ac Iolo yn ei galyn.

Erddreiniog, urddai'r ynys,
Ydd af, wtresaf, at Rys;
Trysorer, treisia'i ariant
64 A'i aur coch, ef a ŵyr cant,
I Rys wyf ai rysyfwr
A'i wir gâr—wi wi o'r gŵr!
Arddelwaf o aur ddolef
68 O olud oll ei wlad ef.

Nid pell Tre'rcastell, cell ced,
Tud nefol, tai Ednyfed;
Ei fenestr fyddaf yno,
72 A'i faer fyth—fy aur yw fo;
Mi a gaf, heb ofwy gwell,
Cystal ag e'n Nhre'rcastell.

Ôl a gwrthol i'r gorthir
76 A wnaf at Rys, gwŷs gwir;
Ar draws Môn o dŷ Rys mwy,
Dierynaig, dŷ Ronwy;
O dŷ Ronwy, da'r ynys,
80 Dir ym ymchwelyd dŷ Rys;
O dŷ Rys, dur ei aesawr,
Dŷ Wilym wych, daw elw mawr;
Llys Wilym, blas llysieulawn,

84   golden leopard, place of ready talent,
     dragon's nature, there will I dwell
     in heaven, and I will do right,
     Clorach's dwelling, brilliant building,
88   I will tarry in Môn as long as I live.

6 Elegy for Tudur Fychan's Sons

     Here is a deserted place now,
     an open court in Penmynydd of Môn;
     here is an Easter when a poet is bare,
4   a harsh place after a splendid colour;
     very similar—the house in which
     Tudur and his children once were, they are good—
     is the court after the casting aside
8   to a bountiful black monastery:
     sad faces of the same demeanour,
     the same appearance as a brother of grim nature,
     and the same form of men's gowns,
12   is everyone from his bright houses,
     the same mournful livery
     as sombre preaching Brothers.
     It was more usual for him from his hand
16   at a festival above to give liveries
     and splendid chequered cloth
     and the best green available
     to bold travelling musicians,
20   to minstrels, than mourning clothes.
     A black course like the sun of the Jews,
     there is a great enchantment all over Môn;
     cold cell, it is losing colour;
24   it is a strange world,
     to see on Rhys and Gwilym
     black habits without knowing anything
     of the monastic life before,
28   or of a convent of fellows.

     May Ednyfed be in heaven,
     Môn has become, alas, escheated land;
     with his brother, harsh upheaval of death,
32   he did leave his country.
     Woe to Môn for her foster sons!

84 Llewpart aur, lle parod dawn,
    Annwyd draig, yno y trigaf
    Yn y nef, ac iawn a wnaf,
    Trafn Glorach, trefn goleuryw,
88 Tariaf i Fôn tra fwyf fyw.

Marwnad Meibion Tudur Fychan

    Llyma le diffaith weithion,
    Llys rydd ym Mhenmynydd Môn;
    Llyma Basg y mae llwm bardd,
 4 Lle dygn gwedy lliw digardd;
    Tebyg iawn, y tŷ bu gynt
    Tudur a'i blant, da ydynt,
    Ydyw'r llys wedy'r llysu
 8 I'r fynachlog ddoniog ddu:
    Wynebau trist un abid,
    Un sud â brawd ansawd brid,
    Ac un wedd gynau i wŷr,
12 Ydyw pawb o'i dai pybyr,
    Un lifrai yn olofrudd
    Â Brodyr pregethwyr prudd.
    Gnodach o'i law iddaw oedd
16 Ar ŵyl fry roi lifreioedd
    A brethynnau brith honnaid
    Ac o'r gwyrdd gorau a gaid
    I gerddorion breisgion brisg,
20 I glerwyr, no galarwisg.
    Hwyl ddu fal haul Iddewon,
    Hud mawr y sydd ar hyd Môn;
    Cell oer, y mae'n colli lliw;
24 Odidog o fyd ydiw,
    Gweled am Rys a Gwilim
    Abid du heb wybod dim
    O ruwl y crefydd erioed,
28 Ac o gwfaint gogyfoed.

    Boed i nef bo Ednyfed,
    Môn aeth, ysywaeth, yn siêd;
    Hwn a wnaeth, marw garw gyffro,
32 Gyda'i frawd gado ei fro.
    Gwae Fôn am ei meibion maeth!

Widespread is the dress of grief
for the fine gentle imposing hawks,
36   men are wearing black clothes;
handsome in the seawind
were the ladies of Môn and her best men;
they have become, cold-lipped pronouncement,
40   all like phantoms now;
there is hardly a single nobleman in Môn
who is not in black clothes.
Green-backed Môn, chamber of song,
44   used to be called the dark island;
most fittingly, united land,
did it get its title and its own name;
the finest day of summer weather
48   will be night forever in Môn;
the shortest night of summer, longer
will it be than the long night of Mawddwy;
there is a cloud like seaweed smoke,
52   there is an eclipse over Môn for a month;
not finely does it darken,
there is nothing more than black fog to be seen,
except a weird image of terrible appearance
56   like looking into a bad mirror;
the earth was without light—
this is dreadful, the darkening of the sun—
on the great day—is there greater darkness?—
60   that he came to the choir of Dindaethwy.

    I am gloomy and distressed
at seeing everyone like a dumb watch.
Quite joyless, lightless
64   came the year to us;
losing a chieftain, hero of Gwynedd,
wise and bold, swift his sword,
lord of Cellan, terrible loss,
68   poets' chamber, court of Celliwig;
oak-shafted shaft-shattering companion,
great grip, lightning-flashing spear—
marvellous was the attack he made,
72   so cold the fate which carried him off!
One of the three great gentle maidens
was his most harmful stepmother:
Atropos, choice pretty goddess,
76   Clotho, Lachesis the colour of sunlight;
it was dreadful that they could terminate,

Gwasgarog yw gwisg hiraeth
Gwasgeddfawr weilch gwaisg addfwyn,
36 Gwasgodion gwŷr duon dwyn;
Heirdd oeddynt ym morwynt mŷr
Gwragedd Môn a'i goreugwyr;
Neur aethant, oerfant arfoll,
40 Weithion mal ellyllon oll;
Nid mawr un gwrda ym Môn
Dieithr mewn gwisgoedd duon.
Yr ynys dywell, cell cerdd,
44 Y gelwid Môn wegilwerdd;
Llwyr y cafas, llawr cyfun,
Ei chyfenw a'i henw ei hun:
Y dydd tecaf haf hinon
48 Nos fyth fydd yn Ynys Fôn;
Y nos ferraf o'r haf, hwy
Fydd no'r nos hir o Fawddwy;
Mae cwmwl fal mwg gwymon,
52 Y mae clipsis fis ar Fôn;
Nid diell yn tywyllu,
Ni wŷl dim mwy no niwl du,
Eithr eilun oeth uthr olwg
56 Megis edrych mewn drych drwg;
Daearen oedd diaraul—
Dihir yw hyn, duo'r haul—
Y dydd mawr—oes duedd mwy?—
60 Y doeth i gôr Dindaethwy.

Gorddu gennym ac arddwl
Gweled pawb fal gwyliad pŵl.
Diwyl iawn, dioleuni
64 Y doeth y flwyddyn i ni;
Colli cun, cyllaig Gwynedd,
Call a glew, cuall ei gledd,
Cellan iôr, coll anwerys,
68 Cell y clêr, Celliwig lys;
Câr paladrddar peleidrddellt,
Gafael fawr, gwayw ufel fellt—
Eres o hwyl a orug,
72 Oered y dynged a'i dug!
Un o'r tair morwyn mwyn mawr
Fu ei lysfam aflesfawr:
Tropos, dewistlos dwywes,
76 Cletis, Letisis liw tes;
Oerffwyr y cawsant orffen,

by work of magic, their white thread.
I would not wonder, I know of a hundred occasions,
80   had he drowned on broad Menai,
or on the North Sea, it was customary
when he was a ruler of the world;
but it was a shock to the people of this world
84   that his body sank in Kent;
in a pitted whirlpool
it happened on a Saturday, grievous accident;
and he was carried on a bier
88   from England to Môn, it will be a grim turn of events,
from London, old dwelling yonder,
to the edge of Môn, the border of the Isle of Man.
There never came to the half-naked Grey Friar
92   to be buried—oh the nightmare!—
to the coffin-burdened ground of Llan-faes
such a body, the grief was entire.

May he go to heaven to Ednyfed
96   his brother of the same family and the same generosity;
may God receive, in a severe plight,
the brothers into Paradise.

7 Elegy for Sir Rhys ap Gruffudd of Llansadwrn

Here are grim tidings for the nations,
the head of Wales's chief has been struck off now;
separated, fitting judgement, are the breast
4   and soul of the book of law;
the fall, heavy dark shame,
of golden Sir Rhys in his war belt.
Woe to those who saw him in Crécy,
8   a fine man like three in the fray,
a pack of watchdogs, of the same spirit as Kay,
brave clear mind in steel livery.
When he put on, free lord of tumult,
12   a steel helmet over Beli's forehead,
there was seen, it was abundant grace,
a mighty man by the shaft of a spear;
and most rare at nightfall

O hud waith, eu hedau wen.
Ni ryfeddwn, gwn ganwaith,
80 Pe boddai ar Fenai faith,
Neu ar Fôr Udd, arfer oedd
Penadur byd pan ydoedd;
Braw eisoes oedd i'r bresent
84 Suddo ei gorff yn Swydd Gent;
Mewn pwll trydwll troëdig
Y bu ar Sadwrn, dwrn dig;
A'i arwain ar elorwydd
88 O Loegr i Fôn, chwŷl garw fydd,
O Gaer Ludd, hen drefrudd draw,
I gwr Môn, goror Manaw.
Ni ddoeth at Frawd llednoeth Llwyd
92 I'w briddo—wb o'r breuddwyd!—
I lawr Llan-faes elorllwyth
Cyfryw gorff, bu cyfa'r gŵyth.

Aed i nef at Ednyfed
96 Ei frawd un giwdawd un ged;
Erbynied Duw, ar bwynt dwys,
Y brodyr i Baradwys.

Marwnad Syr Rhys ap Gruffudd o Lansadwrn

Llyma oerchwedl cenhedlawr,
Llas pen Cymry nen yn awr;
Gwahanwyd, brawd briawd, bron
4 Ac enaid llyfr y ganon;
Syrthio, anghlod swrth anghlaer,
Syr Rhys aur yng ngwregys aer.
Gwae a'i gweles yng Nghresi,
8 Gŵr diwael mewn trafael tri,
Dorgwn gyd, dau gyngyd Gai,
Dewr loywfryd mewn dur lifrai;
Pan wisgawdd, rydd gymlawdd ri,
12 Balaen uwch llethrben Beli,
Yno'i gwelad, nid rhad rhwy,
Gŵr praff wrth baladr saffwy;
Ac aruthr cael yn ael nos

16 was getting cold feet and staying [on the battlefield].
    When he came to France and the heavy slaughter
    with his lance and his fire alarm,
    there was heard there, before kindling fire,
20 a tumult preceding the noise of thunder,
    sign of trumpets, spears of anger,
    and the flash of bright lightning-fire;
    and we were called to his pillared wine-court,
24 praise of the circuit of Lord Rhys's golden sword,
    stout lion ruling with his arm
    the king's host in the place of the Scots.
    Philip of Valois, eager warrior,
28 knew whether he was a soldier,
    Uthr Bendragon, gay splendour,
    all of Paris shook from the blow.
    Image of St George with its hands
32 on the cross urgently pleading yonder;
    he never fled like a coward,
    he never sought the shelter of a cart because of battle;
    he was a wolf with an unflinching face,
36 a wolf was he, and he led a thousand;
    good was his remembrance in tribulation,
    and his spear was full of rage;
    he was high [amongst] the hosts of heaven,
40 and his golden crest over his strong golden helmet.

        I saw him, noble ruler,
    on a day of destruction, there was none like him,
    in a chancel, my stag, under cover,
44 hidden in the fort of Emrys's poet,
    a great body on the floor before me,
    and his kindred mourning him,
    and his spear in its fastening, woe who sees it,
48 and his stallion by his side,
    and his keen blade, jagged look,
    and his shield, all went to the ground,
    and his shining black mantle,
52 lord, and his banner upraised,
    and his funeral rites and his brilliant shroud,
    and his cuirass and his bright grey helmet,
    and his trappings like stars,
56 and his absence in his azure;
    and his soul, he was a lord,
    let that go to the Lord of heaven's fair country.

16   Ac oeri traed ac aros.
       Pan ddoeth at Ffranc a'r tranc trwm
       Â'i lorf a'i engyl larwm,
       Yno y bu, cyn tynnu tân,
20   Cynnwrf ym mlaen twrf taran,
       Arwydd trympau, berau bâr,
       A lluched mellt-dân llachar;
       A'n galw i'w golofn winllys,
24   Glod eurgledd rod Arglwydd Rhys,
       Llew braisg yn llywio â braich
       Llu brenin yn lle Brynaich.
       Gwybu Phylib, aerwib ŵr,
28   O Falois, od oedd filwr,
       Uthr Bendragon, lon lendyd,
       Aeth Paris ar gis i gyd.
       Delw Sain Siôr â'i dwylaw
32   Ar grog drwy fawr annog draw;
       Ni chiliodd yn wacheliad,
       Ni chyrchodd gwart cart er cad;
       Blaidd oedd â threm ddieiddil,
36   Blaidd oedd fo, a blaenodd fil;
       Da oedd ei gof mewn gofid,
       A'i laif yn gyflawn o lid;
       Uchel oedd niferoedd nef,
40   Â'i eurgest uwch helm eurgref.

       Mi a'i gwelais, lednais lyw,
       Dydd anrhaith, nad oedd unrhyw,
       Yng nghôr, fy ngharw, yng nghyhudd,
44   Yng Nghaer fardd Emrys ynghudd,
       Corff mawr ar y llawr gerllaw,
       A'i genedl yn ei gwynaw,
       A'i wayw ar gae, gwae a'i gwŷl,
48   A'i emys yn ei ymyl,
       A'i lem lifaid, drem drydoll,
       A'i aesawr, âi i'r llawr oll,
       A'i bebyll didywyll du,
52   Nêr, a'i faner i fyny,
       A'i arwyl a'i hwyl hyloyw,
       A'i guras a'i helm las loyw,
       A'i seirch yn gyfryw â sŷr,
56   A'i eisiau yn ei asur;
       A'i enaid, ydoedd ener,
       Aed ef i wenwlad nef Nêr.

8   Owain Glyndŵr's Genealogy

I have been considering for a baron
reassuring praise for him;
I will extoll Owain,
4   in metrical words I will gild
daily, not the hacking of alder trees,
the master carpenter's praise of Sirwern's peacock.
Who in all the region of broad Maelor,
8   peacock, lord of the watery land of Glyndyfrdwy,
who rightfully owns, if the world were as it should be,
—who but Owain, faithful peacock?—
the two Maelors of great rent,
12   except him, and Mathrafal?
Who will subdue the land of Powys,
if there were law and right dealing?
Who but the boy of princely stock,
16   Owain Gruffudd, he is a Nudd to us,
son of Gruffudd, red-bladed is the other,
strong-bodied, wise and witty,
great-grandson of Madog, lord who reaped Angles,
20   Fychan trampling Angles,
descendant of swift Gruffudd
Maelor, lord of a true land,
line of old long-lived Madog,
24   a Welshman by the lovely region of the Severn,
helmsman of all the land of the South,
the Lord Rhys's line, summons to battle,
Bleddyn's line, Cynfyn's line of old,
28   Aedd's line, they were of noble stock,
line of Maredudd of the red spear,
sovereign of Carneddau Teon,
line of the Gwinau Dau Freuddwyd,
32   line of Pywer Lew, my brown lion,
Ednyfed's line, honed blade,
holy Uchdryd's line, noble splendid lord,
great Tewdwr's line, ruler of people,
36   hunter with hawks, dispenser of wine,
line of Maig Mygrfras, straight-speared youth,
his poets will always be handsome by his will.
Greetings to a lovely protective lord,
40   a charge yonder in battle, Rhicert's line,
a baron whose lineage I know,
there was never a mightier baron;
worthless is every single baron

Achau Owain Glyndŵr

Myfyrio bûm i farwn
Moliant dyhuddiant i hwn;
Arwyrain Owain a wnaf,
4 Ar eiriau mydr yr euraf
Peunydd, nid naddiad gwŷdd gwern,
Pensaerwawd paun y Sirwern.
Pwy yng nghlawr holl Faelawr hir,
8 Paun, rhwy Glyndyfrdwy dyfrdir,
Pwy a ddylai, ped fai fyd,
—Pwy ond Owain, paun diwyd?—
Y ddwy Faelawr mawr eu mâl,
12 Eithr efo, a Mathrafal?
Pwy a ostwng Powystir,
Pe bai gyfraith a gwaith gwir?
Pwy eithr y mab penaethryw,
16 Owain Gruffudd, Nudd in yw,
Fab Gruffudd, llafnrudd yw'r llall,
Gryfgorff gymen ddigrifgall,
Orwyr Madog, iôr medeingl,
20 Fychan yn ymseingian Eingl,
Goresgynnydd Ruffudd rwydd
Maelawr, gywirglawr arglwydd,
Hil Fadog hiroediog hen,
24 Gymro ger hoywfro Hafren,
Hwyliwr yr holl Ddeheuwlad,
Hil Arglwydd Rhys, gwŷs i gad,
Hil Fleddyn, hil Gynfyn gynt,
28 Hil Aedd, o ryw hael oeddynt,
Hil Faredudd rudd ei rôn,
Tëyrn Carneddau Teon,
Hil y Gwinau Dau Freuddwyd,
32 Hil Bywer Lew, fy llew llwyd,
Hil Ednyfed, lifed lafn,
Hil Uchdryd lwyd, hael wychdrafn,
Hil Dewdwr mawr, gwawr gwerin,
36 Heliwr â gweilch, heiliwr gwin,
Hil Faig Mygrfras, gwas gwaywsyth,
Heirdd fydd ei feirdd o'i fodd fyth.
Hawddamor pôr eurddor pert,
40 Hwyl racw ym mrwydr, hil Ricert,
Barwn mi a wn ei ach,
Ni bu barwn bybyrach;
Anoberi un barwn

44 except the stock from which this one stems;
   great-grandson, indeed, from a fortress of the East,
   of Gwenllian from fair Cynan.

   Our two Gwynedds say,
48 he is good, may God keep him for us,
   to everyone in his patience and his sense,
   bear of fine sense from Deheubarth,
   conqueror of stubborn people,
52 the fierce cub is a young wolf,
   proud and brave, he would hack a shield,
   Beli of the Vale, fair bison,
   lion of Scotland, Peredur's hand,
56 thick-jacketed lion with a steel socket,
   pestle of battle, bold lordly father,
   post of the region of England, thick steel coat,
   he is a prince of an old family
60 from the head of Tref-y-traeth;
   his domain, he requests it,
   [is] Tref-y-garn, and he demands his judgement;
   he will be an heir, overpowering is his judgement,
64 the inheritor of the region of Acharn.

   A good, gentle, exemplary lad
   has he been until now, nobody knew;
   now he is referred to as a man,
68 not an acre of his land shall be taken;
   a stout, regal, swift knight,
   savage in the thick of battle;
   his war-cry, bone of swift strength,
72 rose up, from his foot he is a bold wolf.
   Harsh to the harsh, a man to others,
   humble and gentle to the rest,
   gentle to the weak, he shares his distress,
76 rough to churls.
   Lion of Is Coed, plentiful gifts,
   a hand which does damage to a host,
   feeding the crows, overpowering Scots
80 with a wooden staff greater than an armload.
   If I were to raise, living nourishment,
   a cub for anyone, shoot of a lord,
   fine noble face, course of a flying dragon,
84 for him would I do it, second Maig.

44   Eithr y rhyw yr henyw hwn;
       Gorwyr, dioer, o gaer Dwyrain,
       Gwenllian o Gynan gain.

       Medd y ddwy Wynedd einym,
48   Da yw, a gatwo Duw ym,
       Wrth bawb ei ortho a'i bwyll,
       Arth o Ddeheubarth hoywbwyll,
       Cynyddwr pobl cyneiddwng,
52   Cnyw blaidd ydyw'r cenau blwng,
       Balch a dewr, bylchai darian,
       Beli y Glyn, bual glân,
       Llew Prydain, llaw Peredur,
56   Llew siaced tew soced dur,
       Pestel cad, arglwydd-dad glew,
       Post ardal Lloegr, pais durdew,
       Edling o hen genhedlaeth
60   Yw ef o ben Tref-y-traeth;
       Ei gyfoeth, ef a'i gofyn,
       Tref-y-garn, a'i farn a fyn;
       Gwrthrych fydd, gorthrech ei farn,
64   Gwrthrychiad gorthir Acharn.

       Mab da arab dihaereb
       Hyd hyn fu, ni wybu neb;
       Gŵr bellach a grybwyllir,
68   Ni wneir dwyn un erw o'i dir;
       Marchog ffyrf rhieddog rhwydd,
       Mawrchwyrn lle bu'r ymorchwydd;
       Neur aeth, asgwrn nerth esgud,
72   Ei floedd, o'i droed mae'n flaidd drud.
       Garw wrth arw, gŵr wrth eraill,
       Ufudd a llonydd i'r llaill,
       Llonydd wrth wan, rhan ei raid,
76   Aflonydd i fileiniaid.
       Llew Is Coed, lluosog ged,
       Llaw a wna llu eniwed,
       Llithio'r brain, llethu Brynaich
80   Â llath bren mwy na llwyth braich.
       Be magwn, byw ymogor,
       Genau i neb, egin iôr,
       Hael eurddrem, hwyl awyrddraig,
84   I hwn y magwn, ail Maig.

Let us be quiet, it is best to be quiet,
we will say nothing about him;
good are teeth in front of the tongue, a day will come,
88   in the recess of a clumsy mouth,
when he will get, a belief which is asserted,
the heart of Is Aeron and its cheer,
and health and fine handsome children
92   in Sycharth, enclosure of the poets.
Corwen, Dyfrdwy, Conwy, Cain,
the like of vigorous Kay, Owain's domain;
the same battle, the same eye, the same hand,
96   pure golden fruit of the lord of Aberffraw;
sole head of Wales, bright form,
and Gwynedd's one soul,
one eye, slaughterer of slaves,
100   and one hand is he to Cynllaith.

9 Praise of Owain Glyndŵr

Great movement and strong magic
do we see on nobles.
Let us entreat Mary, it was a good entreaty,
4   to protect the swarthy bison,
fierce lord from the fair Vale
is the Pywer Lew, sovereign of Powys.
Who would recognise a fault in the world,
8   who but Owain, faithful peacock?
The pomp of the proud earl of bloody path,
the charge of Llŷr's son in every path.
Worthless is every single baron
12   except the stock from which this one stems;
Renowned is his grandfather's name,
king over the barons;
his father, everyone knew who,
16   lord of the Vale, cleft in the earth, of the Dee;
Hiriell, exemplum of Wales,
was his father above all others;
whoever the wise Welshman be,
20   what does it matter?—I know something else;
the best boy between man and mother

Tawwn, gorau yw tewi,
Am hwn ni ynganwn ni;
Da daint rhag tafod, daw dydd,
88 Yng nghilfach safn anghelfydd,
Cael o hwn, coel a honnir,
Calon Is Aeron a'i sir,
Ac iechyd a phlant gwycheirdd
92 Yn Sycharth, buarth y beirdd.
Corwen, Dyfrdwy, Conwy, Cain,
Cai fath hoyw, cyfoeth Owain;
Un gad, un llygad, un llaw,
96 Aur burffrwyth iôr Aberffraw;
Un pen ar Gymru, wen wedd,
Ac un enaid gan Wynedd,
Un llygad, cymyniad caith,
100 Ac unllaw yw i Gynllaith.

Moliant Owain Glyndŵr

Mawr o symud a hud hydr
A welwn ni ar welydr.
Archwn i Fair, arch iawn fu,
4 Noddi'r bual gwineuddu,
Arglwydd terwyn o'r Glyn glwys
Yw'r Pywer Lew, iôr Powys.
Pwy adwaenai bai'n y byd,
8 Pwy ond Owain, paun diwyd?
Rhwysg y iarll balch gwyarllwybr,
Rhysgyr mab Llŷr ym mhob llwybr.
Anoberi un barwn
12 Ond y rhyw yr henyw hwn;
Hynod yw henw ei daid,
Brenin ar y barwniaid;
Ei dad, pawb a wyddiad pwy,
16 Iôr Glyn, daeardor, Dyfrdwy;
Hiriell, Cymru ddihaereb,
Oedd ei dad yn anad neb;
Pwy bynnag fo'r Cymro call,
20 Bythorud?—gwn beth arall;
Gorau mab rhwng gŵr a mam

of Powys, ...e-mannered and fortunate;
if a boy, a boy who knows how
24 to love minstrels, thus is praise to be had.
He does not demand that anyone ask boys
their pedigree, he was never a bugbear;
He never took a toy against his will
28 from a boy except what he willingly got;
he never caused him pain
by a blow or a punch with his hands;
he never crooked his finger or uttered
32 so much as a boo, wise prudence.

When he reached strong manhood,
he was a fierce mighty slasher,
he did nothing but ride horses,
36 best time, in dark trappings,
bearing a lance, good bold lord,
a steel socket and a thick jacket,
wearing a rest and a mail cap
40 and a white helmet, a generous man with wine,
and in its peak, fine-plumed summit,
a red wing of the bird of Egypt.
For a while he was the best soldier
44 with Sir Gregory, he was a lord,
in Berwick, stubborn defiant town,
a steward to keep the fortress with him.
Great renown for knocking down a horesman
48 did he win when there was greeting,
and felling him splendidly
to the ground, with his shield in fragments.
And the second rout was a grim battle,
52 and his spear shattered from fury;
this is remembered as a disgrace today,
candle of battle, by the whole of Scotland;
some screaming, some wretched yonder,
56 every bad man, everyone indeed for fear of him
shouting like wild goats,
he caused terror, harsh he was to the Scots.
Great was the path through the froth of blood,
60 a year feeding wolves;
neither grass nor dock grew
nor corn where he had been,
from English-built Berwick
64 to Maesbury, huge was the booty.

O Bowys, foddlwys fuddlam;
Os mab, mab yn adnabod
24 Caru clêr, felly ceir clod.
Ni fyn i un ofyn ach
I feibion, ni bu fwbach;
Ni ddug degan o'i anfodd
28 Gan fab ond a gâi o'i fodd;
Ni pheris drwy gis neu gur
Iddo â'i ddwylo ddolur;
Ni chamodd fys na chymwyll
32 Cymain' â bw, cymen bwyll.

Pan aeth mewn gwroliaeth gwrdd,
Gorugwr fu garw agwrdd,
Ni wnaeth ond marchogaeth meirch,
36 Gorau amser, mewn gwrmseirch,
Dwyn paladr, gwaladr gwiwlew,
Soced dur a siaced dew,
Arwain rhest a phenffestin
40 A helm wen, gŵr hael am win,
Ac yn ei phen, nen iawnraifft,
Adain rudd o edn yr Aifft.
Gorau sawdwr gwrs ydoedd
44 Gyda Syr Grigor, iôr oedd,
Ym Merwig, hirdrig herwdref,
Maer i gadw'r gaer gydag ef.
Gair mawr am fwrw y gŵr march
48 A gafas pan fu gyfarch,
A'i gwympio yno'n gampus
I lawr, a'i aesawr yn us.
A'r ail grwydr a fu brwydr brid,
52 A dryll ei wayw o drallid;
Cof a chyfliw heddiw hyn,
Cannwyll brwydr, can holl Brydyn;
Rhai'n llefain, rhai'n druain draw,
56 Pob drygddyn, pawb dioer rhagddaw
Yn gweiddi megis gwyddeifr,
Gyrrodd ofn, garw fu i Ddeifr.
Mawr fu y llwybr drwy'r crwybr crau,
60 Blwyddyn yn porthi bleiddiau;
Ni thyfodd gwellt na thafol
Hefyd na'r ŷd ar ei ôl,
O Ferwig Seisnig ei sail
64 Hyd Faesbwrch, hydr fu ysbail.

10 Owain Glyndŵr's Court

I have promised twice before now,
fair promise, promising a journey;
let everyone fulfill, as much as is due,
4   his promise which he promises.
A very great pilgrimage,
certain prosperity, such a dear destination,
is going, swift promise,
8   it is beneficial, towards Owain's court;
swiftly will I go there,
not bad, there will I dwell
to bring honour into my life
12   by exchanging greetings with him;
my liege can, highest lineage,
bright golden head, receive an old codger;
it is praiseworthy, though it be but alms,
16   course without shame, to be kind to the old.
I will go to his court in haste,
the most splendid of the two hundred;
a baron's court, place of refinement,
20   where many poets come, place of the good life;
queen of great Powys, Maig's land,
promise of good hope.

This is its manner and its form
24   in a bright circle of water within an embankment:
(isn't the court fine?) a bridge on the lake,
and one gate through which would go a hundred loads;
there are couples, they are couple work,
28   every couple is coupled together;
Patrick's bellhouse, French fruit,
the cloister of Westminster, comfortable enclosure;
each corner is bound together in the same way,
32   golden chancel, it is entirely symmetrical;
bonds side by side above,
cheek-to-cheek like an earthhouse,
and every one looking like a tight knot
36   is tied fast to the next one;
nine-plated buildings on the scale of eighteen mansions,
fair wooden buildings on top of a green hill;
on four wonderful pillars
40   his court is nearer to heaven;
on top of each stout wooden pillar
a loft built firmly on the summit of a croft,

Llys Owain Glyndŵr

Addewais hyd hyn ddwywaith,
Addewid teg, addo taith;
Taled bawb, tâl hyd y bo,
4 Ei addewid a addawo.
Pererindawd, ffawd ffyddlawn,
Perwyl mor annwyl, mawr iawn,
Myned, eidduned oddáin,
8 Lles yw, tua llys Owain;
Yn oddáin yno ydd af,
Nid drwg, yno y trigaf
I gymryd i'm bywyd barch
12 Gydag ef o gydgyfarch;
Fo all fy naf, uchaf ach,
Eurben claer, erbyn cleiriach;
Clod bod, cyd boed alusen,
16 Ddiwarth hwyl, yn dda wrth hen.
I'w lys ar ddyfrys ydd af,
O'r deucant odidocaf;
Llys barwn, lle syberwyd,
20 Lle daw beirdd aml, lle da byd;
Gwawr Bowys fawr, beues Faig,
Gofuned gwiw ofynaig.

Llyna'r modd a'r llun y mae
24 Mewn eurgylch dwfr mewn argae:
(Pand da'r llys?) pont ar y llyn,
Ac unporth lle'r âi ganpyn;
Cyplau sydd, gwaith cwplws ŷnt,
28 Cwpledig pob cwpl ydynt;
Clochdy Padrig, Ffrengig ffrwyth,
Clostr Wesmustr, clostir esmwyth;
Cynglynrhwym pob congl unrhyw,
32 Cangell aur, cyngan oll yw;
Cynglynion yn fronfron fry,
Dordor megis daeardy,
A phob un fal llun llyngwlm
36 Sydd yn ei gilydd yn gwlm;
Tai nawplad fold deunawplas,
Tai pren glân mewn top bryn glas;
Ar bedwar piler eres
40 Mae'i lys ef i nef yn nes;
Ar ben pob piler pren praff
Llofft ar dalgrofft adeilgraff,

and the four lofts of loveliness
44   coupled together where poets sleep;
      the four bright lofts turned,
      a very fair nest load, into eight lofts;
      a tiled roof on every house with frowning forehead,
48   and a chimney from which the smoke would grow;
      nine symmetrical identical halls,
      and nine wardrobes by each one,
      bright fair shops with fine contents,
52   a lovely full shop like London's Cheapside;
      a cross-shaped church with a fair chalk-coloured exterior,
      chapels with splendid glass windows;
      a full bakehouse on every side of the court,
56   an orchard, a vineyàrd by a white court;
      a lovely mill on flowing water,
      and his dovecot with bright stone tower;
      a fishpond, hollow enclosure,
60   what is needed to cast nets;
      place most abounding, not for dispute,
      in pike and fine sewin,
      and his bord-land and his live birds,
64   peacocks, splendid herons;
      bright meadows of grass and hay,
      corn in well-kept fields,
      the rabbit park of our patriarch,
68   ploughs and sturdy horses, great words;
      by the court, outshining the other,
      stags graze in another park;
      his serfs perform all fitting tasks,
72   those are the necessities of an estate,
      bringing the best brew of beer from Shrewsbury,
      liquors of foaming bragget,
      every drink, white bread and wine,
76   and his meat and his fire for his kitchen;
      shelter of poets, everyone wherever he be,
      were it daily, he will have everyone there;
      loveliest wooden court, chief without fault,
80   of the kingdom, may God protect it;
      and the best woman of all women,
      blessed am I by her wine and her mead!
      Fair girl from the line of a knightly ruler,
84   she is dignified and noble by nature;
      and his children come in pairs,
      a fine nestful of chieftains.

A'r pedair llofft o hoffter
44　Yn gydgwplws lle cwsg clêr;
　　Aeth y pedair disgleirlofft,
　　Nyth lwyth teg iawn, yn wyth lofft;
　　To teils ar bob tŷ talwg,
48　A simnai lle magai'r mwg;
　　Naw neuadd gyfladd gyflun,
　　A naw gwardrob ar bob un,
　　Siopau glân glwys cynnwys cain,
52　Siop lawndeg fal Siêp Lundain;
　　Croes eglwys gylchlwys galchliw,
　　Capelau â gwydrau gwiw;
　　Popty llawn poptu i'r llys,
56　Perllan, gwinllan ger gwenllys;
　　Melin deg ar ddifreg ddŵr,
　　A'i glomendy gloyw maendwr;
　　Pysgodlyn, cudduglyn cau,
60　A fo rhaid i fwrw rhwydau;
　　Amlaf lle, nid er ymliw,
　　Penhwyaid a gwyniaid gwiw,
　　A'i dir bwrdd a'i adar byw,
64　Peunod, crehyrod hoywryw;
　　Dolydd glân gwyran a gwair,
　　Ydau mewn caeau cywair,
　　Parc cwning ein pôr cenedl,
68　Erydr a meirch hydr, mawr chwedl;
　　Gerllaw'r llys, gorlliwio'r llall,
　　Y pawr ceirw mewn parc arall;
　　Ei gaith a wna pob gwaith gwiw,
72　Cyfreidiau cyfar ydiw,
　　Dwyn blaendrwyth cwrw Amwythig,
　　Gwirodau bragodau brig,
　　Pob llyn, bara gwyn a gwin,
76　A'i gig a'i dân i'w gegin;
　　Pebyll y beirdd, pawb lle bo,
　　Pe beunydd, caiff pawb yno;
　　Tecaf llys bren, pen heb bai,
80　O'r deyrnas, nawdd Duw arnai;
　　A gwraig orau o'r gwragedd,
　　Gwyn fy myd o'i gwin a'i medd!
　　Merch eglur llin marchoglyw,
84　Urddol hael anianol yw;
　　A'i blant a ddeuant bob ddau,
　　Nythaid teg o benaethau.

Very rarely was bolt or lock
88   to be seen there,
nor did anyone act as porter;
there will be no want, beneficial gift,
nor lack nor hunger nor shame,
92   nor ever thirst in Sycharth.
The best Welshman, valorous feat,
owns the country, of Pywer Lew's line,
slender strong man, best spot,
96   and owns the court, splendid is the place.

11 Thanks for a Knife

Llywelyn, eagle of fine men,
fierce in battle, son of the tawny grey man,
prince and foster-son of praise,
4   refined, proud, virtuous hawk,
is there any better weapon, good is the handgift,
than the one you gave me, renowned gift?
A long knife, swift and sharp,
8   flint-tipped, good for cutting, grim-looking,
with boxwood hilt, hard sombre wood,
French frightener with a red pommel:
abundant shame on my stiff moustache
12   if I ever keep quiet about getting it!
Just as great a disgrace
is for a man to keep quiet about getting an auspicious hour.
What a baselard, it is a
16   leather-coated weapon, it can strike
with its foster-daughter, thorough design,
along its back, good equipment.
What would a valiant man want
20   but a silver chape and a knife?
Moreover, this is bolder,
place of battle, if the host goes to Scotland,
I could shave with it
24   the head of a red Scot—don't I know it?—
shear his beard, valiant weapon,
strike Frenchmen, chop the bodies of some,
shed low blood where I know,
28   cut savagely, fierce deed,
exposed sinews and veins,
hack bones, frail chip.

Anfynych iawn fu yno
88 Weled na chliced na chlo,
Na phorthoriaeth ni wnaeth neb;
Ni bydd eisiau, budd oseb,
Na gwall na newyn na gwarth,
92 Na syched fyth yn Sycharth.
Gorau Cymro, tro trylew,
Piau'r wlad, lin Pywer Lew,
Gŵr meingryf, gorau mangre,
96 A phiau'r llys, hoff yw'r lle.

Diolch am Gyllell

Llywelyn, eryr gwŷr gwych,
Llidfrwydr, fab y gŵr llwydfrych,
Gwahalaeth a mab maeth mawl,
4 Gwalch diwladeiddfalch deddfawl,
Ai gwell arf, gwiw yw'r llawrodd,
Nag a roist im, enwog rodd?
Cyllell hir cuall a llem,
8 Callestrfin holltrin hylltrem,
Bocs ei charn, pren cadarn prudd,
Bygylwraig Ffrainc bogelrudd:
Mefl fflwch i'm trawswch trasyth
12 O chelaf i ei chael fyth!
Cywilydd mawr cywala
Celu ar ddyn cael awr dda.
Wi o'r baslard, arf beisledr
16 Yw hi, arfodi a fedr
Â'i merch faeth, arfaeth yrfa,
Ar hyd ei chefn, dodrefn da.
Beth a geisiai erfai ŵr
20 Eithr arianswch a threinsiwr?
Ychwaethach, hyach yw hyn,
Lle brwydr, od â'r llu Brydyn,
Eillio â hi a allwn
24 Pen Ysgot coch—panis gwn?—
Cneifio ei farf, arf erfai,
Curo Ffrainc, dryllio cyrff rhai,
Lladd adwaed yn lle'dd adwaen,
28 Torri yn chwyrn, terwyn chwaen,
Gïau a gwythau ar gwthr,
Briwio esgyrn, brau ysgwthr.

If the Pictish host comes furtively
32   from the sea yonder, there is no great need for me,
     in order to cause shouts and commotion,
     to seek either sword or battleaxe,
     nor any weapon in my cruel hand
36   except a baselard with a blade on its belly.

     A sister by the same father, router of enemies,
     to fair Durendardd is she;
     cousin, sweet slaughter,
40   to Hawd y Clŷr, lovely bright sword;
     niece, true paragon of treasures,
     to Red Death, she is found in the fray;
     daughter by a wise pure mistress
44   to smooth fine Excalibur;
     if there be anyone who should oppose
     you for so much as an I or an O,
     enthroned man, with the granddaughter of Cwrseus
48   I will draw blood under his lip.
     If you see, my sharp-speared lord,
     golden plume, ask me straightaway,
     in my possession, bright fair weapons
52   or a good jewel in your thronged court,
     take, by Elian Ceimiad,
     carry it off, choice of battle;
     of like grasp to me, of like intent—
56   I own what is yours, son of a fair lord,
     you own, wherever you be,
     anything you wish of what is mine.

     You adorned my thigh, my liege,
60   long life to your head, sweet eloquent language;
     you are indeed brave in a gap,
     and you are very wise in two languages;
     merry is your custom to lively minstrels,
64   grim in battle your manners;
     aristocratic is your loving speech
     and without anger towards poor men;
     you were found firm to the firm,
68   humble and kind to the weak,
     gentle to your friend, shrewd and fond of song,
     a man to a man, harsh to another;
     sweet language, good play,
72   sombre in the fray, constricted field;
     giver of presents, it was a valiant gift
     that you gave me, a famous gift.

O daw dan llaw llu Ffichtiaid
32 O'r môr hwnt, im nid mawr rhaid,
I beri gewri a garm,
Geisio na chledd nac isarm,
Nac arf i'm llaw angiriol
36 Eithr baslard ag ysbard bol.

Chwaer undad, giliad galon,
I Ddurendardd hardd yw hon;
Cyfnitherw, dicherw dachwedd,
40 I Hawd y Clŷr, hoywdeg gledd;
Nith, ddiragrith oreugrair,
I Angau Coch, yn yng y'i cair;
Merch o ordderch ddiweirddoeth
44 I Galedfwlch gyfwlch goeth;
Osid neb a wrthnebo
I ti er nac I nac O,
Gŵr gorsedd, ag ŵyr Gwrseus
48 Y tynnaf waed dan ei weus.

O gweli, fy iôr gwaywlym,
Bluyn aur, arch o'r blaen ym,
Ar fy helw, arfau hoywlwys
52 Neu dlws da yn dy lys dwys,
Cymer, myn Elian Ceimiad,
Dos ag ef, dewis y gad;
Un afael im, un ofeg—
56 Mi biau'r tau, mab iôr teg,
Dithau biau, lle y bych,
O'r man finnau a fynnych.

Herddaist fy nghlun, fy muner,
60 Hoedl i'th ben, huodliaith bêr;
Dewr ar adwy, dioer, ydwyd,
A doeth iawn mewn dwy iaith wyd;
Masw dy arfer wrth glêr glau,
64 Di-fasw ym mrwydr dy foesau;
Dyledog dy serchog sôn
A dilidiog wrth dlodion;
Cadarn wrth gadarn y'th gaid,
68 Gŵyl ac annwyl i'r gweiniaid,
Gwâr wrth dy gâr, cerddgar call,
Gŵr wrth ŵr, garw wrth arall;
Dichwerwiaith, da o chwarae,
72 Prudd yn yr yng, gyfyng gae;
Clenigwr, calonogrodd
A roist im, enwog o rodd.

Oh for a fine diligent goldsmith
76 who would put leaves of red brass
and a splendid fillet of the same kind
with the appearance of gold, it is my booty,
it must be properly fitted across the sheath,
80 the same colour as a silver letter of Arabia,
so that it can more easily, fine sense of a thrust,
be worn on a long weak thigh.

More delightful to an old codger is a sword
84 or a baselard, my lord of constant feast,
more delightful to a slender lover
than to the ape her dumb son.
My heart does not worry
88 lest this should rust or grow old:
ten times, nature of a young lad,
will I draw the grey fine-sheathed blade
to turn it in a whirl around me
92 like a pure white flash of lightning from afar.
This is fun for a sprightly man,
the flashing of Cuhelyn's shield.
You will get, my chieftain of noble blood,
96 'good day' from me daily
as many times as it regularly
comes from its sheath, good place of praise:
health to your dear wise head,
100 cause of my gladdening.

12 To Request a Horse from Ithel ap Robert of Goedymynydd

Who amongst us, our chief trade,
wants, giving God as surety,
twenty marks worth of praise
4 for one horse, and more than a mark?
It is a great profit to get to weave praise
excellently for a stallion.
Only a few have a great deal of money,
8 a gentleman does not wish to bear cash;
another man, he wishes to bear money,
the pure man wishes to bear his praise.
A harp would create a lot of energy
12 leading a dance, one does not tire;

Och fi am eurych gwych gwydn
76 A rôi ddail o rudd elydn
A phenrwym oroff unrhyw
Yn rhith aur, fy anrhaith yw,
Tros y wain rhaid trwsio'n wiw,
80 Arianllythr Afia unlliw,
Fal y bo haws, gwiwnaws gwân,
Ei harwain ar glun hirwan.

Gwychach yw gan gleiriach gledd
84 Neu faslard, fy naf oeswledd,
Gwychach gan serchog achul
No chan yr âb ei fab mul.
Diofal gan fy nghalon
88 Rhag rhydu na henu hon:
Dengwaith, annwyd ieuangwas,
Y tynna'r llafn gloywhafn glas
I droi'n fy nghylch yn dröell
92 Fel mellten burwen o bell.
Digri gan ŵr heini hyn,
Heulo ysgwyd Guhelyn.
Ceffi di, rhi rhywiogwaed,
96 Gennyf i beunydd 'dydd daed'
Cynifer gwaith cynefawd
Y dêl o'i gwain, da le gwawd:
Iechyd i'th ben cymen cu,
100 Achos fy llawenychu.

I Ofyn March gan
Ithel ap Robert o Goedymynydd

Pwy i'n mysg, ein pen masgnach,
A fyn, a rhoi Duw yn fach,
O ganmol werth ugeinmorc
4 Am un march, a mwy na morc?
Elw mawr cael eilio mawl
Er gorwydd yn rhagorawl.
Nid tra ariannog ond rhai,
8 Dyn mwyn ni myn dwyn mwnai;
Dyn arall, myn dwyn arian,
Dwyn ei glod a fyn dyn glân.
Ynni dalm a wnâi delyn
12 O flaen dawns, ni flina dyn;

So does a good faultless dog,
loudly it seeks to the sound of the horn.
Praise lasts longer than a horse,
16 [or even] than iron, firm is my judgement;
the praise of a good tongue does not fail,
it does not spoil on water, it does not jib,
neither spavin nor the heat of a fit
20 of the staggers can cause song to sicken,
nor farcin, it does not graze on draff
like a heavy skinny squinting horse;
neither do its lungs tighten
24 nor disease grow in it.

    This is an exemplum about a hired thing,
it died of the staggers, great retribution;
yesterday it was worth a good deal to me,
28 tonight dead like an old carrion;
look where the carcass is
on a hillside to feed the crows.

    I must, before taking goods on credit,
32 make a petition to Argoed
and send a poem, true memory of artistry,
from me to Coedmynydd;
let rememberance, great fine golden gift,
36 be thrust into the head of the wise magician's wand,
Ithel grandson of Ithel, wonderful man,
great-grandson of terrible Ithel Llwyd,
bright, fair, choice language,
40 Ithel image of fair Michael,
aristocrat, three-fold table,
like a parson, pure and prudent,
a proper prelate, he is a pure member
44 to the church, golden well-bred ruler;
I was in unison, memory of a holy psalm,
with him chanting a while,
with the same teacher, lock of praise,
48 and our old master, it is known that we stem
from the same tribe from Gronwy Llwyd,
post of y Drefrudd, armour riddled with holes;
what is more from Gronwy, quite true,
52 wine-nurtured chieftain, son of Einion;
Uriel, pure angel, of the land of the Eingl,
you were enough for Englefield;
there is no patron saint of the cantref,
56 lamb of God, nor chief justice but him.

Felly gwna ci da diorn,
Llafar y cais gan llef y corn.
Hwy y pery na haearn
16 Gwawd na march, gwydn yw fy marn;
Ni ddiffyg gwawd tafawd da,
Ni lwgr ar ddŵr, ni lwyga,
Na llyngoes, ni all angerdd
20 Rhuthr o'r gysb ddieithrio'r gerdd,
Na ffarsi yw, ni phawr soeg
Fal ceffyl trymgul tremgoeg;
Ni wasg hefyd ysgyfaint
24 Ac ni fag ynddi hi haint.

Pregeth am hurbeth yw hon,
Marw o'r gysb, mawr argosbion;
Talai im ddoe talm o dda,
28 Heno'n farw fal hen furia;
Gwyliwch lle mae y gelain
Ar lethr bryn i lithio'r brain.

Dir im, cyn dwyn da ar oed,
32 Rhoi ergyd cais i'r Argoed
Rhyngof, uniawngof angerdd,
A Choedymynydd â cherdd;
Gyrthied cof, eurged fawrgoeth,
36 Ym mhen y dewinbren doeth,
Ithel ŵyr Ithel, ŵr uthr,
Orwyr Ithel Llwyd aruthr,
Etholedig iaith loywdeg,
40 Ithel delw Fihangel deg,
Pendefig, dridyblig dabl,
Personaidd pur rhesonabl,
Prelad iawn, pur aelod yw
44 I'r eglwys, aur rywioglyw;
Cydwersog, cof diweirsalm,
Fûm ag ef yn dolef dalm,
Gyda'r un athro, clo clod,
48 A'n henfeistr, gwŷs ein hanfod
O'r un llwyth o Ronwy Llwyd,
Post y Drefrudd, pais dryfrwyd;
Peth mwy o Ronwy, wir iawn,
52 Winfaeth bennaeth, fab Einiawn;
Uriel, bur angel, bro Eingl,
Digon oeddud i Degeingl;
Nid oes fabsant o'r cantref,
56 Oen Duw, na phenrhaith ond ef.

He has a herd, pleasant grace,
and stallions; why won't he give me one?
Let him not give a lean shoeless jibbing
60   horse to a sick old man,
lest he lie down, stubborn stance
carrying the burden, under his load.
If I were to receive the tribute of a rouncy
64   without a mane, he would go without me;
I know that by him in the summer
I will get a jittery foal;
Who will hold him while I shoe?
68   Who will stick on him?—I am sluggish;
if the horse runs across the field,
frenzied animal like a long-haired goat,
I would not stay, except at a slant,
72   in my saddle anymore than a goose's egg;
if a sow burrows and turns him,
it's wrong, I would fall on him;
if an old man's bum bruises,
76   if he falls, he'll never get a comfortable night;
if I bite the end of my tongue,
then will praise worsen;
a horse which trots is not good
80   for the curd-filled belly because of very great panting.

Here's how I would form it,
were it to be had this Easter holiday:
a hackney which would go along a causeway,
84   never stumbling, good and lightfooted.
Blessed too would be he in the summer
who should see as I will see
a good stocky faultless lad
88   and a horse in a cord halter
coming by agreement to me
as a present from a lord of true strength;
full joy, I would make
92   his messenger before day,
through God's welcome, take back good grace
to him who honours me.

Gre sy eiddo, gras eiddun,
A meirch; pam na rydd im un?
Na roed farch cul diarchen
60   Llwygus i ŵr heinus hen,
Rhag gorwedd, osgedd ysgwn
Yn dwyn y baich, dan ei bwn.
Pei caffwn ranswn rownsi
64   Heb fwng, ef âi hebof i;
Mi a wn ar hwn yr haf
Mai ebol goffol a gaffaf;
Pwy a'i deil tra pedolwyf?
68   Pwy a lŷn arno?—pŵl wyf;
O rhed march ar hyd y maes,
Gorwylltlwdn fal gafr walltlaes,
Ni thrigwn, eithr ar ogwydd,
72   I'm cyfrwy mwy nag wy gŵydd;
O thuria hwch a throi hwn,
Cam yw, arno y cwympwn;
O siga cloria cleiriach,
76   O syrth, ni ddwg un nos iach;
O brathaf flaen fy nhafawd,
Yna y gwaethyga gwawd;
Nid da i'r cylla ceullawn
80   March â thuth rhag morchwyth iawn.

Llyna megis y lluniwn,
Pes ceid yng ngwyliau'r Pasg hwn:
Hacnai a siwrneiai sarn,
84   Didramgwydd da didrymgarn.
Gwyn ei fyd hefyd yr haf
A'i gwelai modd y gwyliaf
Gwas gogwta da diort
88   Ac eddystr mewn cebystr cort
Yn dyfod dan amod ym
Yn anrheg gan iôn iawnrym;
Mi a wnawn, lawn lawenydd,
92   I'w gennad ef gyn y dydd,
Drwy groeso Duw, droi gras da
Wrtho ef a'm diwartha.

13 Thanks for a Horse

'By great God, spirited grey horse,
you are decaying badly;
you used to be a fine, plump, straight-shanked
4 courser, it's a pity you couldn't always be so;
you were the best racer,
it is distressing and painful for me after you
to see the place where you were reared empty,
8 and your manger without food.
What shall I do, under me to carry me,
for a big fine stallion?
An old man finds it very hard to walk
12 without having a rest, without a gift,
without a horse for me, unless I ask for one—
whom in Is Conwy I don't know.'

'I will give you advice against need,
16 to go to generous old Ithel
ap Robert, the lord is a handsome man,
principal, archdeacon of two choirs.
Some visited him, Ithel was glad,
20 on a bardic circuit, a coming together;
you need not—he will not thank—
either keep a kinsman waiting or visit on a circuit,
nor beg, dear necessity,
24 nor request, but go to him;
you will get a very fine steed
from him from his wine-bearing white hand.'

It was true—is there anyone like him?—
28 prince of the church, when he heard
that my horse had died—great to me was
the grief after losing it—
he sent some fine ones back,
32 it was grand choosing a colt
and leading a steed, spirited, grey,
elegant, fine, lovely, big of stature,
with tightly fitting hoof bound by a rope,
36 swiftly gliding, with a big bridle,
breast like a door, if the lord of York were to buy him
three marks would be an insult to him;
this is the top-class grey horse,
40 with wide-flaring nostrils, white-backed hooves and big reins.
I will be first poet to him,
nor will I be the last to receive from his hand.

I Ddiolch am Farch

'Rho Duw mawr, y march blawr blwng,
Mall yr wyd yn ymollwng;
Teg o gwrser tew garsyth
4 Oeddud, drwg na byddud byth;
Gyrfëydd gorau fuost,
I'th ôl dihir im a thost
Gweled yn wag lle'th fagwyd,
8 A bod dy breseb heb bwyd.
Beth a wnaf, danaf i'm dwyn,
Am orwyddfarch mawr addfwyn?
Gorddin gan gleiriach gerdded
12 Heb gael gorffowys, heb ged,
Heb farch im, onis archwn—
I bwy Is Conwy nis gwn.'

'Rhof gyngor it rhag angen,
16 Myned at Ithael hael hen
Ap Robert, fab pert yw'r pôr,
Iôn, archdiagon deugor.
Dogn a wnaeth, da gan Ithael,
20 Cadw cylch ag ef, cyd cael;
Nid rhaid i ti—ni ddiylch—
Nac oedi câr neu gadw cylch,
Nac erfyniaid, cyfraid cu,
24 Nac erchi, ond ei gyrchu;
Ti a gei eddystr teg iawn
Ganthaw o'i wenllaw winllawn.'

Bu gwir—oes ei debyg ef?—
28 Benaig eglwys, ban giglef
Marw fy march—mawr fu i mi
Edgyllaeth wedi'i golli—
Anfon anwylion yn ôl,
32 Syberw fu ddewis ebol
A hebrwng eddystr blwng blawr
Cain addfwyn teg cynyddfawr,
Carn geugraff mewn rhaff yn rhwym,
36 Buanrhwydd, mawr ei benrhwym,
Bronddor, pes prynai iôr Iorc
Dirmyg oedd arno deirmorc;
Neud hwn yw'r march blaenbarch blawr,
40 Ffroenfoll olwyngarn ffrwynfawr.
Cyntaf bardd fyddaf iddaw,
Nac ola' im gael o'i law.

Here is the field and here is the horse
44 in my possession, greeting of a support;
what good is this, may I urge fiercely,
I am trying to break him in;
in what swift bold manner
48 shall I get onto his back for fear?
A mounting-stone is needed, nimble feat,
heavy is a man bent as if carrying a hump;
I must avoid shepherds,
52 and order those who are dazed
on the road to flee out of my way,
let those who dare be warned,
from afar, not to say boo—
56 that is a loud harsh word;
I must avoid the mill
of Henllan, weak-roofed wizened hag,
and its clap like a floppy sow
60 below the road gobbling beans,
and its millrace, on a winter night,
and its stony road and its ditch;
I must watch out for the trap-filled ford
64 of Glyn Meirchion and the hollow Coedfron;
I must beware of the deep narrow hollow road
with its rocky slope above the church,
an awful road to Denbigh fair,
68 many a thornbush and branchy clumps of hedgerow.

However I fare, I am slow,
whether I fall, or I don't fall,
God's full blessing, true fair pillar,
72 on the man who gave it, best of gifts,
high festival feast, Uchdryd's line,
he is a venerable relic alive in the world.
The lantern of sense and its sanctuary,
76 the eye of the far Perfeddwlad,
patron saint's day of the whole of Englefield,
unconcealed fame—angel of the land of the Eingl,
great surpasser of others—
80 is his compared to the rest;
the colour of his face is more joyful,
my Nudd, and he is more generous than anyone;
wise saintly speech,
84 correctness like a tuning-string;
plumage of a wine-coloured bird laden with foam,
and the appearance of an archangel and his face;

Llyma'r maes a llyma'r march
44 Gwedi'i gael, gafael gyfarch;
Pa dda'r hyn, derwyn dyrrwyf,
Profi ei ddofi ydd wyf;
Pa ffunud ehud eofn
48 Ar ei gefn yr af rhag ofn?
Rhaid esgynfaen, chwaen chwimwth,
Trwm fydd dyn crwm fel dwyn crwth;
Rhaid im ochel bugelydd,
52 A gorchymyn rhai syn sydd
Ar y ffordd erof i ffo,
Rhybuddied rhai a'i beiddio,
O bell, rhag dywedyd bw—
56 Gair honnaid garw yw hwnnw;
Rhaid yw im ochel melin
Henllan, gwrach gronglwydwan grin,
A'i chlap megis hwch lipa
60 Is y ffordd yn ysu ffa,
A'i chafn, gan yr aeafnos,
A'i ffordd garegog a'i ffos;
Rhaid ymoglyd rhyd maglau
64 Glyn Meirchion a'r Goedfron gau;
Rhaid ofn y geuffordd ddofn ddwys
A'i chreiglethr uwch yr eglwys,
Ffordd enbyd ar ffair Ddinbych,
68 Aml draenllwyn a gwrysglwyn gwrych.

Bo a fo ym, aflym wyf,
Ai syrthio, ai na syrthiwyf,
Llwyr fendith Dduw, llorf iawndeg,
72 I'r gŵr a'i rhoes, gorau rheg,
Uchelwyl hwyl, hil Uchdryd,
Uchelgrair yw byw mewn byd.
Llugorn y bwyll a'i llogell,
76 Llygad y Berfeddwlad bell,
Dygwyl mabsant holl Degeingl,
Digel glod, angel gwlad Eingl,
Rhagorwr mawr rhag eraill,
80 Y sydd arnaw gerllaw'r llaill;
Llawenach lliw ei wyneb,
Fy Nudd, a haelach na neb;
Parabl rhesonabl rhyw sant,
84 Cywirdeb mal cyweirdant;
Ffrwyth edn ewynllwyth winlliw,
A phryd archangel a'i ffriw;

my magnanimous generous fosterfather
88   is Ithel to me now,
    and he is my third cousin, and my companion,
    an unbelievable thing, and my serf.
    Easy profit from Ithel
92   is readily obtainable for me,
    a splendid tribute, hawk of a kindred,
    supplying an old man with horses forever,
    and getting on every high festival
96   a gift and an invitation, easy course.
    Worthy body of quiet strength,
    many know it, well does he pay for song;
    he gave silver and burnished gold,
100   I am a horseman, and horses and gold,
    and his food and his drink on his table,
    descendant of Ricart—what a reputation!
    May God grant it, we say,
104   may it be true, long life to him!

14   The Soul's Conversation with the Body

Last night, late wandering to and fro,
the soul did converse
with the body which loved falsity,
4   it made a strange confession;
    the soul said, gracious necessity,
Soul   'Where are you, drunken body?'

Body   'What?' said the incomplete body,
8   hasty sense, at the top of his voice,
    'What evil, wanton, is the reason for this,
    what friend, who asks it?'

Soul   'It is me, my worldly language,
12   your fair soul, which has been travelling.'
Body   'Whereabouts did you go, awful shape?'
Soul   'I wandered throughout the world.
    I walked seeking you
16   across the two Gwynedds yonder,
    the way we went on foot once
    from house to house, they are good;
    I left no refined place
20   in Wales on my progress,

Fy nhadmaeth ehelaeth hael
88 Imi weithian yw Ithael,
A'm caifn ydyw, a'm cyfaillt,
Amau o beth, a'm mab aillt.
Ardreth dichwith gan Ithael
92 Y sydd ym gyflym i'w gael,
Pensiwn balch, gwalch gwehelyth,
Diwallu cleirch ar feirch fyth,
A chael ar bob uchelwyl
96 Anrheg a gwahawdd, hawdd hwyl.
Teilyngorff tawel angerdd,
Talm a'i gŵyr, da y tâl am gerdd;
Rhoddai arian a rhuddaur,
100 Marchog wyf, a meirch ac aur,
A'i fwyd a'i lyn ar ei ford,
Ŵyr Ricart—wi o'r record!
Duw i'w adael, dywedwn,
104 Poed gwir, bywyd hir i hwn!

Ymddiddan yr Enaid â'r Corff

Ymddiddan, bwhwman hwyr,
A wnaeth yr enaid neithiwyr
Â'r corff oedd yn caru ffug,
4 Cyffes eres a orug;
Meddai'r enaid, rhaid rhadlawn,
Enaid 'Mae ydd wyd, y corff meddw iawn?'

Corff 'Beth?' heb y corff anorffen,
8 Ehud bwyll, o hyd ei ben,
'Pa ddrwg, orhëwg, er hyn,
Pa gyfaillt, pwy a'i gofyn?'

Enaid 'Myfi ydyw, mau fydiaith,
12 D'enaid teg a fu'n dwyn taith.'
Corff 'Pa du buost, dost ystum?'
Enaid 'Ar hyd y byd rhodio bûm.
Mi a gerddais i'th geisiaw
16 Ar draws y ddwy Wynedd draw,
Ffordd y buam ar gam gynt
O dŷ i-dŷ, da ydynt;
Ni adewais lednais le
20 Yng Nghymru ar fy nghamre,

nor church, cause of wandering,
of Powys, the way we went,
without asking after you, this is the peace,
24   to the best men and the women.
No one knew where you were,
it is not easy to converse with a dumb man.
You in a feeble condition
28   on a couch, you are a skinny phantom,
snoring like a whirligig,
excessive boo, drunken man, from afar,
whilst I walked, I sent praise,
32   through Ceri, excellent land,
and the smooth-planked Newtown,
borough on the model of Paradise.
In Maelienydd I clung
36   to your track like a hunting dog to a hart,
by the houses of the sons, Lleon's host,
of fine, brave, wise Phylib Dorddu.'

Body   'Magnificent people of great nobility,
40   dear me, were they in good health?'

Soul   Men of Elfael, proud valiant stags,
alive and well, there are no finer hawks.'

Body   Did you go to the land of Buellt,
44   a country of fair trees and grass?'
Soul   'I did, and pleasant it was to be there,
kingly appearance of a famous bright region.
Thick were your tracks,
48   God's vengeance, in Ystrad Tywi,
like Adam's tracks, they were numerous,
when he was driven, he was summoned long ago,
for the apple, harsh punishment,
52   with his tribulation from Paradise.
The rich land was the prosperity of the country,
a country which has always been most renowned.
The three cantrefs are stronger than six,
56   Caeo is better than nine [cantrefs] of heaven.'

Body   'Did you see the men of Kidwelly?'
Soul   'Fine bright street, I saw three;
it was enough for me, good scions,
60   to see the three, princes of battle.'

Na llan, bwhwman baham,
O Bowys, ffordd y buam,
Heb dy ofyn, hyn yw'r hedd,
24   I'r goreugwyr a'r gwragedd.
Ni wyddiad neb p'le'dd oeddud,
Nid hawdd ymadrawdd â mud.
Tithau yn egwan d'annwyd
28   Mewn glwth, ellyll meingul wyd,
Yn chwyrnu megis chwyrnell,
Gormodd bw, gŵr meddw, o bell,
Dra gerddais, anfonais fawl,
32   Drwy Geri, gwlad ragorawl,
A'r Drefnewydd lifwydd lefn,
Bwrdeistref baradwystrefn.
Ymlynais ym Maelienydd
36   Dy ôl di fal helgi hydd,
Ger tai meibion, Lleon llu,
Phylib goeth dewrddoeth Dorddu.'

Corff   'Uchelrwysg bobl wych haelryw,
40   Och fi, a oeddynt iach fyw?'

Enaid 'Gwŷr Elfael, geirw gwrolfeilch,
Byw a iach, nid gwychach gweilch.'

Corff   'A fuost yng ngwlad Fuellt,
44   Elfydd deg ei gwŷdd a'i gwellt?'

Enaid 'Bûm, a gwaith digrif oedd bod,
Brenhinwedd bro wen hynod.
Tew oedd yn Ystrad Tywi,
48   Dial Duw, dy olau di,
Mal ôl Addaf, aml oeddynt,
Pan yrrwyd, gofynnwyd gynt,
Am yr afal, dial dwys,
52   Â'i bryder o Baradwys.
Gwladlwydd fu'r tir goludlawn,
Gwlad fu erioed glodfawr iawn.
Na chwech trech yw'r trychantref,
56   Gwell Caeaw na naw o nef.'

Corff   'A welaist wŷr Cydweli?'
Enaid 'Gwiw olau stryd, gwelais dri;
Digon gennyf, da egin,
60   Gweled o'r tri, gwelydr trin.'

Body   'Did you go, most perfect place,
        to the upper limits of the Taf?'

Soul   'The head, master of monks,
  64   of the White House is there, he is fair and fine;
        saviour of all, it is true,
        the good man is the best of men.'

Body 'What did he ask you,
  68   the abbot of the wine-drinking White House?'

Soul   For you to come to him to Dyfed,
        and if you go you'll get a gift;
        send an authorised messenger
  72   to fetch a mark, and ask for more.
        Wake up, from there we'll go
        towards the duchy of Ceredigion,
        the wealthy land is richly endowed,
  76   and greet Rhydderch the giver
        son of Ieuan Llwyd, nature of a bear,
        provost, fine post of Deheubarth.
        Loving Rhydderch finds it easy
  80   to give away his goods very freely.
        The abbot of the land of Florida will not let you
        suffer any distress, though he give you three florins.
        The lord of Caron, he is very good,
  84   will make up the same sum of money.
        Generous Gruffudd, it will be easy to get a gift,
        heart of the descendants of Gwrwared,
        son of Einion Fychan the chieftain,
  88   he is the soul of men; no worse is
        Dafydd, free flower of Rhos,
        bountifulness, the man of Caerwedros,
        no one finds it easier—I know his nature—
  92   to scatter money in exemplary fashion.
        The descendants of Gruffudd, unconcealed gift,
        may he be in heaven, son of Ednyfed,
        your friends, good faultless honour,
  96   will give you fair presents,
        and others of the best ones
        if I knew them, I know it is not false;
        I warrant, this summer
 100 we will get, this is my opinion,
        everyone will receive, splendid people,
        not one is bad, worth sixty nobles.'

Corff 'A fuost, lle difeiaf,
   Ym mlaenau terfynau Taf?'

Enaid 'Mae yno pen, meistr mynych,
64 Y Tŷ Gwyn, teg yw a gwych;
   Gwaredwr pawb, gwir ydiw,
   Gorau o'r gwŷr yw'r gŵr gwiw.'

Corff 'Beth yw y bu i'th ofyn,
68 Abad y Tŷ gwinllad Gwyn?

Enaid 'It ddyfod ato i Ddyfed,
   Ac od ei ti a gei ged;
   Gyr gennad yn goeladwy
72 I gyrchu morc, ac arch mwy.
   Deffro, oddyno ydd awn
   Ger dugiaeth Geredigiawn,
   Doniog yw'r oludog wlad,
76 Ac annerch Rhydderch rhoddiad
   Ab Ieuan Llwyd, annwyd arth,
   Probost, hoywbost Deheubarth.
   Hawdd gan Rydderch serchlawn
80 Rhoddi ei dda yn rhwydd iawn.
   Abad, ni ad arnad ing,
   Tir Fflur, er rhoi tair fflwring.
   Arglwydd Carawn, da iawn yw,
84 Arianrhif a wna'r unrhyw.
   Gruffudd hael, hawdd fydd cael ced,
   Calon wyrion Gwrwared,
   Ab Einion Fychan bennaeth,
88 Enaid y gwŷr yw; nid gwaeth
   Dafydd, flodeuyn rhydd Rhos,
   Ciriedrwydd, gŵr Caerwedros,
   Nid haws—gwn ei naws—gan neb
92 Hau arian yn ddihaereb.
   Wyrion Gruffudd, ddi-gudd ged,
   Bid yn nef, fab Ednyfed,
   Dy geraint, dafraint difreg,
96 A rydd i ti roddion teg,
   Ac eraill o'r rhai gorau
   Pes adnapwn, gwn nad gau;
   Mi a wrantaf, yr haf hwn
100 Y cawn, hyn a amcanwn,
   Pawb a erbyn, pybyrbobl,
   Nid drwg neb, werth trigain nobl.'

Body   'If you ever go from the land of the South,
104   if well, why not to Sycharth?
           When you go, looking homewards,
           stay, indeed, a while with him.
           God will be a support to an unfailing man,
108   and a help to you to gather everything.
           We will get to collect corn and lambs
           freely through the rich-yielding Perfeddwlad.
           If you do not wish to stay at [the] fair house
112   you need only run,
           make a fine charge at Ithel
           to Coedymynydd furtively.
           Most generous man, he gives his possessions,
116   a poor man would certainly get a gift from his hand.
           The lowest parson or layman,
           he stands on his account, or bows;
           after that, old Culfardd,
120   he sits and plays and laughs.
           It is not fair, nor pleasant, not good
           for an old man to lead the life of a travelling minstrel
               anymore.
           Like a lord's feast the same is ready for you
124   as for him, seek to be present at a festival.

15   Elegy for Ithel ap Robert

           Prodigiously did plants of plague
           break the surface of the earth this hour,
           and prodigiously does it rear terror
4   upon the earth, ball soaked in drips;
           there is a shivering, a cold trembling of fear,
           of the access, hot fit of fever.
           A storm came, it was Tuesday,
8   a great day between the end of March
           and April, profitless for us,
           on Thursday the horror began
           between the new day and the night—
12   few know what cause;
           a great blow, the death of Ithel
           ap Robert, handsome man, generous man
           who gave us burnished gold
16   in plenty and silver and gold;
           virtuous stone, lustre and heat,

Corff   'Od ei byth o'r Deau barth,
104   Os iach, pa waeth i Sycharth?
        Pan elych, edrych adref,
        Trig, od gwn, tro gydag ef.
        Duw fydd porth i ŵr difeth,
108   A help it i hel pob peth.
        Yta ac wyna a gawn,
        Rhad drwy'r Berfeddwlad fuddlawn.
        Oni mynny ddal tŷ teg
112   Nid rhaid i ti ond rhedeg,
        Dwg ruthr deg ar Ithel
        I Goedymynydd dan gêl.
        Rhwyddaf dyn, rhydd yr eiddaw,
116   Neu ry gâi dlawd ged o'i law.
        Lleiaf person a llëyg,
        Cyfyd 'n ei blegyd, neu blyg;
        Gwedy hynny, hen Gulfardd,
120   Eiste a chware a chwardd.
        Nid teg, nac addwyn, nid da
        Bellach i gleiriach glera.
        Parod yw it fal porwyl
124   Cystal ag ef, cais dal gŵyl.'

Marwnad Ithel ap Robert

        Eres y torres terra
        Yr awr hon planhigion pla,
        Ac eres y mag orofn
4   Arni, bellen ddefni ddofn;
        Mae achreth, oergreth ergryd,
        Yr acses, crynwres y cryd.
        Tymestl a ddoeth, neud Diwmawrth,
8   Dydd mawr rhwng diwedd y Mawrth
        Ac Ebrill, di-ennill yn,
        Difiau bu dechrau dychryn
        Rhwng y dydd newydd a'r nos—
12   Bychan a ŵyr ba achos;
        Mawr o wth, marw o Ithael
        Ap Robert, fab pert, fab hael
        A roddes i ni ruddaur
16   Llydan ac arian ac aur;
        Maen rhinweddol, graen a graid,

pure great shining pearl,
angelic miracle-working jewel of the Eingl,
20 pure, good and fair, butterfly of Englefield,
friend of his country, governor of a feast,
Croes Naid and soul of Gwynedd,
brother of an angel, youthful appearance,
24 every good [person] and bad, it pierces everyone;
no one ever passed judgement on him,
the fault was that he did not live on.
Marvellous man, Ithel was the best
28 of scholars, generous old man;
there is hardly any generous man
left in the world since his death.
Woe to them the minstrels in wind and rain
32 and the earth darkened;
there was never on the earth, though it be short,
a storm or any weather
until today, unnatural and terrible,
36 such as this—oh my tall lord!

Holy God is sending angels
as a guard to fetch him,
greatest task, it was agreed,
40 in praise of the thousand thousands,
as God did, clear from heaven,
it was good, after the passion,
when great false empty hell
44 was harrowed, empty swamp,
and the broad pure brown earth
shook—oh the cold;
then He sent Jesus
48 back, he was His beloved son,
and a host of angels like this,
glorious lord, to meet him
and take him without dispute or ostentation
52 safely home to heaven:
that is the magnificent funeral
which God gave him by His strength.

No less now the tumult
56 which came together before the first hour of day
to accompany the worthy fair body
of the apostle without ceasing;
never did so many wise men
60 come together in this island;
this made the weather cold,

Mererid glân mawr euraid,
Glain gwyrthfawr engylawr Eingl,
20   Glân da teg, gloyn Duw Tegeingl,
Câr ei wlad, gwledychiad gwledd,
Croes Naid ac enaid Gwynedd,
Brawd i angel, bryd iangaidd,
24   Pob drwg a da, pawb a draidd;
Neb arno ef ni barnai,
Am na bu fyw ef fu'r bai.
Gŵr uthr, gorau oedd Ithael
28   O'r meibion llên, gŵr hen hael;
Ni bu eto i'r bytwn
Ynemor hael gan marw hwn.
Gwae hwynt glêr mewn gwynt a glaw
32   A'r ddaear wedy'r dduaw;
Ni bu ar honno, cyd bo byr,
Dymestl nac un ardymyr
Hyd heddiw, anwiw enwir,
36   Gyfryw â hyn—gwae f'iôr hir!

Anfon engylion yng ngŵyl
I'w gyrchu, fwya' gorchwyl,
Mae Duw gwyn, amodig oedd,
40   Er moliant i'r fil filioedd,
Mal y gwnaeth, amlwg o nef,
Duw, da oedd, wedi dioddef,
Pan ddarfu, ddirfawr euwag,
44   Ysbeilio uffern, wern wag,
A chrynu—och o'r annwyd—
O'r ddaear lydan lân lwyd;
Yna'r anfones Iesu
48   Yn ôl, ei fab annwyl fu,
A llu o engylion fellýn,
Iôn eurbarch, yn ei erbyn
I'w ddwyn heb grocs, difocsach
52   Adref hyd y nef yn iach:
Llyna dermaint da'i armerth
A wnaeth Duw iddo o'i nerth.

Yr awran nid llai'r owri
56   A ddoeth i gyd cyn pryd pri
I hebrwng corff teilwng teg
Yr abostol heb osteg;
Ni ddoeth i gyd o ddoethion
60   Y sawl yn yr ynys hon;
Hyn a wnaeth yr hin yn oer,

getting hail from the hard moon;
the black earth, driving dust,
64   shaking—how great the trembling!—
mother of all fertile flourishing crops,
cold cloak, because of the size of its load,
when they set off, keen nightmare,
68   to the church, pure scent,
from Coedymynydd with him,
and all his family lamenting,
and the angels, good godly men,
72   before the tumult of the lord's host
were making a great murmuring noise
between the sky and the surface of the road,
and greater men handling horses,
76   prancing and plump trampling the turf,
and noise from fine musicians
and laymen and an enormous host,
and the bells and confusion of clergy and rattling
80   were to be heard, so grievous was the uproar,
and the treble of monks and tumult
and sombre preaching Brothers
chanting a psalm, fine sweet voice,
84   and a litany most solemnly.

    Woe to two thousand after he came
inside the church, lovely praise,
and the lighting, woe to many,
88   three times greater than a cluster of stars,
of bright shining torches of burning wax
like lanterns, total phosphoresence;
beyond number in the church were
92   the proud noblemen, fine crowd,
some wringing their hands, sad sight,
great distress like the grip of death,
some pulling out the hair from
96   every part of their heads like grass from the ground;
maidens, lovely display,
some collapsing, some fainting,
and beggars, grievous men,
100   moaning above all;
many a squire behind
shouting ceaselessly, woe to the weak,
many a tear on a woman's cheek,
104   many a sad nephew, many a niece,
many a feeling of the futility of long life,
oh me if only he were alive and well!

Cael adlaw o'r caledloer;
Y ddaear ddu, dyrru dwst,
64 Yn crynu—faint fu'r crynwst!—
Mam pob cnwd brwd brigogffrwyth,
Mantell oer, rhag maint ei llwyth,
Ban gychwynnwyd, breuddwyd brau,
68 I'r eglwys, lân aroglau,
O Goedymynydd ag ef,
A'i dylwyth oll yn dolef,
A'r engylion, deon da,
72 Rhag twrf y rhi gatyrfa
Oedd yn gwneuthur murmur mawr
Rhwng wybr a'r arllwybr orllawr,
A gwŷr mwy yn gware â meirch,
76 Sathr tew yn sathru tyweirch,
A sôn gan gerddorion gwrdd
A lleygion a llu agwrdd,
A chlywed, tristed fu'r trwst,
80 Clych a chrwydr clêr a chrydwst
A threbl mynaich a thrabludd
A Brodyr pregethwyr prudd
Yn lleisio salm, llais hoywlwys,
84 A letenia yn dda ddwys.

Gwae ddwyfil gwedi'i ddyfod
O fewn yr eglwys, glwys glod,
A goleuo, gwae lawer,
88 Tri mwy na serlwy o sêr,
Torsau hoyw ffloyw fflamgwyr
Fal llugyrn, tân llewyrn llwyr;
Mwy na dim oedd mewn y deml
92 O'r gwyrda beilch, gwiw ardeml,
Rhai'n gwasgu bysedd, gwedd gwael,
Mawr ofid fal marw afael,
Rhai'n tynnu top o boparth
96 Gwallt y pen megis gwellt parth;
Rhiannedd, cymyrredd cu,
Rhai'n llwygo, rhai'n llewygu,
A rheidusion, dynion dig,
100 Yn udo yn enwedig;
Llawer ysgwïer is gil
Yn gweiddi fyth, gwae eiddil,
Llawer deigr ar rudd gwreignith,
104 Llawer nai oer, llawer nith,
Llawer affaith ofer feithfyw,
Och fi na fyddai iach fyw!

Many a hoarse shout, a hundred clerics' bells,
108   and shrieking until evening;
around the body clad in purple
the convent did sing
holy chants beautifully,
112   entertainment by the choir, fair funeral;
the cross-shaped church shook
with the resounding and the heavy sound
like a broad ship at anchor,
116   fraily does it tremble on the sea.

Woe to you Iolo, woe to his family,
from the golden robes to the black pit;
casting fine gravel or grit
120   on top of him was the covering;
and many cries, great utterance,
everyone around him as if there was a battle;
it is known in every court and church
124   that the earth has split into three parts.

Excessive lamentation is unfitting
for a man like him, heaven to us,
after he has had, generous elder,
128   a fair life and state from God,
silence is better than harsh lamenting,
painful loss, for a fine stag;
this is what would be good for him,
132   worshipping Christ without moaning,
giving a resting-place, well would it happen,
to his soul, he was God's lamb,
with Elijah, holy tread,
136   and Enoch in glory;
they will not come, the two sombre saints,
they are brothers, from Paradise
until, the time of the right hand,
140   the Judgement Day comes in the final testing;
then we will see our prince,
woe and wind, strong firm condition;
there will not be on top of the high Mount
144   of Olives, perfect hero,
a fairer lord archdeacon
than will be Ithel of noble lineage.

Aml gwaedd groch, can cloch clêr
108 A diasbad hyd osber;
Ynghylch y corff mewn porffor
Canu, cyfanheddu côr,
Arodion saint yn rhydeg
112 A wnâi'r cwfaint, termaint teg;
Siglo a wnâi'r groes eglwys
Gan y godwrdd a'r dwrdd dwys
Fal llong eang wrth angor,
116 Crin fydd yn crynu ar fôr.

Gwae di Iolo, gwae'i deulu,
O'r pyllaid aur i'r pwll du;
Bwrw mân raean neu ro
120 Ar ei warthaf fu'r ortho;
A llawer gawr, fawr fwriad,
Pawb o'i gylch fal pe bai gad;
Hysbys ymhob llys a llan
124 Dorri'r ddaear yn deirran.

Drwg y gweddai dra gweiddi
Am ŵr fal ef, nef i ni,
Gwedi cael, hael henuriad,
128 Oes deg gan Dduw ac ystad,
Gwell tewi na gweiddi garw,
Amrygoll tost, am rygarw;
Llyma oedd dda iddo ef,
132 Addoli i Grist heb ddolef,
Rhoi gorffwysfa, da daroedd,
I'w enaid ef, oen Duw oedd,
Gydag Eli, sengi sant,
136 Ac Enog mewn gogoniant;
Ni ddeuant, y ddeusant ddwys,
Brodyr ŷnt, o Baradwys
Oni ddêl, hoedl ddeau law,
140 Dyddbrawd yn y diweddbraw;
Yno y gwelwn ein gwaladr,
Gwae a gwynt, cadarnbwynt cadr;
Ni bydd ar ben Mynydd maith
144 Olifer, porffer perffaith,
Iôn archdiagon degach
Nag fydd Ithel uchel ach.

16   The Court of Ieuan, Bishop of St Asaph

Greetings, most noble line of Awr,
rich lord bringing prosperity to his land;
greetings today, amen,
4   to scholars, readers of books,
and squires, handsome company,
nobles, faultless band,
and his chamberlain, fine kernel,
8   that man is my soul of all the handful,
and the chief cook, he was found preparing,
the well-dressed doorman,
and the pantler and the little butler—
12   my soul! Was there ever a gentler man?—
baker, beerman, third turn,
cater—may Good keep him!—
and the man who dispenses oat-fodder
16   and tender hay to the men and their horses,
and the man for me, not a hindering word,
out of respect who opened the gate;
I was a dear companion in good form
20   celebrating a festival with them;
I am a thoroughly joyful Llywarch Hen,
unrestricted, I come and go as I please,
good is my condition, no weak invitation,
24   in the winter with Ieuan;
nothing ever occurred there
to stop me from getting—may he be healthy—
as much as the kernel of a nut,
28   health and life to his head!

I knew, when I met him
in the court, famous home,
I would be welcomed dearly—
32   long life to my fine gracious lord!—
and crossed, where Asaph loves me,
against evil with his two good fingers;
hardly is there, free in every manner,
36   one day when I wouldn't get his blessing;
it came from his mouth twice daily,
by Mary, or three times a day.
A great lovely brilliant mass
40   would I get, and that in song,
mean, treble, quatreble, keenness of repentance,
and constant bourdon, lovely tune;

Llys Ieuan, Esgob Llanelwy

Hawddamawr, hil Awr hael iawn,
Arglwydd gwladlwydd goludlawn;
Hawddamawr heddiw, amen,
4   I feibion, lleodron, llên
Ac ysgwieriaid, haid heirdd,
Dledogion, deulu digeirdd,
A'i siambrlain, gain gnewyllyn,
8   F'enaid o'r dyrnaid yw'r dyn,
A'r pen-cog, darpan y cad,
A'r drysor da ei drwsiad,
A'r pantler a'r bwtler bach—
12   F'enaid! A fu ddyn fwynach?
Pobydd, cyrfydd, trydydd tro,
Cater, poed Duw a'i catwo!
A'r gŵr a ran ebrangeirch
16   A'r gwair mân i'r gwŷr a'u meirch,
A'r gŵr im, nid gair amorth,
Er parch a egorai'r porth;
Cydymaith cu diamwynt
20   Yn cadw gŵyl fûm cydag wynt;
Llywarch Hen llawen oll wyf,
Trwyddedog, treiddio'dd ydwyf,
Da f'ansawdd, nid gwahawdd gwan,
24   Y gaeaf gydag Ieuan;
Ni ddamweiniai ddim yno
Na chawn beth—yn iach y bo—
Cymyn' cnewyllyn cneuen,
28   Iechyd a bywyd i'w ben!

   Gwn, pan gyfarffwn ag ęf
Yn y cwrt, enwog gartref,
Fy nghroesawu'n gu a gawn—
32   Hir hoedl i'm naf hoyw rhadlawn!—
A'm croesi, lle'm câr Asa,
Rhag echrys â'i ddeufys dda;
Odid fydd, rhydd ym mhob rhith,
36   Undydd na chawn ei fendith;
Doeth o'i ben dwywaith beunydd,
Myn Mair, neu dair yn y dydd.
Offeren fawr hoff eirian
40   A gawn, a hynny ar gân,
mên, trebl, chwatrebl, awch atreg,
A byrdwn cyson, tôn teg;

```
        after mass I would go
44      to the well-proportioned wood-filled hall;
        he would have me placed
        at a fitting position in the hall
        to sit up in full view
48      at the high table, fair custom;
        dish after dish the same
        as would come to the lord, he is a Nudd;
        drink after drink will come
52      from his vineyard to me from his white hand.
        I would get eloquent nostalgic poetry,
        string music, splendour;
        pleasant clear sweet harmony,
56      I would have pipes and dance every day.
        There is no great—he's not so mean—
        wardrobe of such a generous bishop,
        nor office in his abode
60      that was not open to all manner of men;
        he does not hinder me from going to the court,
        or coming slowly and unhurriedly;
        Freely in every place does he give
64      me a room, a mead-cellar;
        kitchen, pantry, buttery, food
        when I will; when it is cold
        I would have a turf or log fire,
68      there's none of the dumb sea-coal there.
        In the bishop's room,
        unfailing nature, I would get everything:
        cardamom seeds, rice, raisins,
72      herbs, mead, a fine feast and wine.
        Then to the chamberlain's chamber,
        there I would go at my leisure;
        I would drink for a while,
76      and chat too with him,
        good free-flowing liquor
        in my lord's horns, in a case.
        Sleeping on down or cambric
80      and a hundred sheets and bed-clothes
        amongst a thousand coverlets,
        and the costly purple of the purfil
        and the fur on the cymar and the cope
84      and his robes—oh what a bishop!
        I could have, unselfish grasp,
        every material with him, my generous lord,
        gentle, kind companion,
88      lord of splendid office over a monastic community;
```

Ar ôl offeren yr awn
44 I'r neuadd gydladd goedlawn;
Peri fy rhoddi ar radd
Iawn a wnâi yn y neuadd
I eistedd fry ar osteg
48 Ar y ford dâl, arfer teg;
Anrheg am anrheg unrhyw
A ddôi i'r arglwydd, Nudd yw;
Diod am ddiod a ddaw
52 O'i winllan im o'i wenllaw.
Cerdd dafod ffraeth hiraethlawn,
Cerdd dant, gogoniant a gawn;
Cytgerdd ddiddan lân lonydd,
56 Pibau, dawns, a gawn pob dydd.
Nid mawr un, nid mor anael,
Gwardrob y rhyw esgob hael,
Na swydd yn ei eisyddyn
60 Ni bu rydd i neb rhyw ddyn;
Ni'm lludd i fyned i'r llys,
Neu ddyfod yn araf ddifrys;
Rhydd yw pob lle yn rhoddi
64 Ystafell, meddgell, i mi;
Cegin, pantri, bwtri, bwyd
Pan fynnwyf; pan fo annwyd
Tân mawn a gawn neu gynnud,
68 Ni bydd yno'r morlo mud.
Yn ystafell, naws difeth,
Yr esgob y cawn pob peth:
Grawn de Paris, rhis, rhesin,
72 Llysiau, medd, gwenwledd a gwin.
Yna i siambr y siambrlain,
Yno ydd awn yn ddi-ddain;
Cyfeddach dalm, cyfaddef
76 A gawn hefyd gydag ef,
Diodlyn da diadlaes
Mewn cyrn fy arglwydd, mewn caes.
Cysgu ar blu neu bliant
80 A llennau, cylchedau, cant
Ymysg o gwrlidau mil,
A'r porffor drud o'r pwrffil
A'r gra ar gymar a'r gob
84 A'i wisgoedd—wi o'r esgob!
Pob defnydd, ufudd afael,
Allwn â hwn, fy iôr hael,
Cydymaith mwyn cyweithas,
88 Arglwydd goleuswydd ar glas;

proud to the proud, like a hawk he watches,
prouder, humbler again;
harsh to the harsh—by the strength of the cross!—
92   within three words, a merciful lord;
overbearing his nature, strong and vigorous,
but the teacher's anger does not last;
he is thorough in an honest discussion,
96   I consider his sense to be most wise;
often do I get his gold from his hand,
God's most blessed goodness to him!

17   To Ieuan, Bishop of St Asaph

Ieuan, pure fair apostle,
priest, magnate of the church,
proprietor, poet's friend,
4   poem-book, mass-book of the faith,
you are a primate in Asaph's place,
chieftain of good paternity;
apart from the lord God, you are our head,
8   and our patron saint here in his absence;
no one is a lord, nor a protective hurdle,
except you, you are our father;
my liege, frequent confidence of my faction,
12   my bud, golden crozier,
and my holy spirit and my oaktree
and my greeting and my honour and my head;
a confessor, a hundred officials
16   are yours, Asaph will pay them,
great canons, fine lively hawks,
priors, proud abbots,
monks, brothers, men of true privilege,
20   vicars, parsons, saints;
through their perpetual prayer
will this matter be concluded;
the blessing of your pure good mother
24   will protect you, everyone exalts you;
the blessing of the minstrels and your relations
will take you without misfortune on your way;
the blessings of the good men
28   will protect you as you go;
God before you!—Is there a more burdensome journey?
go safely, day and night.

Balch wrth falch, fal gwalch y gwŷl,
Balchach, difalchach eilchwyl;
Llym wrth lym—myn grym y grog!—
92 Ar dri gair, iôr drugarog;
Uthr ei naws, traws trybelid,
Eithr ni lŷn athro'n ei lid;
Trwyadl yw ar ddadl ddidwyll,
96 Doethaf y barnaf ei bwyll;
Aml yw ei aur im o'i law,
Dedwyddaf da Duw iddaw!

I Ieuan, Esgob Llanelwy

Ieuan, apostol glân glwys,
Periglor, pôr yr eglwys,
Priodor, gyfaill prydydd,
4 Prydlyfr, offerenllyfr ffydd,
Primas wyd yn lle Asa,
Pennaeth o dadwysaeth da;
Onid Duw naf, ti yw'n nen,
8 A'n mabsant yma i'w absen;
Nid arglwydd neb, na dorglwyd,
Onid tydi, ein tad wyd;
Fy nêr, aml hyder fy mhlaid,
12 A'm bagluryn, bagl euraid,
A'm hysbryd glân a'm mesbren
A'm cyfarch a'm parch a'm pen;
Conffesor, can offisial
16 Sy i ti, Asa a'u tâl,
Canonwyr mawr, cain hoywweilch,
Priorau, abadau beilch,
Mynaich, brodyr, gwŷr gwirfraint,
20 Micariaid, personiaid, saint;
Drwy eu gweddi dragwyddawl
Y bydd terfyn hyn o hawl;
Bendith dy fam ddinam dda
24 A'th ddiffer, pawb a'th hoffa;
Bendith y glêr a'th gerynt
Yn ddiddrwg a'th ddwg i'th hynt;
Bendithion y dynion da
28 Wrth fyned a'th ddiffynna;
Duw o'th flaen!—Oes daith flinach?
Dos, y dydd a'r nos, yn iach.

Very often, more than a hundred times,
32 it was very futile, whoever tried
to reconcile—difficult case,
it is a pity that they will not safeguard him—
the English and the Scots, their existence is a burden,
36 and the pact would be a restoration;
a pact of savage foxes
catching chickens on the edge of a field.
Do not, I won't allow it,
40 fear anyone, I will comfort you;
put on the lorica of God, strong bright quality,
when you arise, as long as you live;
say clearly, fine eloquent language,
44 Patrick's easy way to peace;
he was a perfect, faultless, good saint
in Ireland, darkest land;
skilfully did he make, it was a benefit,
48 the vermin go into the stones;
neither toads in streams, he overcame,
nor snakes did he leave alive,
not a little weasel, nasty creature,
52 nor a fine stoat in the land.
So can you put all
the Scots to flight and get rid of them
and turn them into stones
56 in every righteous angry manner
as far as the Isle of Wight, the Picts,
between the shore and the salt sea, great horde.
You need not fear a fierce man,
60 crisis of battle, if you go to Scotland;
I will put a concealing mantle over you,
and I will cover you, Ieuan;
in the shell of the ripe nut
64 during the day I will conceal you,
and at night between the birch, blessed tree,
and its bark, thick is the clothing of the trees.
Curig's excellent hymn
68 will I sing, my lord, correctly,
and God's charm, it is spoken of with gratitude,
as well entirely around you,
you are a bishop with a large retinue,
72 against fierce brigands,
against the roar of the piercing wind, against thunder,
against deceit of Scots, against fire,
against great distress, against a demon,
76 against wind in your face, against sun,

Mynych iawn, mwy na channoed,
32 Ofer iawn oedd, a fu erioed
Yn cysoni, cas anawdd,
Peth truan na wnân' ei nawdd,
Deifr a Brynaich, baich eu bod,
36 Ac adfer fyddai'r gydfod;
Cydfod llwynogod agerw
Yn dal ieir ar dâl erw.
Na fid arnad, ni adaf,
40 Ofn neb, dy ofwy a wnaf;
Gwisg lurig Dduw, gwaisg loywryw,
Pan gyfotych, tra fych fyw;
Dywaid yn groyw, iaith ffloyw fflwch,
44 Rhwyddynt Padrig i'r heddwch;
Sant cyfwlch di-fwlch da fu
Yn Iwerddon, un orddu;
Celfydd y gwnaeth, bu coelfain,
48 I'r pryfed myned i'r main;
Llyffaint mewn naint, maeddu wnâi,
A neidr yn fyw ni adai,
Na bronwen bach, bry' enwir,
52 Na charlwng teilwng i'r tir.
Felly ti a elly oll
Encil Deifr a'u difancoll
A'u gyrru hwynt yn gerrig
56 Ym mhob rhith diragrith dig
Gyr Ynys Wicht, y Ffichtiaid,
Rhwng allt a môr hallt, mawr haid.
Nid rhaid it ofn tanbaid dyn,
60 Adwy brwydr, od ei Brydyn;
Llen gêl drosod a ddodaf,
A'th orchfan, Ieuan, a wnaf;
Ym mhlisg y gneuen wisgi,
64 Y dydd, y'th orchuddiaf di,
A'r nos rhwng bedw, pren dedwydd,
A'i risg, tew yw gwisg y gwŷdd.
Emyn Gurig dda ddigawn
68 A ganaf, fy naf, yn iawn,
A swyn Duw, sôn a'i diylch,
Hefyd i gyd yn dy gylch,
Esgob mawr wyd ei osgordd,
72 Rhag lladron ffyrnigion ffordd,
Rhag twrw chwiblwynt, rhag taran,
Rhag twyll Ysgotiaid, rhag tân,
Rhag cythrudd mawr, rhag cythraul,
76 Rhag gwynt i'th wyneb, rhag haul,

against the hostility of the people, against a noose,
against hail mixed with lightning,
against a man from Scotland, against treachery,
80   against contumely, if it presses upon you,
against the ruining of your oat-eating horses,
against flood and a great stagnant stretch of water,
against the man and against others
84   who can do some small thing outside,
and the dead hand, grim knotted sinews,
raised up and clamped tight;
the all-powerful golden ring
88   and the ruby stone, I praise it,
it will be heavy turning about your finger,
resolute sovereign, to keep you from evil.

Holy God, from Scotland when
92   will you come home, good his lineage?
Come to restore me to life;
to whatever region, whatever part,
you come to your shining land,
96   my curé, you will have my love;
it is a pity you do not know, provider of gifts,
gracious possessor of a crozier;
the welcome of God and man to you,
100   welcomer of poets, the welcome of the world!

18   To Dafydd ap Bleddyn, Bishop of St Asaph

Very good was Mordaf, lord of a great host,
good was Nudd in benefit to the needy,
good was Rhun himself, who was born of love,
4   good was Rhydderch, magnificent man,
good was Rhuawn Befr, good was Efrawg,
very good was Meiriawn, good was Mwrawg,
a prominent noble man was Mynyddawg Eiddin,
8   good Cynin the magician, splendid word,
good was Morien the fine lord, exalted sovereign,
good was Edwin the magician, privileged king,
highest of all I judge Eudaf Oediawg,
12   good without concealing was Coel Godebawg,
good was Gregory's mouth, devotional words,
and better is a steadfast friend, wise man of proud nature,
whose like there never was, powerful ruler;

Rhag cas y bobl, rhag cysellt,
Rhag cenllysg ymysg y mellt,
Rhag dyn o Brydyn, rhag brad,
80   Rhag ysgórn, o gwasg arnad,
Rhag llygru dy feirch ceirchbawr,
Rhag llifddwr a merddwr mawr,
Rhag y gŵr a rhag eraill
84   Peth bychan allan a aill,
A'r llaw farw, arw ïeurwym,
Gwedi'i chodi a'i rhoddi'n rhwym;
Y fodrwy aur anfeidrawl
88   A'r maen rhubi, mi a'i mawl,
Trwm fydd yn troi am ei fys,
Rhi gwychr, i'th gadw rhag echrys.

Duw gwyn, o Brydyn pa bryd
92   Y doi adref, da'i edryd?
Debre wrth fy nadebru;
I ba dir bynnag, ba du,
Y delych i'th lewych wlad,
96   'Ynghire, cei fy nghariad;
Gresyn na wyddost, cost ced,
Grasus berchennog croesed;
Croeso Duw a dyn wrthyd,
100   Croesawwr beirdd, croeso'r byd!

I Ddafydd ap Bleddyn, Esgob Llanelwy

Da iawn fu Fordaf, naf niferawg,
Da fu Nudd o fudd wrth anfoddawg,
Da fu Run ei hun, oedd heniawg—o serch,
4   Da fu Rydderch, gŵr ardderchawg,
Da fu Ruawn Befr, da fu Efrawg,
Da iawn fu Feiriawn, da fu Fwrawg,
Gŵr cyhoedd mwyn oedd Mynyddawg—Eiddin,
8   Da Gynin dewin, gair godidawg,
Da fu Forien hoywner, muner mannawg,
Da fu Edwin ddewin, brenin breiniawg,
Goruchaf barnaf Eudaf Oediawg,
12   Da fu heb gelu Goel Godebawg,
Da Eirioel enau, eiriau oriawg,
Ac ys gwell gâr pell, gŵr pwyllawg—balchryw,
Ni bu ei gyfryw, llyw galluawg;

16   if it is necessary to state further who is the lord,
      Dafydd ap Bleddyn is the generous man,
      a perfect man of good deeds, famous holy face,
      a man of Uchdryd's tribe, no treacherous mind,
20   pleasant man, man of esteem, ruler with extensive family,
      refined, wise man, man with great estate,
      irreproachable man, display of a peacock, fond of a singing
          voice,
      man who loves a main voice, croziered prelate,
24   he is a fitting, humble man, rich man,
      a gentle, loving man, crowned friend,
      fair, wine-drinking, wealthy, unassuming man,
      good-tempered, worthy crown-wearing man,
28   faithful and true and civilized man,
      sensible, joyful man, governor of good family,
      public man who fluently recites verses, singing psalms in
          unison,
      accomplished man, cub of Cynawg,
32   man of divine right, nature which swears no oaths,
      skilful, blessed and splendid man,
      Mary keep the man, all-conquering word,
      good, vigorous, gracious, long-living man,
36   a man very ready with his support, fur-wearing priest,
      good nobleman of large retinue in Asaph's place.

19   The Court of Hywel Cyffin, Dean of St Asaph

      Good is the blessing of a poet and of blessed God
      on a stone house and the mansion, a good place without
          bending,
      and the faultless wise peacock and the prince
4   and he who owns this [court], no layman's sense,
      on generous master Hywel giving diligently,
      and taverns of bright abundant [?] wine,
      and the one who maintains it at Easter and Christmas
8   feeding men where tares do not grow,
      and the holy cardinal and the friend who never refuses,
      on Gwernyglastir, true lovely heaven,
      and the exquisite stronghold and the full garden,
12   and the broad white court abounding in herbs,
      and the most humble lion, no grasping hand,
      and the place where poets are billeted, no miserly hand,

16   Os rhaid mynegi pwy rhi yrhawg,
      Dafydd ap Bleddyn yw'r dyn doniawg,
      Gŵr perffaith iawnwaith, enwawg—santeiddbryd,
      Gŵr o lwyth Uchdryd, nid bryd bradawg,
20   Gŵr digrif, gŵr rhif, rhwyf tylwythawg,
      Gŵr teuluaidd doeth, gŵr cyfoethawg,
      Gŵr digabl, paun chwaen, chwannawg—i gerddlais,
      Gŵr a gâr priflais, prelad baglawg,
24   Gŵr gwiw gŵyl ydiw, gŵr goludawg,
      Gŵr gwâr hygar, câr coronawg,
      Gŵr iesin lladwin lledwawg—cydostwng,
      Gŵr diflwng teilwng talaith wisgawg,
28   Gŵr cywir a gwir a gwareddawg,
      Gŵr cymen llawen, llyw cenhedlawg,
      Gŵr coedd rhwydd wersoedd, cydwersawg—salmau,
      Gŵr cwbl ei gampau, cenau Cynawg,
32   Gŵr dwyfawl ei hawl, hwyl anllyfodawg,
      Gŵr celfydd dedwydd a godidawg,
      Gŵr a gatwo Mair, gair gorfodawg,
      Gŵr iawn hoyw rhadlawn yn hirhoedlawg,
36   Gŵr hyborth ei borth, aberthawg—gwisgra,
      Gwrda'n lle Asa iawn lluosawg.

Llys Hywel Cyffin, Deon Llanelwy

      Da yw bendith bardd a Duw bendig
      Ar faendy a'r plas, fan da heb blŷg,
      A'r paun difai doeth a'r pendefig
4   A'r neb piau hon, nid pwyll llëyg,
      Ar feistr Hywel hael yn rhoi'n ystig,
      A thefyrn o win aur a thefig,
      A'r un a'i deil Basg a Nadolig
8   Yn lluniaethu gwŷr lle ni thyf gwŷg,
      A'r cardinal llwyd a'r câr dinag,
      Ar Wernyglastir, wir nef glwysteg,
      A'r orddewis gaer a'r ardd ddiwag,
12   A'r llys eang wen a'r llyseufag,
      A'r llew ufuddaf, nid llaw fyddag,
      A'r lle y rhennir beirdd, nid llaw rannag,

and the new hall with great tables abounding in poets,
16   and the drinks of mead, fair noble paragon,
and the gentlemanliness of the faultless gentleman,
and his bread and his ale and his beer and his cook,
and the place most frequented by minstrels like a
          prominent host,
20   and the hand of holy Asaph, lord with large retinue,
and the golden goblets, splendid sight,
and every man of the court and everyone bears them,
and the emboldening ale like crying havoc.

20   Praise of Sir Roger Mortimer

Sir Roger of the azure shield,
Sir Roger of great Mortimer,
young Roger, plank of battle,
4   you are a warlike serpent of Sir Ralph's line,
lord of Rhos, golden bright Roger,
hero, conqueror of a hundred forts,
heart of the angels of England
8   and her chief supporter and her bridge,
sweet tree of talent, he causes good below,
white lord, bud of Usk,
princely hawk of worthy blood,
12   eagle of conflict, gilded feet,
heroic is your shapely hand,
descendant of the pure-fruited lord of Aberffraw,
dragon of the islands of the ocean,
16   dragon of war—I am
prophesying truly—it is time for you to come
to Wales where you deserve praise.

You were a boy, you attained land,
20   now you are known as a man;
a man of strength, by the blood of the Cross!
You have no balk, horned buffalo,
except the need to practice
24   arms, beautiful strength of a lord;
the wearing of arms, if pressed,
and increasing them like the long horns of a stag,
and breaking, demand it, in steel,
28   a stout-socketed thrusting battle lance;

A'r neuadd fyrddfawr newydd feirddfag,
16 A'r gwirodau medd, iôr goreudeg,
A gwrdaeiddrwydd y gwrda diddrwg,
A'i fara a'i gwrw a'i fir a'i gog,
A'r lle amlaf clêr mal llu amlwg,
20 A llaw Asa llwyd, iôr lluosog,
A'r ffiolau aur, oroff olwg,
A phob dyn o'r llys a phawb a'u dwg,
A'r cwrw hyfaidd mal crio hafog.

Moliant Syr Rosier Mortimer

Syr Rosier asur aesawr,
Syr Rosier o'r Mortmer mawr,
Rosier ieuanc, planc plymlwyd,
4 Sarff aer o hil Syr Raff wyd,
Rhos arglwydd, Rosier eurglaer,
Rhyswr, cwncwerwr can caer,
Calon engylion Englont
8 A'i phen-cynheiliad a'i phont,
Perbren dawn, pair obry da,
Pôr gwyn, bagluryn Buga,
Edlingwalch o deilyngwaed,
12 Eryr trin, oreuraid draed,
Arwraidd dy luniaidd law,
Ŵyr burffrwyth iôr Aberffraw,
Draig ynysoedd yr eigiawn,
16 Dragwn aer—darogan iawn
Ydd wyf—madws it ddyfod
Gymru lle rhyglyddy glod.

Mab fuost, doethost i dir,
20 Gŵr bellach a grybwyllir;
Gŵr grym, myn gwyar y Grog!
Balc arnad, bual corniog,
Nid oes ond eisiau arfer
24 O arfau, prydferth nerth nêr;
Gwisgo arfau, o gwesgir,
A'u cynnydd fal cyrn hydd hir,
A thorri, myn di, mewn dur,
28 Baladr socetgadr catgur;

bearing iron fiercely and grimly
and riding spirited horses;
jousting with vigorous earls,
32 clashing, engaging with them;
and your squire with your sword before you—
you are a chieftain, who doesn't recognize you?—
and your fine page with your shining lance
36 stands out in front on a courser,
and your bright helmet, and a sizeable host
behind you on horseback, and a retinue,
and awe-inspiring music before you,
40 and the brandishing of palm staffs.

The great estate of the wise Earl of March,
great is the cognomen, greater is the domain;
you are greatly privileged, by Mary above,
44 great bold title, more was given to you:
Earl of March—best earl in the world—
Earl of Ludlow, bloody-handed lord,
Earl of Caerllion, brave warrior,
48 Earl of Ulster, fair brave lord;
another name, the best of these,
from France the famous Duke of Clarence;
a good name, an old man interprets it,
52 grandson of Sir Lionel, angel of the English.

It is prophesied that it's our dragon
which will perform the feats this year:
from the head of the lion with mighty sword
56 will be crowned one of the family of Gwynedd.
Why the strong thick-clawed lion
rather than a bear? Tell me.
With bright gold on your strong arm,
60 descendant of the king of England and the Scots,
you are a sovereign lord, bright valiant peacock,
and scion and line of a lion;
you will be foremost after wardship,
64 second champion after Richard.
Let the earls of England—customary is arrogance—
say what they will about their office,
it would be fitting for you to get the crown
68 of Aberffraw, my tall liege-lord.

It is time, I am a herald,
for you to awake to secure your praise.

Arwain hëyrn yn chwyrn chwerw
A marchogaeth meirch agerw;
Ymwan â ieirll diamwynt,
32 Ymwrdd, ymgyfwrdd ag wynt;
A'th yswain â'th lain o'th flaen—
Pennaeth wyd, pwy ni'th adwaen?—
A'th hengsmon hoyw â'th loyw laif
36 Ar gwrser a ragorsaif,
A'th helm lwys, a thalm o lu
I'th ôl ar feirch, a theulu,
A cherdd o'th flaen o raen rwyf,
40 A chrydr ar belydr balwyf.

   Mawr ystad Iarll y Mars doeth,
Mawr y cyfenw, mwy yw'r cyfoeth;
Mawr o fraint wyd, ym Mair fry,
44 Mawr hy ditl, mwy roed yty:
Iarll Mars—gorau iarll ym myd—
Iarll Llwdlo, iôr llaw waedlyd,
Iarll Caerllion, dragon drud,
48 Iwrl o Wlster, iôr lwystrud;
Henw arall, o hyn orau,
O Ffrens Dug o Clarens clau;
Henw da, gŵr hen a'i dyeingl,
52 Ŵyr Syr Lewnel, angel Eingl.

   Darogan yw mai'n draig ni
A lunia'r gwaith eleni:
O ben y llew glew ei gledd
56 Coronir câr i Wynedd.
Pam mai'r llew crafangdew cryf
Mwy nag arth? Mynag wrthyf.
Yn aur gwaisg ar dy fraisg fraich,
60 Ŵyr brenin Lloegr a'r Brynaich,
Pen-arglwydd wyd, paun eurglew,
Ac eginin a llin llew;
Pennaf fyddy gwedy gwart,
64 Ail rhyswr yn ôl Rhisiart.
Gwnaed ieirll Lloegr—gnawd erllugrwydd—
A fynnon' o sôn i'w swydd,
Teilwng oedd it gael talaith
68 Aberffraw, f'ymandaw maith.

   Amserol, mi sy herod,
It ddeffroi i gloi dy glod.

For what reason, call for silence,
72 were four colours put into
your fair arms? Four earldoms
are yours. To whom does each belong?
Azure is in your shield,
76 Earl of March, with the great gold colour;
cinnabar and pure bright silver
to me is the diagonal shield;
four blameless nations
80 are kin to you: worthy Venedotians,
French, English, fine hawks,
Irish, mother of contention, fine and proud.

The blood of France, worthy and good its fruit,
84 is the gold colour of a pure tribe;
it is an exalted sign,
king in the land of the fine wine
and the whole of Guienne, best of vales,
88 will you be, greater will be your possession.

Yours as far as the borders of Maeloegr,
and may the best place in England be yours;
the silver colour is in the coat of arms
92 of the good white dragon with the flowing mane;
Boo to England and the pupil of its eye,
you are beloved in the country,
lord of great famous Wigmore
96 and Earl of March, great provision.

Inciter of song, the blood of the red dragon
is the cinnabar which is in you;
for that be bold, lively boar,
100 and put on again a gold spur;
your ardour portends the gaining of wealth,
the gaining of victory, may your way be clear!
the grace of Arthur and his cross to you,
104 and his court and all his camp,
the best place, a second Caerllion
which is higher, of this island.

The race of the Irish, noble and fitting,
108 is the azure, colour of bright grey steel;
the toughest hard foundation
is the sharp grey steel, strength of Christendom;
you are tougher, second Galahad,
112 with your fine javelin and your bright spear.

Pa ryw ystyr, pâr osteg,
72 Y rhoed i'r arfau tau teg
Pedwarlliw? Pedair iarlleth
Sy dau. Pwy piau pob peth?
Asur sydd yn dy aesawr,
76 Iarll Mars, gyda'r eurlliw mawr;
Sinobr ac arian glân gloyw
Im yw'r ysgwyd amrosgoyw;
Pedair cenedl diedliw
80 A ddeiryd it: Gwyndyd gwiw,
Ffrancod, Saeson, wychion weilch,
Gwyddyl, mam cynfyl, ceinfeilch.

Gwaed Ffrainc, gwiw a da ei ffrwyth,
84 Ydiw'r eurlliw diweirllwyth;
Urddedig arwydd ydiw,
Brenin yng ngwlad y gwin gwiw
A chwbl o'r Gïen, pen pant,
88 Fyddy, mwy fydd dy feddiant.

Tau hyd ymylau Maeloegr,
A bid tau'r lle gorau'n Lloegr;
Yn achen y ddraig wen wiw
92 Rawnllaes y mae'r arianlliw;
Bw i Loegr a'i mablygad,
Annwyl iawn wyd yn y wlad,
Iôn i Wigmor enwogmawr
96 A Iwrl y Mars, arlwy mawr.

Gwodrudd cerdd, gwaed y ddraig goch
Yw'r sinobr ysy ynoch;
Am hynny bydd hy, baedd hoyw,
100 A rho eto aur otoyw;
Cael da yw coel dy awydd,
Cael gorfod, rhagod poed rhwydd!
Gras Arthur a'i groes wrthyd,
104 A'i lys a'i gadlys i gyd,
Gorau lle, ail Gaerllion
Y sy uwch, o'r ynys hon.

Rhyw Gwyddyl, rhywiog addas,
108 Yw'r asur, liw gloywddur glas;
Glewaf grwndwal gogaled
Yw'r dur glaslym, grym o Gred;
Glewach wyd, ail Galäath,
112 Â'th luchwayw hoyw a'th loyw lath.

By courage, by height of lineage
you will boldly conquer Connaught.
Go across the sea and destroy Meath
116 to the limits of the unruly land;
Trim is your patrimony,
your castle fair of shape,
it was the beauty of the land of Matholwch,
120 the heart of blackest Ireland.
Your task is to raise up
your irresistible standard, splendid sail:
make an ambush, let three hundred be hacked to pieces,
124 great youth, against MacMurrough;
cut, slash, and stab straight ahead
over to Kellistown through his heart;
hurry and claim all
128 the land of Ulster, Elystan's fame;
there's a domain full of false balk,
demand it as yours on the edge of Dundalk.
After capturing Great Nial, my lord,
132 misshapen dog, blockhead of Ulster,
you will cut down, bell-tower of praise,
the people of Ulster with every other stroke.

21   Elegy for Dafydd ap Gwilym

'Dafydd's life was enchanted yesterday,
a fine man had his day been longer,
many-stranded ode, good artistry,
4   son of Gwilym Gam, knot of song.
He fashioned praise straight along the line,
there's a good custom for a man.
My provision, I will make
8   an elegy of love for the man.
He was the jewel of the shires and their tip
and the toy of the country and its beauty,
the mould of entertainment and its manner,
12   my salvation for a fine gift,
the hawk of the girls of Deheubarth,
without him, indeed, let it turn to rubbish.
The *cywydd* of every refined singer
16   is grieving deeply because he has gone.'

O hyder, o uchder ach
Hy goresgynny Gonnach.
Dos drwy'r môr a distryw'r Mydd
116 I flaenau'r wlad aflonydd;
Tref tad i tithau yw'r Trum,
Tau gastell teg ei ystum,
Tegwch gwlad Fatholwch fu,
120 Calon Iwerddon orddu.
Dyrchaf dy stondardd, hardd hwyl,
Diarchar yw dy orchwyl:
Gwna fwysmant, bid trychant trwch,
124 Macwy mawr, â Mac Morwch;
Tor, rhwyg, a brath tu rhag bron
Draw i Galys drwy'i galon;
Brysia a chleimia achlân
128 Gwlad Wlster, glod Elystan;
Llyna gyfoeth llawn geufalc,
Myn di'n dau ym min Dwn-dalc.
'N ôl dal Gred Nïal, fy nêr,
132 Ci ffalstwf, cyff o Wlster,
Ti a leddy, clochdy clod,
Bobl Wlster bob ail ystod.

Marwnad Dafydd ap Gwilym

'Hudol doe fu hoedl Dafydd,
Hoyw o ddyn pe hwy fai'i ddydd,
Diungor awdl, da angerdd,
4 Ap Gwilym Gam, gwlm y gerdd.
Lluniodd wawd wrth y llinyn,
Llyna arfer dda ar ddyn.
Mau ddarpar, mi a ddirpwr
8 Marwnad o gariad y gŵr.
Gem oedd y siroedd a'u swch
A thegan gwlad a'i thegwch,
Mold y digrifwch a'i modd,
12 Ymwared im am wiwrodd,
Hebog merched Deheubarth,
Heb hwn, od gwn, aed yn garth.
Cywydd pob cethlydd coethlawn,
16 Canys aeth, cwynofus iawn.'

'You dog, shut up *cywydd*!
The world is not good, it will not last long.
Whilst Dafydd was alive, skilful song,
20   you were respectable and merry;
and because of this it will not be
fitting to request you after him.
Let whatever praise is woven
24   and its two ends be thrown into the loft.
The pennoncel of language has gone,
if only he were alive he would be everyone's teacher.
Immense is my complaint because of grievous shock,
28   learning was immense in him,
and he was tailor of love to a girl
and the harp of a court and its retinue
and treasurer of minstrels and their praise
32   and trident of battle and conflict,
and pitiful without mitigation
and presumption was the destruction of the man,
and the beam of poets, most sorrowful is the world,
36   and he will not rise up again;
a strong, bold, sharp, clear-voiced teacher
and lord was he, he went to heaven.'

22 Elegy for Llywelyn Goch ap Meurig Hen

'O fair God and his goodness man,
did anyone see Llywelyn
son of noble Meurig Hen,
4   uncle on the father's side to the muse?
Where is he?' 'Who asks after him?
Seek no more, he wants no dealing.'
'It is the loving youths
8   and maidens of Meirionnydd.'
'God knows nothing about an entertainer,
he went to grace as a strong teacher.
Wonderfully in the end did he go
12   to Rome from the shire.
Never did a man go, and God choosing,
with more lamenting after him.
To Paradise did he go
16   to sing to Mary, he was a mighty lord.
Only metre need be taken there,
it is not nasty to receive an entertaining soul.'

'Tydi gi, taw di gywydd!
Nid da'r byd, nid hir y bydd.
Tra fu Ddafydd, gelfydd gân,
20 Ydd oeddud barchus ddiddan;
Ac ni bydd oherwydd hyn
Gwedy ef gwiw dy ofyn.
Bwrier a wëer o wawd
24 A'i deuflaen ar y daflawd.
Ethyw pensel yr ieithoedd,
Eithr pe byw athro pawb oedd.
Uthr fy nghwyn o frwyn fraw,
28 Athronddysg oedd uthr ynddaw,
A thaeliwr serch i ferch fu
A thelyn llys a'i theulu
A thrysorer clêr a'u clod
32 A thryfer brwydr a thrafod,
A thruan heb athrywyn
A thraha fu difa'r dyn,
A thrawst beirdd, athrist y byd,
36 A thrachefn ni thrachyfyd;
Athro grym glewlym gloywlef
A thëyrn oedd, aeth i'r nef.'

Marwnad Llywelyn Goch ap Meurig Hen

'O Dduw teg a'i ddäed dyn,
A welai neb Lywelyn
Amheurig fonheddig Hen,
4 Ewythr frawd tad yr awen?
Mae ef?' 'Pwy a'i hymofyn?
Na chais mwy, achos ni myn.'
'Meibion serchogion y sydd
8 A morynion Meirionnydd.'
'Nis gŵyr Duw am deuluwas,
Yn athro grym aeth i'r gras.
Rhyfedd o ddiwedd ydd aeth
12 I Rufain o'r siryfiaeth.
Dyn nid aeth, a Duw'n dethol,
Erioed fwy cwyn ar ei ôl.
I Baradwys i brydu
16 Yr aeth i Fair, iôr uthr fu.
Nid rhaid dwyn yno ond rhif,
Nid hagr cael enaid digrif.'

It is a serious matter if the chief poet is dead,
20 Mary knows that the poetry will not die.
When there are requests, it was the custom
of the voices in the courts,
the first request, true work,
24 to the minstrels, sweet recital,
is the lovesong of the old red man,
a multitude hears it like the voice of a bell.
There is no song to a tune,
28 it's true, where young men are,
nothing unaccompanied is pleasant
nor any accent at the finger's end
but the *cywydd* of the fine-voiced singer,
32 no one wants any *cywydd* but his.
Not a single word is to be found, crude skill,
falsely placed in the poetry;
Never did Tydai Father of the Muse,
36 nor could fair old Culfardd
make the pure poetry which he made,
mighty and brilliant his poetic art,
true, refined master-poet,
40 prophet of poetry, how great the lament!
Highway and guardian of praise,
judge of every chief composition,
he was the top master of the Ovidian *cywydd*,
44 qualified, he was an expert;
my great brother in the faith was full of song,
a song-book for all sweet rhymes;
from smooth-lipped Taliesin,
48 in his sleep, not bad his gathering,
he learnt—what a pupil!—
fine biblical praise in song.
Artistry, not feeble,
52 good teacher, he took learning
to the place where the wide peace is,
and let poetry go with him;
there is no need for it in summer,
56 well does he know the most entertaining.

There was no one, dear partnership,
reciting in Gwynedd
except what we two did,
60 he and I, he was a second Amig,
I am Amlyn; there are not very many
of the old ones left on its face.

Mawr yw'r pwnc os marw'r pencerdd,
20 Mair a'i gŵyr na bydd marw'r gerdd.
Pan ofynner, arfer oedd
Y lleisiau yn y llysoedd,
Cyntaf gofynnir, wir waith,
24 I'r purorion, pêr araith,
Rhieingerdd y gŵr hengoch,
Lliaws a'i clyw fal llais cloch.
Nid oes erddigan gan gainc,
28 Gwir yw, lle bo gwŷr ieuainc,
Ni bydd digrif ar ddifys
Nac un acen ar ben bys
Ond cywydd cethlydd coethlef,
32 Ni myn neb gywydd namn ef.
Ni cheir ungair, chwerw angerdd,
Ar gam yn lle ar y gerdd;
Ni wnâi Dydai Dad Awen,
36 Ni wyddiad Gulfardd hardd hen
O gerdd bur wneuthur a wnaeth,
Gwrdd eurwych ei gerddwriaeth,
Prydyddfardd priod addfwyn,
40 Proffwyd cerdd, praffed yw cwyn!
Priffordd a gwelygordd gwawd,
Profestydd pob prif ystawd,
Prifeistr cywydd Ofydd oedd,
44 Profedig, prifai ydoedd;
Prydfawr fu'r ffyddfrawd mawr mau,
Prydlyfr i bob pêr odlau;
I gan Daliesin finrhasgl,
48 Trwy ei gwsg, nid drwg ei gasgl,
Y dysgodd—wi o'r disgibl!—
Ar draethawd bybyrwawd bibl.
Ethrylith, nid ethrylysg,
52 Athro da, neur aeth â'r dysg
I'r lle mae'r eang dangnef,
Ac aed y gerdd gydag ef;
Nid rhaid wrthi hi yr haf,
56 Da y gŵyr ef y digrifaf.

Nid oedd neb, cyfundeb cu,
Yng Ngwynedd yn ynganu
Dieithr a wnaem ein deuoedd,
60 Mi ac ef, ail Amig oedd,
Amlyn wyf; nid aml iawn neb
O rai hen ar ei hwyneb.

Pure teacher of poetry, sweet strength of language,
64   he was adept, who knows anything?
I am bearing a long yoke alone,
sleepless, I cannot
thresh, nor weave praise,
68   with one flail—oh the misfortune!
The same nature as the fair turtle dove,
I am weak, and the same will;
the gentle bird does not descend,
72   it does not sing on a green birch, pure voice,
when its mate, it is harsh that I live on,
is dead, I am mute;
Me, I do not wish to sing
76   ever after him, what shall I do?

    I have been praying to Peter, eager manner,
I will sing a song for support,
to bring Llywelyn, good man,
80   noble master of heaven, to the stronghold
amongst, people of learned life,
the prophets of heaven, they are strong;
David the Prophet will like
84   the recital of Lleucu Llwyd's song;
David was a poet to God,
the praise of the Trinity and the One God;
my lord composed the poetry
88   of the psalter every syllable;
he was unchaste during his lifetime,
sinful and amorously inclined;
harpist, head of a retinue,
92   he was a lover, he repented.
God forgave it him, easy grief,
at the end of his life.
He will forgive his poet
96   his foolishness, uncomely fault.
There is an open court, high office,
for a poet by day wherever he comes.
Neither door—no man complains—
100   nor gate shuts before him, it is not fitting.
It's not easy to keep, grim punishment,
a poet from the gate of Paradise.

Pur athro cerdd, pêr ieithrym,
64   Parod oedd, pwy a ŵyr dym?
    Minnau'n dal hiriau fy hun,
    Mi ni wn, i mewn anun,
    Na dyrnu, na gwëu gwawd,
68   Ag unffust—och rhag anffawd!
    Un natur â'r turtur teg,
    Egwan wyf, ac un ofeg;
    Ni ddisgyn yr edn llednais,
72   Ni chân ar irfedw, lân lais,
    Pan fo marw, garw y gorwyf,
    Ei gymar, aflafar wyf;
    Minnau, canu ni mynnaf
76   Byth yn ei ôl, beth a wnaf?

    Gweddïo Pedr, gwedd eorth,
    Y bûm, canaf gerdd am borth,
    Ar ddwyn Llywelyn, dyn da,
80   Urddolfeistr nef, i'r ddalfa
    Ym mysg, pobl hyddysg eu hynt,
    Proffwydi nef, praff ydynt;
    Hoff fydd gan Ddafydd Broffwyd
84   Ddatganu cerdd Lleucu Llwyd;
    Prydydd oedd Ddafydd i Dduw,
    Clod y Drindod a'r Unduw;
    Prydyddiaeth a wnaeth fy naf
88   Y sallwyr bob esillaf;
    Anniwair fu yn ei oes,
    Careddfawr carueiddfoes;
    Puror telyn, pôr teulu,
92   Serchog, edifeiriog fu.
    Duw a'i maddeuawdd, hawdd hoed,
    Iddo yn ei ddiweddoed.
    Yntau a faddau i'w fardd
96   Ei ffolineb, ffael anardd.
    Llys rydd y sydd, swydd uchel,
    I brydydd lliw dydd lle dêl.
    Ni chae na dôr—ni chŵyn dyn—
100   Na phorth rhagddo, ni pherthyn.
    Ni hawdd atal, dial dwys,
    Prydydd i borth Paradwys.

23   Elegy for Ithel Ddu

It is grievous for the land of mottled Meilir—
a brave splendid man has died;
from a spear thrust a handsome lord went
4 to an earth-house, black cold time;
wise man's woe, it was a baneful spear,
that God did—it was vicious slaughter,
very worst thing for the hard veins—
8 thrust a spear under Ithel's brooch,
a spear of Irish pain,
God did a vicious deed,
surreptitiously shedding streams
12 by stabbing him with the head of a short spear
without a challenge, plain anger,
right through him crossways, evil auger.
An Irishman would not commit against his enemy
16 such an evil deed of hatred as this.
The death of Ithel, prominent golden stag,
is a cause of great lament in Is Conwy.
Song is finished, the land above yr Eifl
20 has become a wilderness—oh the disaster!
The rule of entertaining verse has been overturned,
poet, chief and foremost judge;
he was a famous amorous poet,
24 and his deeds were excellent:
the lad's feats were throwing a girl down,
accomplishing praise, feat of lively love,
lampooning the ugly-faced dry Brem
28 and slate-featured Gwyddelyn,
drinking emboldening mead, fierce wolf,
fine singing voice, on an empty stomach,
chasing girls and drinking horns,
32 and hunting with dogs, vigorous noble man.
Why didn't—harsh heather girdle—
Gwyddelyn die, stammering lichen?
He will get no shout where he comes
36 now, since Ithel is not alive;
blessed and rejoicing is
the little Brem, at the first hour
he died before him this year,
40 he did right, this I know.

What is the world? Who took the ball?
Wise head, who but Ithel?

Marwnad Ithel Ddu

Dihir i fro Feilir frych—
Deryw marw gŵr dewr mawrwych;
O ruthr gwayw yr aeth iôr gwymp
4 I ddaeardy, ddu oerdymp;
Gwae doeth, bu gwayw adwythig,
Y gwnaeth Duw, bu gwyniaith dig,
Gwaethaf dim i'r gwythi del,
8 Gwthio gwayw dan gae Ithel,
Gwayw o ddolur Gwyddelig,
Gweithio o Dduw gwaith oedd ddig,
Dan anwybod dwyn ebyr
12 O'i wân â phen bilan byr
Heb air ymladd, bâr amlwg,
Trwyddo ar draws, trwyddew drwg.
Ni wnâi Wyddel â'i elyn
16 Cynddrwg o hirwg â hyn.
Cwyn mawr Is Conwy yw marw
Ithel, ddiargel eurgarw.
Deryw'r gerdd, aeth yn dir gŵydd
20 Uwch yr Eifl—och o'r aflwydd!
Troed awgrym gwawd tra digrif,
Prydydd, pen profestydd prif;
Prydydd serchog enwog oedd,
24 A thrada ei weithredoedd:
Campau'r mab oedd cwympo merch,
Cwmpasu gwawd, camp hoywserch,
Dychanu'r Brem salwdrem sych
28 A Gwyddelyn gwedd elych,
Yfed medd hyfaidd, blaidd blwng,
Aur gathlef, ar ei gythlwng,
Helgud merched a heilgyrn,
32 A hely â chŵn, ŵr hael chwyrn.
Pam na bu farw, garw gaerug,
Gwyddelyn, march cregyn cryg?
Ni chaiff ef dolef lle dêl
36 Weithian, gan nad byw Ithel;
Gwyn ei fyd yn gwynfydu
Y Brem bach, awr brim y bu
O'i flaen farw ef eleni,
40 Iawn a wnaeth, hyn a wn i.

Peth yw'r byd? Pwy aeth a'r bêl?
Pen doeth, pwy onid Ithel?

Who was the best, man's talents,
44   reader in the land of Lleyn?
Who knew secret love?
Who, except what Ithel knew?
It was astonishing that he was interred,
48   that God chose Ithel Ddu.
If he needed a poet
and a minstrel and a hunter of the hart,
there is grief as far as Ynys Bir,
52   Ithel Ddu went in hunting garb,
and his houndsman, I would not mock him,
and his horns with him, and his dogs;
and by ship he was loosed
56   from his country to the land of holy Lleudad
to hunt the rabbits of Cynon's line,
to a thousand saints with his words of praise.
No ship's load ever went
60   from sea's bane to Bardsey Island—
this I swear, fullest oath—
half as good as that one!
The load is my golden shining soul,
64   and my black supple favourite;
a man who could elegantly
lie where there is a colloquium of saints,
and hear Talbod Talba
68   and Iolyn Ddu calling finely,
and praise the psalm, frequent is the chase,
God is glad to get a minstrel
of faultless courtesy,
72   he would make a splendid sheriff.
There is no grim demon
that comes there, bright land of wine,
a good dwelling were one to come to it,
76   no one would ever leave it;
there he entered a religious order,
there for ever—will it not be right?—
his eloquent body rests
80   until judgement, good rich ode;
no more amusing man of noble lineage
ever entered a religious order.

Pwy oedd orau, doniau dyn,
44 Darlleawdr ar dir Llëyn?
Pwy a wyddiad cariad cêl?
Pwy, eithr a wypai Ithel?
Oedd eres ei ddaearu,
48 Ethol o Dduw Ithel Ddu.
O bai raid iddo brydydd
A cherddwr a heliwr hydd,
I Ynys Bir mae hiraeth,
52 Ithel Ddu'n rhith hely ydd aeth,
A'i gynydd, nis goganwn,
A'i gyrn gydag ef, a'i gŵn;
Ac â llong y gollyngwyd
56 O'i wlad i dir Lleudad llwyd
I hely cwning hil Cynon,
I fil o saint a'i fawl sôn.
Nid aeth llwyth o adwyth lli
60 Unllong i Ynys Enlli—
Hyn a dyngaf, llwyraf llw—
Hanner cystal â hwnnw!
F'enaid aur llathraid yw'r llwyth,
64 A'm dewisdyn du ystwyth;
Gŵr a fedrodd yn gywraint
Gorwedd lle mae senedd saint,
A chlybod Talbod Talba
68 Ac Iolyn Ddu'n galw yn dda,
A moli'r salm, aml yw'r siâs,
Da gan Dduw gael teuluwas
Diddrwg ei ddiwladeiddrwydd,
72 Digrif pe sirif ei swydd.
Nid oes gythraul disgethrin
A ddêl yno, gwenfro gwin,
Da dyddyn o doid iddi,
76 Nid âi neb ohonai hi;
Yno'dd aeth ef yng nghrefydd,
Yno byth—pand iawn y bydd?—
Gorffowys mae'i gorff huawdl
80 Hyd frawd, ddiodlawd dda awdl;
Nid aeth o uchafiaeth ach
I grefydd wr ddigrifach.

24   Description of a Girl

I love, she is lovable,
coral cheek like the rowan,
proud friend, she dispensed mead,
4   a loving girl of Tegfedd's court;
a faultless branch with bright chin,
the bristling foam of clear rippling waves;
flourishing shining-white hemlock,
8   dear blameless body like a distaff;
bright colour of the wave like sunlight on a tower,
reed-like body which no man has ever known;
colour of shallow snow on pale rock,
12   radiance of rippling water against a rock's swelling.
She has caused me complete anguish, many groans,
tender sapling, red-cheeked Llywy,
moon-like face the colour of January snow,
16   she is gentle and fine, light of dawn;
very good is the timid girl's face
and her exquisite head, Isolde's form;
pretty, well was she formed,
20   she is proud, by holy David;
a forehead with gold coins of the best mould,
primrose hair of a gold-coloured crest;
the same colour as Eigr, good bright treasure,
24   slender black brow like Mary's image;
eye like the jewel of a fine clasp,
similar to the Tiboeth stone;
an easy smile like the colour of gossamer on ice,
28   a white, shapely, rounded nose which sneezes lightly,
and sweet pretty little teeth and a smiling
lovely wine-drinking mouth;
a long throat, beautifully shaped,
32   like a swan's, finely rounded, slender and smooth;
a thumb which counts a burden of rosary beads,
and an apple-shaped bosom and an arm;
a slender hand like the colour of the glove,
36   long baselard, fair, bright, tender finger;
a pink fingernail on it
and a golden ring here and there;
a flank shaped like that of a pretty, smooth goddess,
40   straight as a timber of tender condition;
a rounded leg the colour of snow on a hillside path,
pale white under a scarlet gown;
a slender ankle beneath miniver fur,
44   a foot white and shapely although short;

I Ferch

Caru'dd wyf, caruaidd yw,
Cwrelrudd cyriwalryw,
Cares falch, hepgores fedd,
4   Caredigferch caer Degfedd;
Cangen ddifethl aelgethloyw,
Ceginwrych geirwddwfr crych croyw;
Cegiden bebyrwen babl,
8   Cogeilgorff cu ogelgabl;
Hoywliw'r don fel haul ar dŵr,
Brwynengorff heb rin ungwr;
Lliw eira bas ar lasgraig,
12   Llewych dŵr crych ar dor craig.
Llwyr ing y'm gwnaeth, llawer och,
Llarieiddgainc, Llywy ruddgoch,
Lloer wyneb lliw eira Ionawr,
16   Llary yw a gwiw, lleuer gwawr;
Da iawn yw gwedd y dyn gwyllt
A'i dewisiad, dwf Esyllt;
Dillyniaidd, da y lluniwyd,
20   Diwyl hon, myn Dewi lwyd;
Tâl ag aur mâl gorau mold,
Brialluwallt bre lliwold;
Deuliw Eigr, da oleugrair,
24   Du ael fain megis delw Fair;
Llygad fel glain caead coeth,
Tebyg i faen y Tiboeth;
Gwên rwydd fel lliw gwawn ar rew,
28   Gwyndrwyn cyfladdgrwn gwandrew,
A deintws mwyndlws a min
Digrifwymp diagr yfwin;
Tagell hir, teg oll ei himp,
32   Alarchwedd gronwiw lerwchwimp;
Bawd a rif badereufaich,
A bron afaldwf a braich;
Llaw fain fel lliw y faneg,
36   Baslart hir, bys hoywlary teg;
Ewin ballasarn arnaw
A modrwy aur yma draw;
Ystlyslun dwywes dlosleddf,
40   Ystudfwm modd ystad meddf;
Esgair gron lliw eira bron brisg
Lwydwen dan ysgarladwisg;
Ffêr fain is ffwrri fenfyr,
44   Ffurfeiddwen droed cyd boed byr;

fair, sweet, chuckling Welsh,
wise progression, beautiful Welsh woman.
If a finger is crooked suddenly
48   in front of her, rounded eye like a pebble,
white-nailed delicate reed,
she almost falls like an ear of barley.
Smooth-templed girl the lovely colour of snow,
52   white hem on fine golden sleeves;
happy is she, her cheek is white,
who wears, my red-lipped girl,
a pale head-dress, wise peerless girl,
56   a pennoncel of cambric, fine-browed peacock.
Who could, even if he were a master craftsman,
paint with chalk my darling's condition?
God made her, golden son's purpose,
60   by Peter's image, for His son.
I have heaped up poetry, helpless state,
pencil of love, is it not presumptuous of me
to imagine getting, it was a noble reason,
64   to sleep with my girl with the lowered eyes?

25   The Poet's Beard

'Was it you, beard, who scared off
the girl who was willingly kissing me?
You were planted too thickly in place,
4   you are a great crop on my flesh;
Irish, harsh, black and sharp,
on looking at my countenance and my face
my mug and my visage became,
8   chin's beard of corn, all shag!'

No matter how thoroughly it is trimmed,
and the way it is shaved for me,
it is no smoother, indisputable fact,
12   than a skate's rough-ended tail.
A beauty has little desire
for my lips, because of my beard;
She of the fair hue finds it harsh
16   like a teasel of the skin.
The edge of the cheek was always harsh,
painful bristles, harsher every day.

Cymräeg lwyschweg laschwardd,
Camre syw, Cymräes hardd.
O chemir bys yn chwimwth
48 O'i blaen, lygad crynfaen crwth,
Brwynen ewinwen wanwyrth,
Braidd fel tywys haidd na syrth.
Arleislefn ddyn eira lwysliw,
52 Wrls gwyn ar eurlewys gwiw;
Gwyn ei byd, gwen yw ei boch,
A wisg, fy nyn weüsgoch,
Penwisg welw, ddyn ddiddelw ddoeth,
56 Penselgombr, peunes aelgoeth.
Pwy a allai, pei pensaer,
Peintio â chalch pwynt fy chwaer?
Duw a'i gwnaeth, arfaeth eurfab,
60 Myn delw Bedr, ar fedr ei Fab.
Pentyriais gerdd, pwynt dirym,
Puntur serch, pond trahaus ym
Dybio cael, bu hael baham,
64 Gytgwsg â'm dyn lygatgam?

I'r Farf

'Ai dydy, farf, a darfodd
Y ferch a'm cusanai o fodd?
Rhydew'n y fan y'th blannwyd,
4 Cnwd mawr ar y cnawd im wyd;
Wyddelig arw ddulem,
Wrth edrych i'm drych a'm drem
Aeth fy ngwep a'm hwynepryd,
8 Gol gên, yn geden i gyd!'

Er llwyred darffo'i llori,
A'r modd yr eillier i mi,
Nid llyfnach, ddianach ddysg,
12 Na chloren gwrwben garwbysg.
Nid oes gan wen i'm genau
Fawr o fodd, am y farf fau;
Garw gan deg ei goroen
16 Fal llysiau cribau y croen.
Garw erioed oedd gwr y rudd,
Gwrych boeni, garwach beunydd.

There's gain for a woman if a hag has
20 a heap of toothless wool combs;
there is on my cheek, so they say,
material for a thousand little teeth.
It is the coat of an old hedgehog,
24 it's a burden on the chin like a muzzle;
nastiest beard of corn, holly tips,
steel goads goading a girl.

'Old sow's bristles, where did you come from?
28 You're a crop of gorse shoots!
Every bristle is sharp and tough,
hard heather stabbing a girl,
like—so harshly do they grow—
32 a thousand points of tiny thistles.
You are like stubble on ice,
without any covering, straight-tipped arrow-like bristles.
Flee from deep insult,
36 chin's covering like the root of a horse's mane!'

If it makes my chin look old,
with hot water it will come from its root.

26 A Game of 'Nuts in my Hand'

The girl who dresses nobly,
she is slender-browed and tender;
there was no cause nor reason
4 for striking the fair girl, she hindered men,
except that the two of them went,
it was the Jealous One's idea,
to play the silly game, bitter was the sense,
8 of 'Nuts in my hand'—better to chew them all up!

'Nuts in my hand to hear truth.'
'They are mine without delay.'
'Why yours?' Sensible words,
12 'I doubt this.' 'Because they were sent.'
'Who sent them, such gain?'
'Iolo Goch and his provoking hand.'
'Why does the lad love you from where he is?
16 Whether he loves or not, play.'

Budd i wraig o bydd i wrach
20   Mintai o ardiau mantach;
Mae ar fy llechwedd, meddan',
Ddeunydd mil o ddannedd mân.
Pais draenog oediog ydyw,
24   Pwn ar ên fal penwar yw;
Blina' col, blaenau celyn,
Symlau dur yn symlu dyn.

   'Blew henwch, o ble'r hanwyd?
28   Cnwd o egin eithin wyd!
Llym a glew yw pob blewyn,
Grug del yn gorugo dyn,
Megis—mor arw y magan'—
32   Esgyll mil o ysgall mân.
Yr wyd fal y sofl ar rew,
Heb haen, yn sythflaen saethflew.
Dos ymaith rhag dwys amarch,
36   Do gên fel bôn myngen march!'

   O gwna fy ngên yn henaidd,
Â dŵr gwres y daw o'r gwraidd.

Chwarae Cnau i'm Llaw

Y ferch a wisg yn sientli,
Main ei hael a mwyn yw hi;
Ni bu achos nac ystyr
4   Er lladd gwen, fo'u lluddiodd gwŷr,
Ond eu myned ill deuoedd,
O ddychymig Eiddig oedd,
Chwarae syn, chwerw fu'r synnwyr,
8   Cnau i'm llaw—gwell eu cnoi'n llwyr!

   'Cnau i'm llaw er gwrandaw gwir.'
'Minnau biau heb ohir.'
'Pam y tau?' Synhwyrau sôn,
12   'Amau hyn.' 'Am eu hanfon.'
'Pwy a'u hanfones, lles llyn?'
'Iolo Goch a'i law gychwyn.'
'Pam y câr mab o'r lle mae?
16   Cared na chared, chwarae.'

'Leave there,' said the fine girl,
'an odd number for me, love does not disappoint me.'
When he opened his hands,
20 by heaven! no more than nine.
In the palm of his hand there were nine
nuts, he is made a cuckold!

The Jealous One threw the nuts from his hand
24 amongst peat ashes, and raged.
'Iolo has been with you.'
'Who will prove that? When?'
'He has been with you often.'
28 'No he hasn't, if he has may you never be.'
'You were seen on St Mary's eve,
you and he, in a hay-barn,
and you were seen on Shrove eve,
32 you and he, in a corn-barn.
My faith! if I had come upon you
I would have made the red fox flee.'
'The good faultless lad wouldn't run away
36 from any man as far as India.'
'That's a lie,' said the narrow-browed man,
'He would run away, or he would deny having you.
Get out this minute.'
40 'I will not, indeed, if you are a fine lad.'
'Go to the devil,' deadly fate,
'I will not, sirrah,' unnecessary statement.
The nasty harsh-bearded Jealous One took
44 a great staff, a big stout rod;
he laid the weight of the staff on her
over her head—she had to flee.

A thick-clawed cat would not love
48 an old bundle of hair beyond its first year.
Oh tonight the girl from Gwynedd,
woe is me a hundredfold that she is not mine!

'Gad yna,' heb y geinferch,
'Amnifer ym, ni'm sym serch.'
Pan agorodd ei ddwylaw,
20 Myn y nef! nid mwy na naw.
Naw oedd ynghwr ei neddair
O gnau, yn gwcwallt y gwnair!

Bwrw o Eiddig cnau o'i law
24 Ymysg lludw mawn, a llidiaw.
'Fo a fu Iolo gennyd.'
'Pwy a braw hynny? Pa bryd?'
'Fo fu gennyd yn fynych.'
28 'Na fu, o bu fyth na bych.'
'Fo a'th welad nos Ŵyl Fair,
Ti ac ef, mewn tŷ a gwair,
Ac a'th welad nos Ynyd,
32 Ti ac ef, mewn tŷ ac ŷd.
Fy nghred! pe doethwn atoch
Gwnaethwn ffo i'r cadno coch.'
'Ni chiliai'r gwas difai da
36 Er undyn hyd yr India.'
'Celwydd!' heb y gŵr culael,
'Ciliai, neu gelai dy gael.
Dos allan gynta' y gellych.'
40 'Nac af, 'sgwir, od wyd was gwych.'
'Dos i ddiawl,' wenwynawl naid,
'Nac af, syre,' neges afraid.
Cael o Eiddig, farfddig ferf,
44 Crynffon, wialenffon lawnfferf;
Rhoi pwys y ffon ar honno
Ar hyd ei phen—bu rhaid ffo.

Ni charai gath ewindew
48 Dros ei blwydd hen drwsa blew.
Och heno'r ferch o Wynedd,
Can gwae fi nad mi a'i medd!

27 The Twelve Apostles and the Judgement

I will sing, greatest praise,
to wise learned Peter,
splendid gate-keeper of a pleasant dwelling,
4 head of the Lord of heaven's host
The second is pure gentle John,
the Apostle whose faith is not foolish,
eagle's form in a lovely cloak,
8 shining treasure, the youth is Mary's nephew.
The third most wise apostle
is fine kind Andrew;
he suffered, God's will,
12 good was his memory, faultless lord,
golden forehead, in agonising pain,
the golden treasure, on the crooked cross.
The fourth, warrant of the world,
16 apostle who is a divine saint
to give ready access to heaven,
is Bartholomew, fitting praise;
for truly believing through long pain
20 in Christ he was flayed,
and the pain turned, sharp stabbing pang,
into constant joy forever.
Chief and truest warrant,
24 fifth, sixth, seventh saint,
solemn Philip, he is beneficial,
virgin's delight, and two Jameses.
When I count, ever-increasing praise,
28 the eighth and ninth heavenly ones,
Saint Simon, of fine Edmund's line,
and brilliant zealous Saint Jude;
I know, they are two cousins
32 to the true God and gentle man.
The tenth is Thomas, long vigorous grace,
and India is his territory;
when Mary went, utterance of a beneficial word,
36 with the Lord's host to heaven,
from her legion she let fall
from heaven to Thomas her protection,
her belt, good maiden,
40 finest form of gold and jewels;
that is, gift of good kind,
his warrant, fine fair payment.
They would come with their graceful speech,

Y Deuddeg Apostol a'r Farn

Prydu a wnaf, mwyaf mawl,
I Bedr ddoeth wybodawl,
Porthor cun eiddun addef,
4   Pen ar nifer Nêr o nef.
Ail yw Ieuan lân lonydd,
Ebostol nid ffôl ei ffydd,
Llun eryr mewn llen arab,
8   Llewych grair, nai Mair yw'r mab.
Trydydd ebostol tradoeth
Yw Andras gyweithas goeth;
Dioddef a wnaeth, Duw eiddun,
12   Da fu ei gof, difai gun,
Dâl eurliw, mewn dolurloes,
Yr aur grair, ar yr ŵyr groes.
Yn bedwerydd, byd warant,
16   Ebostol sy ddwyfol sant
I beri nef yn barawd,
Barthlomëus, weddus wawd;
Am gredu'n wir drwy hirboen
20   I Grist y tynnwyd ei groen,
A'r boen a droes, loes.loywsyth,
Yn llawenydd beunydd byth.
Pennaf a gwiraf gwarant,
24   Pumed, chweched, seithfed sant,
Phylib brudd, fudd yw efô,
Degan gwyry, a dau Iago.
Pan gyfrifwy', fwyfwy fawl,
28   Wythfed a nawfed nefawl,
Sain Simwnt, hil Edmwnt hoyw,
A Sain Sud awchlud wychloyw;
Adwen, dau gefnderw ydyn'
32   I wir Dduw ac i wâr ddyn.
Degfed Tomas, hoywras hir,
A'r India yw ei randir;
Pan aeth Mair, fuddair addef,
36   Gyda nifer Nêr i nef,
O'i lleng hi a ollyngawdd
O nef i Domas ei nawdd,
Ei gwregys hi, wiw riain,
40   Orau modd o aur a main;
Hwnnw yw, iawnrhyw anrheg,
Ei warant ef, wiw rent teg.
Döent â'u dadl yn rhadlawn,

44   two apostles, divine talent,
      Matthew, strength of prayers of grace,
      great inspiration, and Mathias.
      There they are, pinnacle of heaven's protection,
48   the twelve, by the passion,
      who will judge, oath of golden lips,
      hour of salvation, the whole world;
      and blessed is he, firm union,
52   fine strong [?] manner, before the Judgement Day,
      who honours, fair kingdom,
      the festivals, the days of the twelve.

      When the horns of resurrection, united voice,
56   where praise is heard, are sounded,
      everyone together will rise
      up from the four corners of the world
      to the place where the Lord of a host suffered,
60   Prince of ages, the true Jesus.
      And there our good lord will come,
      Adam and his children, lord of nine hundred,
      and old Noah's host, it was a necessity,
64   early, and his troops—
      it will be a joy to his mother,
      heavenly colour—and Abraham's host,
      and the leader of these with a free host,
68   Moses filling the fields,
      and all the splendid host of David
      the Prophet, the psalter was chanted,
      and Paul the apostle of the faith,
72   gentle lord, will come to the mountain,
      he and his sweet ready troop
      which he converted to the faith, treasure of fate;
      and the sun's disc, immense destruction,
76   and the moon will fall to the ground,
      and the seven fine planets and the stars
      from the heavens above and their number;
      and from hell, long marsh of exile,
80   from prison they will be fetched,
      angry, terrible, double-edged plague,
      Satan's host in the colour of soot.
      Every man at his summons will come
84   on the one day there to listen
      to the terrible judgement, strong shout,
      and the thundering of their deeds.
      Higher is its grace, oh true Jesus,
88   eternal fear of the black day.

44   Dau ebostol, ddwyfol ddawn,
     Mathau, grym gweddïau gras,
     Maith awen, a Mathïas.
     Weldyna hwynt, nawddbwynt nef,
48   Y deuddeg, myn dioddef,
     A farnant, eurfant arfoll,
     Arbed awr, ar y byd oll;
     A gwyn ei fyd, cyd cadarn,
52   Cain dawdd fodd, cyn dydd y Farn,
     A wnêl urddas, deyrnas deg,
     Yng ngwyliau, dyddiau'r deuddeg.

     Pan ganer, lle clywer clod,
56   Cyfun lef, y cyrn cyfod,
     Pob un cyfun a gyfyd
     I'r lan o bedwar ban byd
     I'r lle goddefodd Nêr llu,
60   Gwawr oesoedd, y gwir Iesu.
     Ac yno daw ein gwiwner,
     Adda a'i blant, nawcant nêr,
     A llu Noe hen, angen oedd,
64   Yn fore, a'i niferoedd—
     Llawenydd a fydd i'w fam,
     Lliw wybrol—a llu Abram,
     A llyw y rhain â llu rhydd,
68   Moesen yn llenwi'r meysydd,
     A llu hardd Dafydd, yn llwyr,
     Broffwyd, lleiswyd y llaswyr,
     A Phawl ebostol y ffydd,
72   Iôr mwyn, a ddaw i'r mynydd,
     Ef a'i nifer pêr parawd
     A droes i'r ffydd, drysor ffawd;
     A rhod yr haul, draul dramawr,
76   A'r lloer a ddisgyn i'r llawr,
     A'r saith wiw blaned a'r sêr
     O'r nefoedd fry a'u nifer;
     Ac o uffern, herwwern hir,
80   O garchar hwynt a gyrchir,
     Llidiog blin daufiniog bla,
     Llu Satan mewn lliw swta.
     Pob dyn o'i ddyfyn a ddaw
84   Yr undydd yno i wrandaw
     Ar y farn flin, gadarn floedd,
     A thrydar eu gweithredoedd.
     Uwch ei ras, och wir Iesu,
88   Tragywydd ofn y dydd du.

Then we will see our fine ruler
showing, he is holy,
how on the cross, lord who suffered for salvation,
92   he was pierced on Friday,
and the crown, gripping spikes,
of thorns harsh on his brow,
and the agonising nails yonder,
96   and pain in feet and hands,
and the wounds, fair gushing
floods of flowing blood.
Then woe to them the foolish ones,
100   and then will every wise man tremble,
the soul that God put in me,
when the reckoning is made, correctness of memory;
Michael, bright Uriel,
104   with the swords, waves of fire,
he is sure beside the Lord God
picking out the wise ones;
then the imprisoned host of devils in hell
108   will suffer terrible longing;
then there will be, by the faith of Christendom,
wailing on the Mount of Olives;
then Mary, bright word,
112   will be on her pure knees
lifting up, supportive complaint,
her hands to beseech
her son and her lord and her protector,
116   golden her voice for her task,
our golden sister, and requesting
heaven and mercy for us.
We will get a place through the strength of Anna's daughter,
120   colour of day, amongst the good host;
and because of that, wise word,
it is best for me to adore Mary.

Yno gwelwn ein gwiwlyw
Yn ymddangos, aedsios yw,
Modd ar y groes, nawddloes nêr,
90 Y gwanwyd ef ddyw Gwener,
A'r goron, hoelion hylud,
O ddrain am y tâl yn ddrud,
A'r cethri dur drwy gur draw,
96 A dolur draed a dwylaw,
A'r gwelïau, tonnau teg
Rhydaer o waed yn rhedeg.
Yno gwae hwy rhai annoeth,
100 Ac yno y crŷn pob dyn doeth,
Enaid a roes Duw ynof,
Pan gyfrifer, c'wirder cof;
Mihangel, Uriel eirian,
104 Â'r cleddyfau, tonnau tân,
Diau yw gerllaw Duw Iôn
Yn dethol y rhai doethion;
Yno y bydd dir hiraeth
108 Yn uffern ar gethern gaeth;
Yno bydd, myn crefydd Cred,
Lefain ym Mwnd Olifed;
Yno bydd Mair, air eirian,
112 Ar dalau ei gliniau glân
Yn dyrchafael, gafael gŵyn,
Ei dwylo i adolwyn
I'w mab a'i harglwydd a'i mur,
116 Aur ei llef er ei llafur,
Ein eurchwaer, ac yn erchi
Nef a thrugaredd i ni.
Cawn ran drwy nerth merch Anna,
120 Lliw dydd, ymysg y llu da;
Ac am hynny, gymhennair,
Gorau i mi garu Mair.

28   The Ploughman

When the people of the world, lively host of Christendom,
   show, some free time,
   before the Lord God, it would be [His] will,
4   fine bold language, their deeds,
   on top of the strong Mount of Olives,
   where judgement will be, all of them,
   joyful will be the unhesitating speech

8   of the ploughman, traverser of the field,
   if he gave, generously to the good God,
   his offering and tithe to God,
   a good true soul then
12   will he pay to God, he deserves reward.
   Easy for the ploughman of the fine meadow
   is trust in the Lord God afterwards:
   he does not refuse anyone charity,
16   in his righteousness, or lodging;
   he does not pass judgement except on a ploughbeam,
   he does not like anger amongst his fellow labourers;
   he does not wage war, he does not persecute,
20   he does not rob a man of his goods by force;
   he is never harsh towards us,
   he makes no claim, forbearing fault;
   it would not be right, by the passion,
24   there would be no life, no world without him.
   I know that he far prefers,
   placid constant manner,
   to follow, I care not, with little blame,
28   the curved plough with the goad
   than if he were, when he was breaking a tower,
   in the shape of Arthur the ravager.
   Except through his work Christ's sacrifice
32   is not to be had to feed Christendom,
   nor the life—why should I blame?—
   of pope or emperor without him,
   nor king, fine wine-dispensing ruler,
36   perfect his sense, nor any man alive.
   Clever old Lucidarius
   said this truly:
   'Blessed is he, against hardship beyond,
40   who holds the plough with his hands.'

    Low flat broom-tearing cradle,
   fine creel cutting a field into strips;

Cywydd y Llafurwr

Pan ddangoso, rhywdro rhydd,
Pobl y byd, peibl lu bedydd,
Garbron Duw cun, eiddun oedd,
4 Gwiw iaith ddrud, eu gweithredoedd,
Ar ben Mynydd, lle bydd barn,
I gyd, Olifer gadarn,
Llawen fydd chwedl diledlaes
8 Llafurwr, dramwywr maes,
O rhoddes, hael i'r Hoywdduw,
Offrwm a'i ddegwm i Dduw,
Enaid da yna uniawn
12 A dâl i Dduw, dyly ddawn.
Hawdd i lafurwr hoywddol
Hyder ar Dduw Nêr yn ôl:
O gardod drwy gywirdeb,
16 O lety ni necy neb;
Ni rydd farn eithr ar arnawdd,
Ni châr yn ei gyfar gawdd;
Ni ddeily ryfel, ni ddilyn,
20 Ni threisia am ei dda ddyn;
Ni bydd ry gadarn arnam,
Ni yrr hawl, gymedrawl gam;
Nid addas, myn dioddef,
24 Nid bywyd, nid byd heb ef.
Gwn mai digrifach ganwaith
Gantho, modd digyffro maith,
Galyn, ni'm dawr, heb fawr fai,
28 Yr aradr crwm â'r irai
Na phe bai, pan dorrai dŵr,
Yn rhith Arthur anrheithiwr.
Ni cheffir eithr o'i weithred
32 Aberth Crist i borthi Cred,
Na bywyd—pam y beiwn?—
Pab nac ymherodr heb hwn,
Na brenin, heilwin hoywlyw,
36 Dien ei bwyll, na dyn byw.
Lusudarus hwylus hen
A ddywod hyn yn ddien:
'Gwyn ei fyd, rhag trymfyd draw,
40 A ddeily aradr â'i ddwylaw.'

Crud rhwygfanadl gwastadlaes,
Cryw mwyn yn careio maes;

its praise is proclaimed, the fair treasure,
44 a share which opens up a bright furrow,
swift basket of uncultivated land for a long while,
noble and well-designed with a coulter,
gander of overgrown acres,
48 well is grain to be had by its craft;
it seeks a crop in rich soil,
good foal biting earth,
a man with an aversion to pebbles,
52 a lad who flays with his leg before him;
he wants his knife and his food
and his table under the base of his thigh;
his head is hard at it every day,
56 a healthy road under oxen's feet;
often will I sing his song of praise,
he wishes to pursue the plough-chain;
a root-chopper bearing fruit in the valley,
60 sticking out a rigid neck;
train-bearer of a mighty lord,
earth-scattering, fine, wooden-legged.

Hu the Strong, master of a fine nation,
64 a king who gave wine for praise,
emperor of land and seas,
he was the golden constable of Constantinople,
after the flood he held
68 a good strong plough with sturdy beam;
he never sought, healthy-living lord,
turner of soil, any bread
except, good was his teacher,
72 by his own hard labour, creator of a land,
in order to show, finely-gifted eagle,
to the proud and the humbly wise
that the most treasured Father prizes
76 one craft above all, no false word,
a sign that this is foremost,
ploughing, it is a learnèd art.

As far as Christendom and baptism extends
80 and everyone maintains the faith,
the hand of the Lord God, best of men,
the hand of Mary over every ploughman.

Crïir ei glod, y crair glwys,
44 Crehyr a'i hegyr hoywgwys,
Cawell tir gŵydd rhwydd yrhawg,
Calltrefn urddedig cylltrawg,
Ceiliagwydd erwi gwyddiawn,
48 Cywir o'i grefft y ceir grawn;
Cnwd a gyrch mewn cnodig âr,
Cnyw diwael yn cnoi daear,
Gŵr a'i anfodd ar grynfaen,
52 Gwas a fling a'i goes o'i flaen;
E fyn ei gyllell a'i fwyd
A'i fwrdd dan fôn ei forddwyd;
Ystig fydd beunydd ei ben,
56 Ystryd iach is traed ychen;
Aml y canaf ei emyn,
Ymlid y fondid a fyn;
Un dryllwraidd dyffrynnaidd ffrwyth
60 Yn estyn gwddw anystwyth;
Gwas pwrffil aneiddil nen,
Gwasgarbridd gwiw esgeirbren.

Hu Gadarn, feistr hoyw giwdawd,
64 Brenin a roes gwin er gwawd,
Ymherodr tir a moroedd,
Cwnstabl aur Constinobl oedd,
Daliodd ef wedi diliw
68 Aradr gwaisg arnoddgadr gwiw;
Ni cheisiodd, naf iachusoed,
Fwriwr âr, fara erioed
Oddieithr, da oedd ei athro,
72 O'i lafur braisg, awdur bro,
Er dangos, eryr dawngoeth,
I ddyn balch a difalch doeth
Bod yn orau, nid gau gair,
76 Ungrefft gan y Tad iawngrair,
Arwydd mai hyn a oryw,
Aredig, dysgedig yw.

Hyd y mae Cred a bedydd
80 A phawb yn cynnal y ffydd,
Llaw Dduw cun, gorau un gŵr,
Llaw Fair dros bob llafurwr.

29   To Saint David

Desiring good to my soul,
I am getting old, this was necessary,
to go to the place where Christ was crucified
4   although my two sad black feet
are stuck here in fetters,
the feet do not wish to go there.
It is just as beneficial for me
8   to go three times to Menevia
as to go, fine dignity,
in the summers as far as Rome.
I knew where I would wish to be,
12   it is a virtuous residence,
in the manor of David of Menevia,
it is a fine spot, by the cross;
in Glyn Rhosyn is the beautiful [place],
16   and olive trees and vines
and excellence of music and manner
and the sound of men and a clock
and lively harmony, shining brilliance,
20   between an entire organ and bells,
and a great heavy golden thuribulum
emitting incense to give a sweet odour.
Fine heaven of heavens open to all,
24   it's a good town after the fashion of Rome,
fair smooth paradise of Wales,
choice sovereign town laid out like paradise.

Saint Patrick was reluctant
28   because of God's displeasure, angry time,
because this was commanded, it was an insult,
that he should go from the place which he had made,
away from Menevia
32   before David's birth, he's good.
He was a saint from heaven to us
inherent before his birth;
he was a pure saint when he was born
36   because of the splitting of the stone, marvellous his faith;
he restored his sight
to the sick man's eyes, overcoming bad disease,
his godfather, worldly family,
40   without eyes or nose, great was the praise;
Sant was his father, it was undeniable
that he was the chief of the saints;

I Ddewi Sant

Dymuno da i'm enaid,
Heneiddio'r wyf, hyn oedd rhaid,
Myned i'r lle croged Crist
4 Cyd boed y ddeudroed ddudrist
Mewn trygyff yma'n trigaw,
Ni myn y traed myned draw.
Cystal ymofal im yw
8 Fyned deirgwaith i Fynyw
Â myned, cymyrred cain,
Yr hafoedd hyd yn Rhufain.
Gwyddwn lle mynnwn fy mod,
12 Ys deddfol yw'r eisteddfod,
Ym maenol Ddewi Mynyw,
Mangre gain, myn y grog, yw;
Yng Nglyn Rhosyn mae'r iesin,
16 Ac olewydd a gwŷdd gwin
Ac edmig musig a moes
A gwrle gwŷr ac orloes
A chytgerdd hoyw, loyw lewych,
20 Rhwng organ achlân a chlych,
A thrwblwm aur trwm tramawr
Yn bwrw sens i beri sawr.
Nef nefoedd yn gyhoedd gain,
24 Ys da dref ystad Rufain,
Paradwys Gymru lwys lefn,
Pôr dewistref p'radwystrefn.

Petrus fu gan Sain Patrig
28 Am sorri Duw, amser dig,
Am erchi hyn, amarch oedd,
Iddo o'r lle a wnaddoedd,
Fyned ymaith o Fynyw
32 Cyn geni Dewi, da yw.
Sant oedd ef o nef i ni
Cynhwynol cyn ei eni;
Sant glân oedd ef pan aned
36 Am hollti'r maen, graen ei gred;
Eilwaith y rhoes ei olwg
I'r claf drem rhag clefyd drwg,
Ei dad bedydd, dud bydawl,
40 Dall wynepglawr, mawr fu'r mawl;
Sant ei dad, diymwad oedd
Penadur saint pan ydoedd;

a beneficial bright-eyed saint
44   was Non his good pure mother
daughter of Ynyr of great family,
fine nun, it is a wonderful tale.
One food went into his mouth,
48   cold bread and cress
and black water as long as he lived,
manner of a gift, of the same kind
as went into bright fine Non's mouth
52   since he was conceived, he is sovereign.

All the saints of the world, joint journey,
came to the fine senate long ago
to listen on the same day
56   to his sermon and some of his faith;
there rose up, it was no misfortune,
a hill under David of Brefi's feet
where he taught a splendid host,
60   where he delivered a fine sermon
six thousand, seven score thousand saints
and one thousand, what a congregation!
It was given to him to be, praise of purity,
64   head of all the saints of the world.
He blessed fairly,
the cantref of heaven was his refuge,
the warm fresh bath,
68   it will not cease, it will remain forever.
Firmly did he permit,
good grace of the black Lent,
to the Britons above all others,
72   honour of the *brut*, the herring.
God transformed, harsh angry rage,
two wolves of devilish nature,
two old men who were from the land of magic,
76   cunning Gwydre and Odrud,
for committing, evil exploit long ago,
some sin which they willed;
and their mother—why should she be?—
80   was a wolverine, a curse on her;
and good David released them
from their long suffering and from their exile.
God stocked his altar,
84   his net performed a great miracle;
he drove the wild birds in flight
to the houses, my fair lord;

Santes gydles lygadlon
44 Ei fam dda ddi-nam oedd Non
Ferch Ynyr fawr ei chenedl,
Lleian wiw, gwych ydiw'r chwedl.
Un bwyd a aeth yn ei ben,
48 Bara oer a beryren
A dwfr du tra fu fyw,
Waneg anrheg, o'r unrhyw
Ag aeth ym mhen Non wen wiw
52 Er pan gad, penaig ydiw.

Holl saint y byd, gyd gerrynt,
A ddoeth i'r senedd goeth gynt
I wrando yn yr undydd
56 Ei bregeth a pheth o'i ffydd;
Cyfodes, nid oedd resyn,
Dan draed Dewi Frefi fryn
Lle dysgodd llu dewisgoeth,
60 Lle bu yn pregethu'n goeth,
Chwemil, saith ugeinmil saint
Ac unfil, wi o'r genfaint.
Rhoed iddo fod, glod glendyd,
64 Yn ben ar holl saint y byd.
Ef yn deg a fendigawdd,
Cantref o nef oedd ei nawdd,
Yr ennaint twymn wyrennig,
68 Ni dderfydd, tragywydd trig.
Hydr y gwnaeth ef genhiadu,
Gras da y Garawys du,
I'r Brytaniaid, brut wyneb,
72 Y gwynad yn anad neb.
Duw a rithiawdd, dygngawdd dig,
Ddeuflaidd anian ddieflig,
Deuwr hen oedd o dir hud,
76 Gwydre astrus ac Odrud,
Am wneuthur, drwg antur gynt,
Ryw bechod a rybuchynt;
A'u mam—baham y bai hi?—
80 Yn fleiddiast, oerfel iddi;
A Dewi goeth a'u dug wynt
O'u hirboen ac o'u herwbwynt.
Diwallodd Duw ei allawr,
84 Ei fagl a wnaeth miragl mawr;
Yr adar gwyllt o'r hedeg
A yrrai i'r tai, fy iôr teg;

and the spirited, swift, hard-antlered stags,
88   wonderful servants, served him.
On Tuesday the first day of March in the grave
to die he went to lie.
There were on his grave, good end,
92   fine clergy singing a gloria,
angels of heaven on the bank of a stream
after his funeral.
The soul of a man who is buried
96   in the cemetry of David of Menevia
above all other land, it is not vain,
will not be condemned to the pit of hell;
no filthy devil will ever tread
100   on his land for all the world's wealth.

If there were in a book of paper
every day as on a long summer's day
one of the same nature as a public notary
104 with pen and ink with a steel tip
writing, it was profit,
his famous life,
hardly, however good he were,
108 would he ever manage to write
in three days and a full year
all the miracles which he performed.

30 A Prayer

Christ hear us, sovereign lord,
lest I should suffer some oppression;
lamb-lion, alpha and omega,
4 god-man eternally true,
redeeming king you must dispense
true council to us against death.

He was not sown, he was not born,
8 he was not clearly seen,
he is not seen on sea or land,
he tormented, he certain,
he is the retribution for the apple,
12 one whose properties are changeable,

A'r ceirw osglgyrn chwyrn chwai,
88 Gweision uthr, a'i gwasnaethai.
    Dyw Mawrth Galan Mawrth ym medd
    I farw'r aeth ef i orwedd.
    Bu ar ei fedd, diwedd da,
92 Cain glêr yn canu gloria,
    Engylion nef yng nglan nant
    Ar ôl bod ei arwyliant.
    I bwll uffern ni fernir
96 Enaid dyn, yn anad tir,
    A gladder, diofer yw,
    Ym mynwent Dewi Mynyw;
    Ni saing cythraul brycheulyd
100 Ar ei dir byth er da'r byd.

    Pebai mewn llyfr o'r pabir
    Beunydd mal ar hafddydd hir
    Noter pyblig un natur
104 Â phin a du â phen dur
    Yn ysgrifennu, bu budd,
    Ei fuchedd ef ddiachudd,
    Odid fyth, er däed fai,
108 Ennyd yr ysgrifennai
    Dridiau a blwyddyn drydoll
    A wnaeth ef o wyniaith oll.

Gweddi

    Crist audi nos, craton cyrios,
    Rhag im aros rhyw gamwriau;
    Agnus leo, alffa et o,
4   Deus homo dioesamau,
    Rex redemptor rhaid it hepgor
    Iawn rhyw gyngor in rhag angau.

    Ef ni hëed, ef ni aned,
8   Ef ni weled yn iawn olau,
    Ar fôr na thir ef ni welir,
    Ef yn ddyir, ef yn ddiau,
    Ef yw'r dial am yr afal,
12 Un anwadal ei anwydau,

he high, he quiet,
he low, he clumsy,
he well-known through his will,
16 he swift, he wants no rewards,
coming and going very quickly
here and there by his steps,
he will be no older in the year,
20 no man knows, he will be no younger,
and he trembles and he does not freeze,
and he pulls and he is silent;
not sluggish where he comes, sparks do not burn him,
24 cold does not hinder him, weapons do not kill him,
no coward dares face him, no brave man waits for him,
flowing water does not drown him, swords do not stand
         against him,
he does not run hard, he does not rest,
28 he is not contained, no diseases carry him off,
not dead not alive, I know not what he is,
one does not feel him under cold protruding ribs,
a shower does not wet him, no eye sees him,
32 our pure father who listens to us.

True king of heaven for your peace,
for your suffering, for your passion,
for your agonies for mankind,
36 for your crown, best nobleman,
for your torment, for your distress,
bright scarlet language, and your wounds,
for your fast for the people of the world,
40 for your penance, for your pains,
for your virtue and the ten commandments,
man of pure nature, for your true blood,
for all your saints, for your wound,
44 for your pierced breast, for your honours,
for your torment and your bloody breast,
man of pure faith, for your true blood,
for your tribulation on Friday,
48 and your true light and your wounds,
for your praise, heavenly king,
valiant teacher, and your surpassing qualities
give me understanding to withstand evil,
52 pure wise lord, for your true blood:
this I wish, this I will get,
this I seek, fine objectives,
the protection of the true cross and the protection of Idloes,
56 and giving me life, me and mine,

Ef yn uchel, ef yn dawel,
Ef yn isel, ef yn asau,
Ef o'i awydd yn gyfarwydd,
16 Ef yn ebrwydd, ni fyn obrau,
Yn bwhwman yn dra buan
Draw ac yman drwy ei gamau,
Ef ni bydd hŷn yn y flwyddyn,
20 Ni wybydd dyn, ef ni bydd iau,
Ac ef a grŷn ac ef ni ryn,
Ac ef a dynn ac ef a dau;
Nid llesg lle dêl, nis llysg ufel,
24 Nis lludd oerfel, nis lladd arfau,
Nis baidd llwfr, nis ery dilwfr,
Nis bawdd cleuddwfr, nis baidd cleddau,
Ni red yn ddwys, ni orffowys,
28 Nis daw cynnwys, nis dwg heiniau,
Nid marw nid byw, nis gwn beth yw,
Dyn nis erglyw dan ais oerglau,
Nis gwlych cawad, nis gwŷl llygad,
32 Ein gwiriawndad a'n gwarendau.

Gwir frenin nef er dy dangnef,
Er dy oddef, er dioddau,
Er dy loesion er dyniaddon,
36 Er dy goron, wrda gorau,
Er dy gystudd, er dy gythrudd,
Iaith oloywrudd, a'th ddoluriau,
Er dy ympryd er pobl y byd,
40 Er dy benyd, er dy boenau,
Er dy gynneddf a'r dengair deddf,
Ŵr diweirgreddf, er dy wirgrau,
Er dy saint oll, er dy archoll,
44 Er dy fron holl, er dy freiniau,
Er dy godded a'th fron waedled,
Ŵr diweirgred, er dy wirgrau,
Er dy bryder at dduw Gwener,
48 A'th wir leufer a'th welïau,
Er dy ganmol, frenin nefol,
Athro gwrol, a'th ragorau,
Moes im ddeall i wrthladd ball,
52 Iôr diweirgall, er dy wirgrau:
Hyn a fynnaf, hyn a gaffaf,
Hyn a geisiaf, hoyw negesau,
Nawdd y wirgroes a nawdd Idloes
56 A rhoi im oes, mi a'r rhai mau,

the protection of Maria and the protection of Anna,
and the saints of Asaph and the saintesses,
the protection of the saints of Bardsey and of Cybi,
60   and of David, Nudd of the South,
and of Ieuan and of Cadfan,
and of Sanan, Nudd of the saints,
the protection of Michael and of Gabriel,
64   and of Uriel, the best protection,
the protection of the saints of the world be with me
to safeguard me against the snares.

31   Ode to Mary

Wisely did Jesus choose you,
lovely jewel, as his mother.
The Lord said 'ave'
4   against the retribution for Eve's apple.

Eve did not take the forbidden
apple without encountering trouble;
evil does not go without heavy retribution
8   any more than good goes without payment.

Fair was the enlivening payment from the word of the Trinity,
    from the coronet of the chair,
      when Christ became—sweet cherished lord,
12   lamb of God the highest—Mary's son.

Mary look upon me o empress,
you are the highest of maidens, sovereign Mary,
Mary you are blameless, queen Mary,
16   noble bright-faced Mary, mistress Mary,
have mercy on me, manner of a hen-eagle;
you are the virgins' songbook and their own benefactor,
glass window of heaven and its peacock,
20   you are the angels' moon and their lioness,
and mother to God comprehending,
and daughter to your one brother, declaration of greatest
    fortune,
and you are sister to your one son and kinsman,
24   very closely, princess,
is your son related to you, no wonder.
It was a good womb-load, [yours] was the condition of a
    countess,

Nawdd Maria a nawdd Anna,
A saint Asa a santesau,
Nawdd saint Enlli a nawdd Cybi,
60   A nawdd Dewi, Nudd y Deau,
A nawdd Ieuan a nawdd Cadfan,
A nawdd Sanan, Nudd y seiniau,
Nawdd Mihangel a nawdd Gabriel,
64   A nawdd Uriel, y nawdd orau,
Nawdd saint y byd i'm cymhlegyd
I ymoglyd rhag y maglau.

Awdl i Fair

Doeth y'th etholes Iesu,
Em addwyn, yn fam iddo.
Dofydd a ddyfod 'afi'
4   Rhag dial afal Efa.

Ni chymerth Efa'r afal
Gwardd heb gyfwrdd â gofal;
Nid â'r drwg heb drwm dial
8   Mwy nag yr â'r da heb dâl.

Teg fu'r tâl eirial o air—y Drindod,
    O drendal y gadair,
     Pan ddoeth Crist, naf arafgrair,
12   Oen Duw pab, yn fab i Fair.

Mair edrych arnaf ymerodres,
Morwyn bennaf wyd, Mair unbennes,
Mair diornair wyd, Mair deÿrnes,
16   Mair oleudrem hael, Mair lywodres,
Miserere mei, moes eryres;
Prydlyfr gweryddon wyd a'u priodles,
Ffenestr wydrin nef a'i pheunes,
20   Lleuad engylion wyd a'u llewes,
A mam i Dduw yn ymoddiwes,
A merch i'th unbrawd, briffawd broffes,
A chwaer i'th unmab wyd a chares,
24   Ys agos o beth, dywysoges,
Y deiryd dy fab it, nid eres.
Ys da dorllwyth, fu ystad iarlles,

my soul, from the angel whom the spirit
28 sent to you, warm messenger,
he with a sweet word made you pregnant,
and God went into your bosom
as the sunbeam goes through glass,
32 like a cluster of splendid grace,
three ripe nuts, into three did it turn,
father, he excelled through love,
holy, tender, sweet, warm son,
36 spirit of purity, pure fair prophecy.
It is proverbial how easily the lord of perfect benefit
was delivered without birth pains,
without any wound from bearing him, prioress of heaven,
40 without any fornication with anyone intimately,
or disgrace from any man, there was no contact.
After the birth of the boy, well did he act,
a round constant star appeared
44 to the three holy kings, this was what happened,
to bring you an offering against misfortune,
gold and frankincense and myrrh, the saint is not angry.
Joseph from the manger, true was the declaration,
48 it is remembered, was the first who lifted him.
John the Baptist, may he save us,
the sinless mighty godfather bathed him
through faith and baptism, he did not mind,
52 in the water of the Jordan, there did he swim.
Well did you suckle him like a goddess
on your dear breast, queen on high.
From there you were a sorceress,
56 you fled with him towards a land,
to Egypt to escape punishment and persecution.
Marvellous was the power of Mary the companion,
a virgin bearing child, Mary my lady,
60 a virgin before bearing, tender nun,
a virgin whilst bearing, lying-in of a beneficial name,
still virginal and a mistress.
You are alive in heaven like an abbess
64 in your bodily form, radiant body beneficial like the sun,
with the brotherly man who married you,
and fittingly did he choose you.

F'enaid, o'r angel a'i hanfones
28 Yr ysbryd atad, gennad gynnes,
Efo â chwegair a'th feichioges,
A Duw o fewn aeth yn dy fynwes
Fal yr â drwy'r gwydr y terydr tes,
32 Megis bagad o rad rodres,
Tair cneuen gwisgi, tri y tröes
Yn dad, drwy gariad y rhagores,
Yn fab gwyn arab araf cynnes,
36 Yn ysbryd glendyd, glandeg armes.
Dihareb rhwydded y dehores
Heb boen yn esgor pôr perffeithles,
Heb friw o'i arwain, nef briores,
40 Heb ddim godineb â neb yn nes,
Neu ogan o ŵr, nid oedd neges.
Gwedi geni'r mab, gwiw digones,
Seren gron gyson a ymddangoses
44 I'r tri brenin gwyn, hyn fu'r hanes,
I ddwyn rhyw gyflwyn it rhag afles,
Aur a thus a myrr, ni syrr santes.
Sioseb o'r preseb, gwir fu'r proffes,
48 Cof ydyw, fu'r cyntaf a'i cyfodes.
Ieuan Fedyddiwr, gŵr a'n gwares,
Tad bedydd dibech trech a'i troches
Drwy ffydd a bedydd, ni ddarbodes,
52 Yn nwfr Urddonen, yna nofies.
Da y megaist ef megis duwies
Ar dy fron hygu, fry frenhines.
Oddyno y buost yn ddewines,
56 Ti a ffoaist ag ef tua pheues,
I'r Aifft rhag anghraifft a rhag yngres.
Rhyfedd fu'r gallu o Fair gyfeilles,
Ymddŵyn yn forwyn, Fair f'arglwyddes,
60 Morwyn cyn ymddŵyn, fwyn fynaches,
Morwyn yn ymddŵyn, gorllwyn geirlles,
Morwynaidd eto a meiriones.
Byw ydwyd yn nef fal abades
64 Yn dy gorffolaeth, hoywgorff heules,
Gyda'r gŵr brawdwr a'th briodes,
A theilwng o beth y'th etholes.

32   Praise of the Horsehair Harp
and Satire on the Leather Harp

By the noble God, a course of graces,
lord of host, once merry Wales,
the best place, vineyard of lavishness,
4   in the living world were you
whilst there was time for minstrelsy
and the learning of the good old Welsh people;
now, God knows, cold knowledge,
8   there is noisy song in our midst,
a weak-framed incomplete plank,
harps, gates of leather.

David did not have, flourishing of faith,
12   a single string made from dead sheep;
the virtuous Prophet David
never made, swift magic of minstrels,
any harp, entertaining skill,
16   except of horsehair, proper song.
Wise is the easy lively expression
of the harp of shining black horsehair.
The horsehair harp, profound gift,
20   by the blessing of the Trinity and its grace,
told David all
that was beforehand and will be
from the world's beginning, mighty purpose,
24   to the day of judgement, great meditation.
No yearning devil will ever reach
the status of the horsehair harp.

No one of our nation desires,
28   if he knows a tune or its semblance,
to make sound, fie on the job,
anything but a leather harp, not felicitous,
and a curved-tipped nail, nasty thorn,
32   and some base lad to carry it.
It will be hard for an apprentice in a month
to string a brass greyhound bitch,
evil plague shaped like a bare bow,
36   a rainbow and a crooked abomination.
I never loved, true attempt of art,
its studded sounding board nor its song
nor its gutty sound, harsh misfortune,

Cywydd Moliant i'r Delyn Rawn
a Dychan i'r Delyn Ledr

Rho Duw hael, rhadau helynt,
Gwawr rhif, Gymru ddigrif gynt,
Gorau man, gwinllan y gost,
4 Ar fyd o fywyd fuost
Tra fu amser i glera
A dysg yr hen Gymry da;
Weithian, dioer, oer addysg,
8 Y mae cerdd seiniog i'n mysg,
Diflo anghyfan wangledr,
Telynau, llidiardau lledr.

Nid oedd un tant, ffyniant ffydd,
12 O ddefaid meirw i Ddafydd;
Ni wnaeth, clau ddewiniaeth clêr,
Dafydd Broffwyd diofer
Un delyn, ddiddan angerdd,
16 Onid o rawn, gyfiawn gerdd.
Doeth yw ymadrawdd hawdd hoyw
Y delyn o rawn duloyw.
Y delyn rawn, dawn difas,
20 O rad y Drindod a'i ras,
A ddyfod oll i Ddafydd
A fu rhagllaw ac a fydd
O ddechrau byd, bryd breisgfawr,
24 Hyd dydd brawd, myfyrdawd mawr.
Ni ddaw cythraul hiraethlawn
I'r radd y bo telyn rawn.

Nid oes a fynno o'n iaith,
28 O gwybydd gainc na'i gobaith,
I beri sôn, wb o'r swydd,
Ond telyn ledr, nid hylwydd,
Ac ewingorn, dorn difwyn,
32 A rhyw was diras i'w dwyn.
Anodd i brentis fis fydd
Ystofi miliast efydd,
Anfad bla llun bwa llwm,
36 Enfys ac echrys gochrwm.
Ni cherais, iawngais angerdd,
Na'i chafn botymog na'i cherdd
Na'i choludd sain, damwain dig,

40   nor its jaundiced colour nor its insolence
     nor its bow-legged rough comb
     nor its bent column, a coward loves it.
     Bad under the stitching of the eight fingers is
44   the shape of its womb, the linen of its shirt.
     The wild neighing, false roaring,
     of a yellow mare for stallions.
     Sister by the same father, long night's wandering song,
48   to the cold yellow plague of Rhos.
     Sound of a nasty lame goose in corn,
     noisy crazy Irishwoman,
     the thud of a mill, trouser-crumpling leap,
52   screeching crooked-necked ear,
     shrivelled-looking witches,
     geese squabbling over territory,
     young crows wallowing,
56   a rabble feeling rain,
     a hailstorm gathering
     flanked by lightning on a stone roof.
     Its column and its hoarse voice
60   were made only for an old Englishman.
     It was a wooden sickle for a silly girl,
     an old hag's crooked shin.

     Let every true apprentice
64   from the march of the land of England to Môn
     seek a bright harp of black horsehair
     to play and spread learning
     as it was, my declaration,
68   in the time of our ancestors.
     Let not, favourless double complaint,
     the day-apprentices seek to bear it.

33   The Ship

     It is hard for me to give a single greeting
     on the ship, cold is its deck,
     stream's saddle, hollow its boast,
4   prisonhouse of the vile bitter beer
     and the black ale, cold harsh gaol,
     and the sparkling, cold, puked cider;
     greetings, golden pronouncement,

40   Na'i rhifwnt liw na'i rhyfig
    Na'i chwr bergam disgamar
    Na'i llorf cam, un llwrf a'i câr.
    Drwg yw dan bwyth yr wythmys
44   Llun ei chroth, lliain ei chrys.
    Gweryrad gwyllt, rhuad gau,
    Gwilff felen am geffylau.
    Chwaer undad, herwnad hirnos,
48   I'r oer fad felen o Ros.
    Sain gŵydd gloff an-hoff yn ŷd,
    Sonfawr Wyddeles ynfyd,
    Ysgwd melin, lowdrgrin lam,
52   Ysgyfar waeddgar yddgam,
    Gwiddonod mewn gwedd anir,
    Gwyddau yn dadlau am dir,
    Cywion brain yn ymgreiniaw,
56   Ciwed yn ymglywed â glaw,
    Cawod genllysg yn cywain
    O du mellt ar do main.
    Ni luniwyd ei pharwyden
60   Na'i chreglais ond i Sais hen.
    Cryman pren i fursen fu,
    Crimog henwrach yn crymu.

    Ceisied pob prentis cyson
64   O fars tir Lloegr i Fôn
    Telyn eirian i'w chanu
    I rannu dysg o rawn du
    Fal yr oedd, mau gyhoeddi,
68   Yn oes ein henafiaid ni.
    Na cheisied, ddiged ddeugwyn,
    Y dydd brentisiaid i'w dwyn.

Cywydd y Llong

    Anodd im un hawddamawr
    Ar y llong, oer yw ei llawr,
    Cyfrwy ffrwd, ceufawr ei ffrost,
4   Carchardy y cwrw chwerwdost
    A'r âl ddu, oer eol ddig,
    A'r gloyw seidr oer gloesiedig;
    Hawddamawr, eurfawr arfoll,

8   to my lord and all my comrades;
let there be no greeting, no pregnant hollow grim,
phantom on the deck of the ship.

Great punishment, it was painful for me,
12 for a feeble thin man to live in it;
it would rock, faulty thing,
on its side, cold its shivering;
it was a hateful house for me, cheese-house of the seas,
16 castle of torment, the sailors' coffin,
most hateful dame, frequent its mis-steering,
it is a filthy Noah's ark,
oaken soot-pan, bitter its sweat,
20 frisky round-walled pale-shirted old cow,
coal cart, no good clean court,
with canvas sails, hollow bulging nature,
high-nosed hag, scabby-edged board,
24 with hollow nostril, rope-reined saddle,
breadth of a kneading trough, shape of a new moon,
it lurches like an old churn,
swift tower of swollen appearance,
28 a box seven straight cubits long,
bucking mud-stirring mare,
erratically jumping scale-pan,
gaol of scabby wood like crabs' guts,
32 swollen mare, everyone sees her from France;
she grimaced in seaweed,
a skate skewered under its breast,
her rent pays more than a mark,
36 crooked-edged basket of bouncy cork.
She will frolic, Arthur's confession,
in the hollow stone, stone like a wall,
and also, good renunciation,
40 I will never go to my destruction,
cold black chest in rough condition,
to her, old cupboard of the sea,
dull churlish lass, she was in Greece,
44 broad cold black anchorage,
vile rushing sow's refuge,
seed dish with a row of masts and a swelling breast,
broad creaking gravel sled,
48 it would leap over the furrow, cold bare mare,
rounded conspicious dung-ridden cart,
cold serpent like Sir Fulk's horse,
fat barrow, it pours out yeast,
52 stone-bellied serpent, salty negress,

8   I'm iôn a'm cyfeillion oll;
     Ni bo, wyll gyflo geuflong,
     Hawddamawr ar llawr y llong.

     Cerydd mawr, cur oedd i mi,
12   O feinddyn llesg fyw ynddi;
     Rhocian a wnâi, bai o beth,
     Ar ei hochr, oer ei hachreth;
     Casty im oedd, cawsty mŷr,
16   Castell ing, cist y llongwyr,
     Casaf dâm, aml ei chamlyw,
     Alch Noe olychwin yw,
     Huddyglgrud derw, chwerw ei chwŷs,
20   Henfon hoyw walgron welwgrys,
     Certwain glo, nid cwrt iawn glân,
     Carthennwyl, ceuroth anian,
     Ffriwuchel wrach, fingrach fort,
24   Ffroengau, ystrodur ffrwyngort,
     Lled noe, llun lleuad newydd,
     Lletpai fal hen fuddai fydd,
     Esgud dŵr ysgod toreth,
28   Ysgrîn saith gyfelin seth,
     Esgudlam wilff ysgydlaid,
     Ysgâl anwadal ei naid,
     Geol wyddgrach goluddgrainc,
32   Gwilff roth, pawb a'i gwŷl o Ffrainc;
     Mingamai hi mewn gwymon,
     Morcath a'i brath dan ei bron,
     Mwy a dâl ei mâl na morc,
36   Mwys gyrgam ymwasgargorc.
     Caiff serthedd, cyffes Arthur,
     Yn y tyllfaen, maen fal mur,
     A hefyd, diofryd da,
40   Nid af fyth i'm difetha,
     Oer ddugest arw arddigor,
     Iddi, hen almari môr,
     Iangwraig bôl, yng Ngroeg y bu,
44   Angorddwr eang oerddu,
     Hwch ddinas ddiras oddáin,
     Hadlestr hwylbrenrhestr bronrhain,
     Llydan yslêd graean greg,
48   Llamai'r gŵys, llom oer gaseg,
     Sarred groth domled amlwg,
     Sarff oer megis march Syr Ffwg,
     Berwa dew, burm a dywallt,
52   Bolmaen sarff, blowmones hallt,

harrow raking the ocean,
very crooked hind of the sea.

Many times, God knows, cold border,
56   when the wild bare sea was in full flood,
I sent greetings, fine noble lord,
golden helmet, to Cilmael,
where Rhys ap Robert was,
60   another Lazarus's court, prominent kinsman;
there I would get, unstinting gift,
a drink of his golden foaming bragget;
it's there, praiseworthy seal of comfort,
64   I'd be were I where I'd be.

34   Satire on the Grey Friar of Chester

Hywel, fine hawk in holy orders,
son of Madog, proud priest,
you know more about love,
4   cause of trouble, from Taliesin's words,
than anyone, you do not practise
fornication, but lead a loving life.
Yours is a complaint which pertains
8   to every cleric in the world;
you complained, fair lord,
to me about one the colour of snow, my liege,
and your complaint, most wise sovereign,
12   is my complaint, fine ruler:
expression of anger, you know grief,
this is the fierce complaint, is it not harsh?
The descendant of an angel makes, dark image,
16   a passionate complaint against a Grey Friar from Chester;
the barefooted cub came angrily
where there was the wife of many a Jealous One
and gentle maidens on a bench,
20   our most beloved, young ones;
he was the very worst friar
to preach his morals to a cleric;
no one would go to heaven, he said,
24   if she loved a man with a tonsure;
that man's office is higher, a curse on his pate,
if only he knew the truth.
Should a cleric, shooter of love,
28   not be freely allowed a wife or concubine,

Og yn gorllyfnu eigiawn,
Ewig y môr ogam iawn.

Llawer gwaith, dioer, oer oror,
56 Pan fai lanw gwyllt moelwyllt môr,
Rhois hawddamor, hoywior hael,
Eurog helm, ar y Cilmael,
Lle'r oedd Rys, ail lys Lasar,
60 Ap Robert, ddiguert gâr;
Yno cawn, dawn diennig,
Wirod o'i aur fragod frig;
Yno, dyhuddglo haeddglod,
64 Petwn y mynnwn fy mod.

Dychan i'r Brawd Llwyd o Gaer

Hywel, urddedig hoywwalch,
Amhadog, aberthog balch,
Mwy wrth gariad, lle cad cost,
4 O addau Taliesin a wyddost
No neb, godineb nid oes
Gennyd ond serchog einioes.
Ergwyn yw'r tau a ergyd
8 Ar bob ysgolhaig o'r byd;
Ti a gwynaist, teg ener,
Wrthyf am liw nyf, fy nêr,
A'r cwyn tau di, rhi rhyddoeth,
12 Yw'r cwyn mau finnau, iôr coeth:
Llid addau, lled a wyddost,
Llyma'r cwyn terrwyn, pand tost?
Llin engl a wna, llun anghlaer,
16 Llid gŵyn rhag Brawd Llwyd o Gaer;
Llwdn troednoeth a ddoeth yn ddig
Lle'r oedd wraig llawer Eiddig
A mwyn rianedd uwch mainc,
20 Mwyaf a gerym, ieuainc;
Gwaethaf Brawd i bregethu
Ei foes wrth urddol a fu;
Nid âi nef, meddai ef, un
24 O charai ŵr a chorun;
Uwch yw'r swydd, och ar ei siâd,
Eiddo ond gwir a wyddiad.
Pan na bai rydd, seythydd serch,
28 I urddol wraig neu ordderch,

then let a free permit, grace preserves him,
be given, in the name of day, in the leaves.

Vile deed for a vain pompous thief,
32 the impetuous Friar had a bitter tongue,
to take it upon himself, nasty double shock,
nit-ridden beam, for the reward of a jealous man,
burden of cold terror, to pass judgement in haste
36 on the soul of anyone of the island.
God the Father, true power of wisdom,
holds the wife of a holy cleric, if she is humble,
in greater honour in his guileless house,
40 and he would do more for her,
than the keen Grey Friar
from Chester said, angry words.
The Friar was a big strong lad,
44 out of lechery he often struck a blow
furtively with his cock, if he got the chance
to play with a lovely fine girl.
May no better fate, old crooked basket,
48 befall the dreadful Friar
than to be caught, circle-haired thief with a wild cock,
wicked one roaming around us,
with his grey cowl in the hot crotch
52 of a randy sour Englishwoman.
Course cloth in the shape of a basket, cold form,
scabby skin, crier of the punishment for everything,
plaguey arse, feeding ground for a crop of lice,
56 crooked-balled dirty dog with a hood like a bag,
shrine of a rotten sick frail hag,
shape of an old bald empty scrotum,
bent stubble, smirking burden,
60 flank like a headless pea-brush,
rascally idiot, by Gregory,
let him consider, bald Mahomet,
that a girl could not, nor would she wish to
64 turn a cleric from his lust.
If the young man could borrow a habit
from this bearer of a full burden of rage,
he would preach much better
68 than a thousand of him in May,
and get a bright-handed girl
to listen in true wonder.
Base sombrely fervent slanderer,
72 say, poor Friar from Chester,

Rhoed cennad, rhad a'i cynnail,
Rhydd, myn y dydd, mewn y dail.

Chwaen hagr i leidr gorwagrwysg,
32 Chwerw dafawd oedd i'r Brawd brwysg,
Gymryd arnaw, ddeufraw ddig,
Geibr nedd, er gobr un eiddig,
Fwrw oer fraw, farnu ar frys
36 Ar enaid neb o'r ynys.
Gwell y peirch, gwiw allu pwyll,
Duw Dad, yn ei dŷ didwyll,
Gwraig ysgolhaig, os gŵyl hi,
40 Urddol, a mwy y gwnâi erddi,
Nag a ddyfawd y Brawd brau
Llwyd o Gaer, llidiog eiriau.
Mawr o was bras oedd y Brawd,
44 O ddirnwyf aml ei ddyrnawd
Â chal yn lledrad, o chae
Â chain wiw riain warae.
Ni bo well, hen gawell gŵyr,
48 Y darffo i'r Brawd oerffwyr
No'i ddal, leidr gwylltgal gwalltgylch,
Un cas yn rhodio i'n cylch,
A'i gwfl llwyd mewn gafl llodur
52 Cynhaig o Seisnigwraig sur.
Cri ar wisg cryw, oer wasgeth,
Clawr croen, crïwr poen pob peth,
Cwthr pla, lle cnofa llau cnwd,
56 Ci ceillgam budr cwcyllgwd,
Ysgrîn gwrach fraen afiach frau,
Ysgod hen felgod foelgau,
Ystum ar sofl, gofl gowen,
60 Ystlys ysgub pys heb ben,
Ystelff dihir, myn Sirioel,
Ystyried, Myhumed moel,
Na allai, na fynnai ferch
64 Drosi urddol o'i draserch.
Pe câi'r mab fenthyg abid
Gan hwn yn dwyn llawnbwn llid,
Gwell o beth y pregethai
68 No mil ohono ym Mai,
A chael gan fun loywlun law
O wir wnder i wrandaw.
Distadl athrodwr dwystaer,
72 Dywed, Frawd godlawd o Gaer,

kite of the grave deserving hanging,
of what did you falsely accuse the women,
with the soul, prelates of the region,
76 of Gwynedd and Powys there?

    Watch out, if you see the man,
in an urgent hurry like a stout knave,
vigorous trot on one sole or two,
80 grey and swollen, without the price of a pair of trousers,
let one club be given, we must kill him,
like a watery dough, destitute and base,
let another be given in the wretch's need,
84 a blow as alms to the man.
May God cause chaos in his way, filthy thing,
bundle of malt, because of his sermon.

35   Satire on the Grey Friar

Fair is the product, famous and fine,
of Taliesin, eloquent-lipped fruitful poet,
on loving one the colour of hillside snow,
4 a seagull by the sea strand;
he would be the foremost poet, were it not for
the English Friar, twisted grey coat,
and his sermon, filthy thing from the bible,
8 unpleasant pungent churl,
who said, bad [would be] twice his worth,
harsh words about clerics,
putrid dog, stinking feet,
12 canvas, ragged lad of bad blood,
great ugly bald-scabby burdock,
wolf with a knotted belt and a scabby shirt,
stiff-trousered seal full of cabbage,
16 son of an old man by a rotten old hag.
The licentious dirty Friar
ordered this, old beggar,
to the women, by twisted slander,
20 to keep away from lovely pure priests.
Who would seek—no one would—
licentiousness from noblemen?
The body's nature urges it
24 to create children, treasures of the womb,

Beth a holud, barcud bedd,
Grogwr, ar gam i'r gwragedd,
Ac enaid, breladiaid bro,
76 Wynedd a Phowys yno?

    Gwyliwch, o gwelwch y gŵr,
Â brys yng fal bras iangwr,
Gwydn duth ar un gwadn ai dau,
80 Llwydrwth, heb warthol llodrau,
Rhoed un lysg, rhaid in ei ladd,
Rhyw does dŵr, rheidus diradd,
Rhoed arall yn rhaid oerwr,
84 Ffonnod yn gardod i'r gŵr.
Drysid Duw rhagddaw, baw beth,
Drwsa brag, dros ei bregeth.

Dychan i'r Brawd Llwyd

Teg o gynnyrch, hygyrch hardd,
Taliesin, ffraethfin ffrwythfardd,
Ar garu hoen eiry goror,
4 Gwylan gerllaw marian môr;
Pennaf bardd oedd, pe ni bai
Y Brawd Sais, llwytpais lletpai,
A'i bregeth, bawbeth o'r bibl,
8 Taeog anserchog surchwibl,
A ddywod, drwg ei ddeuwerth,
Am ysgolheigion sôn serth,
Ci brynnig, drewedig draed,
12 Cynfas, dragwas o'r drygwaed,
Cedowrach hagr foelgrach fawr,
Cidwm gwregysglwm grysglawr,
Moelrhawn bresychlawn sychlodr,
16 Mab cleiriach o'r bwdrwrach bodr.
Gorchymyn hyn, hen glermwnt,
A wnâi'r Brawd anniwair brwnt
I'r gwragedd, o'r gŵyr ogan,
20 Rhag offeiriaid glwysiaid glân.
Pwy a geisiai—ni wnâi neb—
O wyrda anniweirdeb?
Anian y corff a'i ennyg
24 I grëu plant, greiriau plyg,

to increase, at the edge of the road,
the people of the dear world later.
A minor, groundless defamation
28 would it be for a slender pretty girl,
golden body, to make love to a priest,
it would be no reproach to hear it anywhere,
quite thoughtless, not acceptable
32 to God, although it be so to man.
The rank of the priest is high,
God's work, his estate is higher still.
For this reason truly, a beauty's profit,
36 John the treasure is known
without falsehood as the Blessed,
his father and his grandfather were priests;
what was he, best man,
40 lovely John the Baptist?
A fine son from the body of a priest,
wise manners, the same way as his father;
the wise father of Gwynnog and Noethan
44 was a bishop in an imposing white cope;
the finest bishop of all nations
was the pure father of Elian again.
No one is openly reproached
48 for his father's fornication;
the gentle wise son does not bear
the father's burden for an old sin;
for this reason truly, greatest consolation of the saints,
52 men pay homage to one honour.

If one seeks christianity and baptism
priests and faith are necessary;
the priest's office, the Father swears it,
56 is the power to bind and release
any man who comes under his hands,
if he comes—whatever he may do before he comes;
to forgive deed and thought,
60 to do away with the hardship of sin;
if he gets communion and confession
he will go to heaven, may it be closer;
if he comes into contact with him
64 no devil will know him, evil tribulation.
The Friar's honour was not as great,
nor his forgiveness which he pronounced,
and he is not fit, false releasing,
68 he is not able to give communion to another,

I amlhau, ymyl heol,
Pobl fyd anwylyd yn ôl.
Gogan bychan heb achos
28 Oedd i riain dlysfain dlos,
Gorff aur, garu offeiriad,
Nid dannod glybod mewn gwlad,
Diddarbod iawn, didderbyn
32 Gan Dduw, er ei bod gan ddyn.
Uchel yw gradd offeiriad,
Achos Duw, mae'n uwch ei stad.
Am hyn yn wir, feinir fudd,
36 Y gelwir yn ddigelwydd
Ieuan degan Fendigaid,
Offeiriad ei dad a'i daid;
Beth oedd yntau, gorau gŵr,
40 Ieuan diddan Fedyddiwr?
Mab hoff o gorff offeiriad,
Ffyrdd doeth, unffordd â ei dad;
Tad doeth Gwynnog a Noethan
44 Oedd esgob mewn cadrgob can;
Tecaf esgob ar bob iaith
Oedd dad glân Elian eilwaith.
Ni liwir yn oleuad
48 I neb odineb ei dad;
Ni ddwg mab arab aren
Baich y tad am bechod hen;
Am hyn yn wir, gorau sir saint,
52 Y gofreinia gwŷr unfraint.

    O cheisir cred a bedydd
    Rhaid yw offeiriaid a ffydd;
    Swydd offeiriad, Tad a'i twng,
56 Gallu rhwymo a gollwng
Dyn a ddêl dan ei ddwylaw
Er a wnêl—o dêl—cyn daw;
Maddau gweithred a meddwl,
60 Diffoddi caledi cŵl;
O chaiff gymun a chyffes
Ef â i nef, a fo nes;
Ag ef od â i gyfrwch
64 Nis gŵyr cythrel, trafel trwch.
Nid oedd gymaint braint y Brawd
Na'i faddeuaint a ddywawd,
Ac nid teilwng, gollwng gwall,
68 Ni ŵyr gymuno arall,

nor baptize, worthless consent,
he was vile, he doesn't know anything
more than a bald heap of toadstools,
72   pigs' manners, he devours more than a horse!

36   Satire on Hersdin Hogl

Ithel Ddu I am calling you,
I am a mighty slanderer of poets,
you are made master of poetry over a hundred,
4   they call you the choice hawk of poets,
and you are excellent, no man denies it,
and minstrel of the nation of Llŷn;
you demanded a great feat of poets,
8   an unnecessary demand before the snow of February,
to commemorate the vile sinews,
a grumbling woman, one who squabbles over barley,
stinking Hersdin Hogl,
12   old phlegm-covered breeches with rotten ankles;
there are inside her as one disease
two fierce hags ridden with ringworm,
Meheldyn, fleshless goat,
16   thin-skinned snake with trembling lip,
and Russel's daughter, draff of sorel,
frail dry squinting cabbage-shitting hag;
we will soon have to—empty is her pate—
20   forge her two elegies:
mentioning her haunch with a back like a rake,
wrinkled scabby shed on a withered leg,
old mother of amber-coloured Gwyddelyn,
24   haunch with bulging arse and far-extending buttocks,
buttocks with scabs numbering as many as [the teeth of]
       a comb,
smock holding in piss like a urine pipe.

   Why, faultless Ithel Ddu,
28   if she had to be praised,
my soul, why did you not send
her foot measurement, awful swelling bulge,
whilst her bones, horns sticking right out,
32   and her black sinews were all in one piece,
while some part of her ribs
was still intact, leanness of a bear?

Na bedyddio, bodd diddim,
Anardd oedd, ni ŵyr ef ddim
Mwy no mwdwl moel madarch,
72 Moes moch, mwy a ŷs no march!

Dychan i Hersdin Hogl

Ithel Ddu i'th alw ydd wyf,
Athrodwr beirdd uthr ydwyf,
Athro'r gerdd y'th roir ar gant,
4 Etholwalch beirdd y'th alwant,
A thra da wyd, ni thry dyn,
A theuluwr iaith Lëyn;
Erchaist i feirdd orchest fawr,
8 Arch afraid cyn eiry Chwefrawr,
Goffáu y gïau ffiaidd,
Gythwraig, ymddanheddwraig haidd,
Hersdin Hogl a'r arogl oer,
12 Henllodr figyrnbodr garnboer;
Mae yni'i hun yn un haint
Dwy daerwrach dew eu derwraint,
Meheldyn, gefryn heb gig,
16 Meingroen neidr min grynedig,
A merch Rwsel, sorel soeg,
Gwrach fresychgach frau sechgoeg;
Rhaid ynn gyda hyn, gau ei hiad,
20 Furnio iddi ddwy farwnad:
Grybwyll ei hers gefngribin,
Grepach hogl grach ar hegl grin,
Henddyn fam Wyddelyn wefr,
24 Hers dinroth hir estynrefr,
Rhefr grach gwedy rhifo'r grib,
Hefis ystrethbis droethbib.

Paham, Ithel ddinam Ddu,
28 O bai raid iddi brydu,
F'enaid, pam nad anfonud
Fesur ei throed, fos roth ddrud,
Tra fai'i hesgyrn, cyrn carnfoll,
32 A'i gïau du i gyd oll,
Tra fai ddryll o'i hesgyll hi
Wrth ei gilydd, arth guli?

It's not easy to find pure abundant praise
36   in the absence of a sour-faced mare;
      I would hold her memorial day splendidly
      if I were to see her with a load of beans.
      I have, I am a slim lad,
40   bitch's belly, as best I could,
      hacked out the sole for her,
      her name was a name without honour;
      let her have a prayer—who was she?—
44   let it be soon, she was rotting;
      it used to be asserted that she lived a long while
      in the time of old Ceridfen long ago,
      lecherous wild woman, I know her greed,
48   crab-eating sow with withered thumbs,
      nasty catapult in two scabs,
      begging for flour, wool, wax, a night's lodging,
      cheese, meat, blandishment,
52   vilest matter, seeking everything;
      many a bagful of old wheat,
      many a burden on her mottled arm,
      many a piece of meat, stuffing for sausage,
56   and a cheese under her armpit,
      many a skewer, her appearance is mocked,
      did she pull out with her teeth;
      woe to the lad with the twisted mouth
60   who lost her, horrid black she-devil.

      By night she was bound, broken gate,
      with her arms on her breast,
      and the sow was thrown into a reed barrow
64   with many blocks and earth mixed
      in the corner of a hut, filthy mess,
      with her litter watching her.
      Wild and savage, tattered hempen bag,
68   let a coffin be put over the corpse,
      and a big net over the mother,
      bow-legged spokeshave gathering cheese to her chest,
      lest the split of her mare's arse be seen
72   and the fleece of her pate above her arse.
      In her rag, food-begging old hag,
      she went to the grave, old man's slave.
      Silly cow, there was no manner
76   of mass or offering
      over her, false peevish witch,
      nor any share, nor banner, bare fiend,

Nid hawdd cael gwawd barawd bur
36 Yn absen gwilff wynebsur;
Gwnawn yn hoff ei dydd coffa
Pes gwelswn â phwn o ffa.
Minnau y sydd, meinwas wyf,
40 Foly gellast, fal y gallwyf,
Gwedy naddu'r gwadn iddi,
Enw heb senw oedd ei henw hi;
Pader i hon—pwy ydoedd?—
44 Poed ar awr dda, pydru'dd oedd;
Haeru a wneid ei bod hirynt
Yn oes hen Geridfen gynt,
Rhyswraig gynhaig, gwn ei hainc,
48 Rhysywin fawdgrin fwydgrainc,
Blif annigrif yn neugrest,
Blota, gwlana, gwera, gwest,
Cawsa, cica, mincoceth,
52 Casa' pwnc, ceisio pob peth;
Llawer cydaid hen wenith,
Llawer baich ar ei braich brith,
Llawer dryll cig, selsig sail,
56 A chosyn dan ei chesail,
Llawer gwaell, lliwir ei gwedd,
A dynnai hi â'i dannedd;
Gwae'r mab gwedy gwyro'r min
60 A'i colles, ddiefles dduflin.

Nos y rhwymwyd, dorglwyd don,
A'i deufraich ar ei dwyfron,
A bwrw'r hwch mewn berwa wrysg
64 Â phloc aml a phlwyw cymysg
Yng nghwr bwth, anghywair baw,
A'i gwaling yn ei gwyliaw.
Rhull gyrchgas, rhwyll gywarchgwd,
68 Rhoed ysgrîn ar hyd ysgrŵd,
A rhwyd fawr ar hyd y fam,
Rhasgl fynwes gawsgasgl goesgam,
Rhag gweled rhwyg ei gwilers
72 A chnu'i hiad yn uwch no'i hers.
Yn ei brat, henwrach gateirch,
Yr aeth i'r cladd, caeth y cleirch.
Buwch ffôl, ni bu uwch ei phen
76 O ffurf gaffael offeren
Nac offrwm, widdon geuffrom,
Na rhan, na lluman, ŵyll lom,

except her magic cauldron and her flail handle,
80 the ear could hardly hear a thing;
there was never before her this year,
alternating with her arse,
anywhere in Gwynedd, nasty ship,
84 such a knell after a lame goat;
her wool and her cup and her cap
and her two lepers giving two claps.
She bore a son to the devil,
88 the devil take him, Gwyddelyn.

Do not make her funeral feast
with her old bread, lame bear's thigh;
let her flour and her oats be shared out
92 amongst clergy, and her pinner and her stick
and her canvas sheet and her coarse ragged smock
and her brass buckle and her rags
and her bag and her sieve, horrible cow,
96 and her dog and her cat, fie on her cheek,
and her milk pail and her weeding hook,
and her bag, Hersdin scarecrow Hogl,
and her old handkerchief and her stick,
100 and her halter and her spitting dish
to pray, withered jaws,
with her, mouth like an old privy,
for a share of heaven lest anyone freeze
104 for she of the dirty face;
pitchfork case, wave of terror,
woe to us that she was such a long time dying.

37   Satire on the Irishman

Filthy rump-eating Irishman,
dogs' lees-bowl, amber wyvern,
woe to you old bulls' byre,
4 long-helmed goose, appearance of the sun of the dead,
peevish cowardly withered saffrony lad,
his face is like a dirty cowshed,
heap of brass, rotten bronze horn,
8 tithe cart of a band of serfs,
stag with an insect inside its nostril,
scabby-browed rowan-skinned giant,

Eithr ei hudffat a'i throedffust,
80 Odid o chlywid â chlust;
O'i blaen ni bu eleni,
Bob eilwers gyda'i hers hi,
Lle yng Ngwynedd, llong anoff,
84 Gyfryw glul ar ôl gafr gloff;
Ei gwlan a'i chwpan a'i chap
A'i deuglaf yn rhoi dwyglap.
I ddiawl oedd ohoni ddyn,
88 I ddiawl yntau Wyddelyn.

Na wna o'i hen fara hi
Ei harwyl, arthglun heri;
Rhanned ei blawd a'i rhynion
92 Rhwng clêr, a'i phiner a'i ffon
A'i chynfas a'i chrys bras brau
A'i chae latwm a'i chlytiau
A'i chwd a'i gogr, fuwch edern,
96 A'i chi a'i chath, och i'w chern,
A'i chunnog laeth a'i chwynnogl,
A'i chwd, Hersdin hwgwd Hogl,
A'i ffunen hen a'i ffon hi,
100 A'i burwy a'i mail boeri
Er gweddïo, gwyw ddwyen,
Gyda hi, safn geudy hen,
Rhan o nef rhag rhynnu neb
104 I honno fudr ei hwyneb;
Gwain gweirfforch, gwaneg oerffwyr,
Gwae ni ei marw hi mor hwyr.

Dychan i'r Gwyddelyn

Gwyddelyn fudryn fwydrefr,
Gwaddodlestr cŵn, gwifrwn gwefr,
Gwae dydy hundy hendeirw,
4 Gŵydd helm hir, gwedd haul y meirw,
Gwas ffromlwrf gwyw saffrymlyd,
Gwiws brwnt gisa ei bryd,
Carnedd bres, corn efydd brau,
8 Car degwm côr daeogau,
Carw â phryf mewn cwr ei ffroen,
Cawr aelgrach cyriwalgroen,

crab snatcher, wrinkled copper knave,
12   minstrels' tannery with pickled arse,
      stink of a sow's guts, rider over barley,
      brass stump copper-coloured like a horse,
      base churl with his hut by the edge of the Soch,
16   silly hollow long red muscley body,
      you are a squabbler, Ronald's cock,
      hollow red basin, skin of a salty dogfish,
      sea-hornets jest with your skin,
20   vain stiff bristles, many cockles for your children,
      bald cuckold, dumb fat-balled dog,
      exiled meat beggar with tattered hood.
      You are a bellower giving
24   me some mockery—you are alder bark—
      for making, carrier of lice,
      for your bowlegged mother with an arse like a hollow shed
      great praise, land is not given to a dumb man,
28   you acted like a churl, you were a cow-pat.
      You call to mind, you're going to come a cropper,
      a swanking hollow coffer made from a rotten stump.
      What sort of man are you, proper singer?
32   Rusty beard, vain hubbub,
      filth and gold, flabby and fat-navelled,
      bran-bread, icy morning face,
      marten's breast, crossed shins,
36   rottenness of an old briar bush,
      you follow without dragging
      from one side to the other like a sledge.
      Is there no place open [to you], old stableman's lad,
40   except in Llŷn or Dinllaen?

      It's easier for you, heavy-shitting red-urined thief,
      to dry wise Ithel Ddu's horse
      and throw out, country wool sack,
44   its dung, abbot's serf,
      great feat, than to compete
      with him, it is good to tolerate the Black One,
      or with Madog, learned lover,
48   Dwygraig, man of noble nature;
      and me, why should I not wish
      the dirt of a hundred dogs down your throat?
      No foolish sense at the top of our voices,
52   no minstrels of the marketplace coloured like the three stars,
      no flour-begging poets, powerless judgement,
      we are proven master poets.

Cipiwr crainc, iangwr copr crin,
12 Cyffeithdy clêr cyffeithdin,
Ceufflair hwch, ceffylwr haidd,
Cyff elydn copr ceffylaidd,
Carl serth a'i fwth car ael Soch,
16 Cyhyrgorff syml cau hirgoch,
Cecr ohonot coc Rhonallt,
Cawg cau coch, croen ci coeg hallt,
Cacwn môr â'th bil coecant,
20 Coecsyth blew, aml cocs i'th blant,
Cwcwallt moel, ci ceilltew mud,
Cocylltwn cicai alltud.
Rhuadwr yn rhoi ydwyd
24 Rhyw ysgórn im, rhisgwern wyd,
Am wneuthur, llywiadur llau,
I'th fam heglgam din hoglgau
Glod fawr, ni roir gwlad i fud,
28 Gwladeiddiaist, gleuad oeddud.
Coffáu yr wyd, ceffi rus,
Coffor o wystn cau ffrostus.
Ba ryw ŵr wyd, buror iawn?
32 Barf rydlyd, berw afradlawn,
Baw a gold, mwygl bogeldew,
Bara rhudd, bryd bore rhew,
Bron belau, crimogau croes,
36 Brynhigrwydd hen bren egroes,
Dilyd yr wyd a dilusg
O'r cwr i'r llall fal car llusg.
Oes le rhydd, was osler hen,
40 Ond yn Llëyn neu Dinlläen?

    Haws it, leidr cachdraws cochdroeth,
Sychu march Ithel Ddu ddoeth
A bwrw allan, sach gwlân gwlad,
44 Ei ebodn, taeog abad,
Gorchest fawr, nag ymgyrchu
Ag ef, da goddef y Du,
Neu â Madog, serchog syw,
48 Dwygraig, gŵr dyledogryw;
A minnau, pam na mynnwn
I'th freuant faw cant o'r cŵn?
Nid synnwyr ffôl wrth ddolef,
52 Nid clêr lliw'r tryser llawr tref,
Nid beirdd y blawd, brawd heb rym,
Profedig feirdd prif ydym.

We will not, indeed, all
56   be inferior to a single thief like a diseased bear;
    a wild male eagle is not—
    unless he be deaf—inferior to tame hens;
    a lion is not inferior to a young hind,
60   even a red simpleton would be angry;
    a young healthy wolf is not
    inferior to a woolly-skinned scabby-kneed lamb;
    greyhounds—brass pig-trough—
64   are not inferior to a bald red cur.

    You will never come with safe conduct by day
    from Llŷn to joy;
    a blind man does not come out of his house,
68   the mole does not come out of the weak earth;
    you would never come from your mother's house,
    an anchorite does not go a single step from his house.
    Unwise head, were I to go
72   to your land, falsely shitting knave,
    I would be branded like an animal
    if I were to be found in the fold,
    as you did, troublesome affliction,
76   brand your wife, red wart;
    your randy pauper of a wife
    has only one finger and a third of a thumb
    and a tendon, honest Gwerfyl,
80   woe to her kindred if it's true.
    It's not easy for her to cook food
    thus, you son of a bald grey hag.
    Get yourself, if you are driven out together,
84   every so often, son of the long arse,
    a toncuer on your sharp pointed tongue,
    peddler of poetry, face like an alderwood tankard.
    Does your poetry, sour your smile,
88   if it be asked, need any salt?
    You make song below Bardsey
    from a very chaffy material, wretched dog.
    Lice-ridden knave of great sourness,
92   eat devil's dirt, clumsy was your language.

Ni byddwn, od gwn, i gyd
56 Wrth unlleidr fal arth heinllyd;
Ni bydd gŵr, onid byddar,
Eryr gwyllt wrth yr ieir gwâr;
Ni bydd llew wrth lo ewig,
60 Ni bu ddelff coch na bai ddig;
Ni bydd blaidd ifancaidd iach
Wrth oen â gwlangroen glingrach;
Ni bydd, cafn efydd i foch,
64 Milgwn wrth gostog moelgoch.

Ni ddoi di ar nawdd y dydd
O Lŷn fyth i lawenydd;
Ni ddaw dall o'i dŷ allan,
68 Ni ddaw'r wadd o'r ddaear wan;
Nid aud fyth o dŷ dy fam,
Nid â ancr o'i dŷ uncam.
Pen annoeth, pei awn innau
72 I'th wlad, iangwr cachiad cau,
Fy neifio fal anifail
A wneid o'm ceid yn y cail,
Fal y gwnaethost, gost gystudd,
76 Deifio dy wraig, dafad rudd;
Nid oes i'th wraig gynheigdlawd
Eithr un bys a thraean bawd
A gewyn, Werfyl gywir,
80 Ys gwae ei chenedl os gwir.
Nid hawdd iddi bobi bwyd
Felly, fab i wrach foel-llwyd.
Gad atad, o'th gyd-wtir,
84 Bob eilwers, fab yr hers hir,
Twncl ar y tafod tancern,
Tincer gwawd, wyneb tancr gwern.
Oes ar dy wawd, sur dy wên,
88 Os holir, eisiau halen?
Eisinllyd iawn is Enlli
Y seili gerdd, salw o gi.
Yswain morchwain mawrchwaith,
92 Ŷs faw diawl, aswy fu d'iaith.

38   Satire on Madog ap Hywel

I will provide for Madog, one-legged scoundrel,
    grasping cur, grabbing cream,
    Hywel's troublesome son, he had to be avoided,
4   low-browed flagon, no second Asaph,
    keeper of store cattle, guarding cheeseries,
    fetid tattered bag of rust, feeble overweight mole,
    flacid tub, bucket whining like a sack of farts,
8   churlish sheep trough, it's a grasping nature,
    carved knot, funnel, Mahomet's heart,
    hard despite his shortness, he doesn't know what a
        paragraph is,
    blunt-pricked boxwood bacon as wide as a pack of wool,
12   cauldron of mallows full of deceit, may he be hanged by a rope,
    neck of Peter's shepherd, collars like a wizened trellice,
    skill in lying, leather cowl, young animal in a boat,
    pile of scummy yeast, pincers could not seize
16   so much as a halfpenny from the filthy wretch.

Satirical Englynion

A gaping gob is the contorted gob of the dirty dog,
    the beak, crooked-edged gap,
    piper's gob, rush scum,
4   calf's gob, lad who drinks every drop.

It is a wide gob, bent and twittering,
    a gob which puked last night,
    a gob full of filth which pukes air,
8   cheese trough gob, it will be long before it is more pleasant.

Otter's gob, crooked-backed dirty dog, damp little
    beggars with weak crooked lips,
    bull-ape's gob, twisted little gob,
12   it's a gob which knows how to slang.

Gob of a wretched raven with very crooked jaws,
    a gob which never sang psalms,
    evil gob like a smoke-hole in a wall,
16   false gob which will not stand its ground in battle.

Puny horrible flabby churl with a big gob,
    protruding beam, dog [fed on] deer's fat;
    insulting everyone is his sense,
20   dead bitch's gob, rough crooked gob.

Dychan i Fadog ap Hywel

Costiaf i Fadog, castyn untroediog,
Costog cynghafog, hufen amcaff,
Cystuddfab Hywel, costiai ei ochel,
4   Costrel aelisel, nid ail Asaff,
Custos gwartheg cadw, cawstyau achadw,
Cwd rhwd brwd bradw, breudwrch rhybraff,
Cildwrnel gwanleddf, celwrn bramsachleddf,
8   Cail mail mileinddeddf, neud cynneddf caff,
Cwlm ysgwthr, twnffed, calon Mahumed,
Caled er byrred, ni ŵyr barraff,
Calgrwn bacwn bocs cyfled fflaced fflocs,
12 Cawldrwm hocs llawn crocs, crocer wrth raff,
Colwydd bugail Pedr, colerau wystn gledr,
Celwydd fedr, cwffl lledr, llwdn mewn ysgraff,
Cymwrn burm ysgai, cymaint â dimai
16 I gan y bawai ni graffai'r graff.

Englynion Dychan

Safn agored yw safn gorwyr—bawci,
   Y bici, gwthr cannwyr,
   Safn pibydd, swyfen pabwyr,
4   Safn llo, gwas a yf yn llwyr.

Safn llydan ydyw lledwyr—chwidach,
   Safn a chwydodd neithiwyr,
   Safn llawn baw a chwyd awyr,
8   Safn cafn caws, bydd haws hwyr.

Safn dyfrgi, bawci bacwyr,— rheidusion
   Mân lleithion min lliethwyr,
   Safn gwrab, sefnig erwyr,
12   Safn yw ymsennu a ŵyr.

Safn cigfran druan drawyr—ei genau,
   Safn ni ganodd sallwyr,
   Safn drwg mal twll mwg magwyr,
16   Safn ffals ni saif o fewn ffwyr.

Safnog digorffog daeog oerffwyr—lleibr,
   Cyhoeddgeibr, ci hyddgwyr;
   Sennu pawb yw ei synnwyr,
20   Safn gellast farw, safn garw gŵyr.

Notes

1

The precise purpose of this unusual poem is a matter for speculation, but it seems likely that the direct address to King Edward is a purely rhetorical device (despite the claim in ll. 17-18 that he possesses every angelic language), and that the poem was a piece of political propaganda intended to increase Welsh support for the King and his wars. In LlC ix, 62, D J Bowen made the very plausible suggestion that the poem was composed at the instigation of Sir Rhys ap Gruffudd (subject of poem no 7), one of the Crown's most prominent supporters in south Wales. CMCS 12, 81-85, shows that Iolo's poem is influenced by a work known as 'The Prophecy of the Six Kings to Follow John', which is based on Geoffrey of Monmouth's Merlin prophecies, using animal symbolism to refer to each of the six kings from Henry III to Henry IV. The several prose and verse versions of that prophecy, in French, English, Latin and Welsh, have been discussed by T. M. Smallwood in *Speculum* 60, 571-92, and in view of his conclusions about their dating it now seems unlikely that the 'English Couplet Version' was composed early enough to have been a source for Iolo's poem, as I postulated. His source therefore seems to have been the Anglo-Norman French prose version, written soon after 1312. The prophecy predicts the events of Edward III's reign in very vague terms, referring to him as a boar, as Iolo does in I. 13 here. Iolo of course gives a much more specific account of events up to the taking of Calais in August 1347, and his poem must have been composed sometime between then and the next significant English victory, at the battle of Poitiers in 1356. Edward's glory as a warrior king was at its height at that time. The prophecy has left its mark on his description of Edward in the first part of the poem, but its influence is clearest on the second part, where a 'darogan' is specifically referred to, that is the successful crusade which concludes the account of the boar's reign in the prophecy. The implication is clearly that Edward has fulfilled the first part of the prophecy, and should now go on to fulfill the rest.

5. *ririaist:* this is a borrowing from the English verb *rear*, which was used especially in the context of war with the meaning 'commence'.

8. *eryr Gwynsor:* Edward was born at Windsor in 1312.

11-12. The French prophecy refers to 'un sengler que avera la teste sen et quoer de leon'.

13. *baedd y gyfnewid:* this phrase occurs in Welsh versions of Geoffrey of Monmouth, corresponding to 'aper commerciae', see *BD* 108. The addition of the adjective 'didwyll' may reflect ecclesiastical disapproval of the usury involved in commerce.

21-24. At the beginning of his reign Edward had to overcome his mother, Isabella of France, and Roger Mortimer before taking the crown himself.

30. David II of Scotland was captured at the battle of Neville's Cross, near Durham, in 1346.

Brynaich: originally the inhabitants of the land of Bernicia, between the rivers Tees and Forth. It is often used by the poets to refer to the English in general, but Iolo seems to be aware of the old meaning, since he consistently uses it to refer to the Scots. Cf. *Deifr* in 9.58.

33-34. Edward besieged Berwick in 1333.

35-36. This refers to the naval battle of Sluys against the French in 1340.

37-38. The siege of Calais lasted from 1346 to August 1347.

39-42. The King of Bohemia was killed at the battle of Crécy in 1346. Edward went very close to the city of Paris on his way to the battlefield.

57. The emendation suggested tentatively in GIG has been adopted. The cause of the corruption in the manuscripts seems to have been the rare verb *gorestwng*, 'subdue, conquer', which was replaced by its more common synonym *goresgyn*, necessitating further changes to maintain the *cynghanedd*. The compound *crwystaith* is composed of the plural form of *croes*, 'cross', and *taith*, 'journey'. The standard Modern Welsh word for crusade, 'croesgad', is not attested until 1852 (although Iolo Morganwg has *crwysgad*). The Middle Welsh expression for the undertaking of a crusade was *mynd â chroes*, see GPC 604.

67-74. The bodies of the Three Kings were believed to be buried at Cologne.

75-76. According to the Prophecy of the Six Kings the boar would not return from his crusade.

2

Sir Hywel ap Gruffudd gained the nickname 'Hywel of the Axe' because of his deeds on the field of battle at Poitiers in 1356, for which he was knighted and made constable of Cricieth castle, an office which he held until his death in 1381. The reference to the young king Richard II ('Lionheart's heir'), who came to the throne at the age of ten in June 1377, enables us to date this poem to the last years of Sir Hywel's life. The poem is based on the story *The Dream of Macsen Wledig* (trans. in Jones and Jones, *The Mabinogion*), in which the Roman emperor has a dream vision of a splendid court, located at Caernarfon. Iolo's description of the court at Cricieth is strongly reminiscent of the idealised courts of chivalric romance. The device of the dream and its subsequent explanation serves to emphasize the visual, even visionary, aspect of the poem, and gives it a highly dramatic quality. The impressive rhetorical peroration, culminating in a toast to the lord of the castle, reminds us that oral performance was an essential part of this sort of praise poetry. The audience in the hall of Cricieth castle would no doubt have responded warmly to the idealised portrait of themselves, and to the bloodthirsty recital of the heroic deeds of their lord.

13. *carawl*: from the English *carol*, which had a wider application than it does today, meaning any light song, especially those accompanying dancing.

19. *Twrch Trwyd*: the legendary boar of the story *Culhwch and Olwen*. *Trwyth* is the form used in the story, but *Trwyd* is the normal form in poetry.

20. *farneiswin*: from the English *vernage wine*, a kind of sweet white wine from Italy.

23-26. Sir Hywel's coat of arms was three fleurs-de-lis on a black background, see ll. 50-52 below, and E J Jones, *Medieval Heraldry* (Cardiff, 1943), plate XXX.

38. Cricieth castle was built by Llywelyn the Great of Gwynedd in the 1230s, and was captured by Edward I in 1283.

40. *mangnel:* from the English, a machine for hurling stones. Such a machine was a permanent part of the defence of Cricieth castle.

50. *Beuno:* the patron saint of Clynnog Fawr, where Sir Hywel was buried.

51. *oris:* from English *orris* (= iris), this refers to the fleurs-de-lis. The term *erw* is used figuratively for the background in the coat of arms (more commonly *maes* in Welsh).

60. A reference to an old Welsh proverb, 'asgwrn hen yn angen' (see B, iv, 2).

61. *rhwysgainc:* I take this to be a compound of *rhwysg*, 'rule', and *cainc*, 'strand'.

62. The King of France was captured at the battle of Poitiers.

63. *mab Erbin:* Geraint, hero of one of the Welsh Arthurian romances.

65-68. These lines refer to the work of the barber, who used to let blood for medicinal purposes as well as shaving and cutting hair. The image is grimly ironic, since the blood-letting performed by Sir Hywel was far from medicinal.

69. *ŵyr Leinort:* this reading does not occur in any of the 52 manuscript copies, but it seems to be the only way to make sense of an otherwise meaningless line. Lit. 'grandson', *ŵyr* is commonly used in the sense of 'heir'. Richard II was not in fact the heir of Richard I, who died childless, but he was of the same family, and his name would no doubt have called to mind his heroic predecessor. Since Richard II was only a boy at this time, the use of the future tense is appropriate.

77. *loensiamp:* from the French *longchamp*, this may be a placename, possibly connected with the battle of Poitiers, but I have not managed to locate it.

79. *mordarw:* the only known example of this word, lit. 'sea-bull'. It seems to be in contrast to *mordrai* in the following line.

3

Ieuan ab Einion had his court at Chwilog, some six miles north-east of Pwllheli. He was nephew to the Sir Hywel of the previous poem, and held the office of sheriff of Caernarfon 1385-90. The reference to him as sheriff in l.13 enables us to date this poem to that period. His father before him held the same office 1351-59, and was praised by Gruffudd Gryg, see DGG[2] LXXVIII. The concluding lines of this poem suggest some threat to Ieuan's authority.

6. *pinagl:* an image drawn from castle architecture, 'a small ornamental turret, usually terminating in a turret or cone, crowning a buttress, or rising above the roof or coping of a building' (OED).

12. *Cadell:* one of the sons of Rhodri Mawr, and father of Hywel Dda.

16. Ieuan's family were descended from Collwyn ap Tangno, Lord of Eifionydd and Ardudwy.

23-28. Pasgen and Owain were sons of Urien Rheged, from whom Collwyn's line claimed descent.

30. *secr:* from Middle English *escheker*, 'treasury'.

34. An echo of the old proverb, 'a fo ben bid bont', see PKM 40-41.

41. Fulk fitz Waryn was an outlaw in the reign of King John who later became the hero of a popular romance, in the course of which he turns the main road aside to go through his court, so that he can offer hospitality to travellers. See Dr Bromwich's note in YB, xii, 76, and cp. 33.43.

44. *Celliwig:* Arthur's court in Cornwall.

57. The *troedog*, or *hual*, some sort of torque, seems to have been a traditional insignia of the royal house of Gwynedd, see TYP, triads 17 and 62.

60. *fei:* from the English *vie*, 'challenge (in card playing); sum ventured or staked; challenge to contest or rivalry' (OED). This example predates the earliest in English.

64. Beli Fawr fab Manogan was an ancestor deity from whom the ruling dynasties of early Wales claimed descent, see TYP 281-83.

67-68. 'Gwell rydraus no rydruan' is another old proverb, see B iv, 10.

67. Rhodri Mawr was king of Gwynedd in the 9th century.

4

On the Tudor family of Penmynydd in Anglesey, descendants of Llywelyn Fawr's seneschal Ednyfed Fychan, see the article by Glyn Roberts, 'Wyrion Eden', in his *Aspects of Welsh History* (Cardiff, 1969). Tudur Fychan ap Goronwy had houses at Trecastell in Anglesey and Brynbyrddau in the parish of Llandygái. He and his brother Hywel, Archdeacon of Anglesey, are known to have been involved in the murder in 1345 of the English official Henry de Shaldeforde, one of the Prince's attorneys in North Wales. This is interesting in view of Iolo's portrait of him as a defender of the legal rights of the Welsh in ll. 79-82. Tudur's second wife, Margaret daughter of Thomas ap Llywelyn of Cardiganshire, was sister to Owain Glyndŵr's mother. Tudur died in 1367, a year after his brother Hywel. This elegy opens in dramatic fashion with a series of questions and answers about the lamentation on Tudur's death.

22. *Dindaethwy:* one of the commotes of Anglesey.

23. *Egryn*: patron saint of the church of Llanegryn in Meirionethshire, see LBS, ii, 415.

26. *Ricart:* grandson of Gruffudd ap Cynan, from whom Tudur was descended through his paternal grandmother.

28. I have emended the readng given in GIG, and followed the best manuscripts in omitting the *a* before *fydd*, giving better grammar, but a six-syllable line. The line-length may deceive the ear because of the possibility of an epenthetic vowel between the *d* and the *l* of *dlodion*.

33. *brwydr gyfaddef:* a legal term which seems to refer to a court case in which both sides brought claims against one another, see WLW, 193.

35-36. Tudur's first wife, Mallt, mother of the four sons praised in the next poem, was the great-great-granddaughter of Rhirid Flaidd of Powys, but I have been unable to trace Tudur's own ancestry to him (although he was descended from another Rhirid through his grandmother). His sons are quite legitimately linked to Rhirid Flaidd in 5.31-32.

39-40. There was a prophecy that a Norse fleet would come to the Traeth Coch to the north of Penmynydd, see M E Griffiths, *Early Vaticination in Welsh* (Cardiff, 1937), 150.

48. Ednyfed Fychan was lord of Brynffanugl near Abergele.

54. *dellt:* lit. 'lattice', a common image for a shattered shield.

58. *dwy Wynedd:* Uwch Conwy and Is Conwy, that is to the west and east of the river Conway.

65. *Hirerw:* location of the priory where the Penmynydd family were buried, today a part of Bangor known as Hirael. Note that Tudur's son Gronwy was buried at Llan-faes in Anglesey, 6.91-94.

5

This poem can be dated between the death of the father in 1367 (note the tense in l. 35) and Gronwy's death in 1382. At this time Gronwy, the eldest son, lived at Penmynydd, Ednyfed at Trecastell, Rhys at Erddreiniog, and Gwilym at Clorach. The reference to staying at Clorach at the end of the poem suggests that it was first performed at a feast held by Gwilym, in the presence of all four brothers. No mention is made of their half-brother Maredudd, father of Owain Tudur, who was Tudur Fychan's son by his second wife. There is a good deal of evidence to suggest that Tudur's sons were loyal servants of the Crown. Gronwy is known to have fought in France, probably in the service of the Black Prince. He held the office of Forester of Snowdon, in which he appears to have been succeeded by his brother Rhys. Rhys and Gwilym both seem to have been in some kind of personal relationship to King Richard II. Iolo's claims that he will be squire, treasurer, and cup-bearer to three of the brothers are not to be taken literally. They are a hyperbolical expression of the brothers' prowess and generosity towards the poet.

9. *Rhun:* there were several traditional heroes of this name, but the son of Maelgwn Gwynedd is probably meant here and in 18.3.

10. Alun Dyfed is mentioned in the Stanzas of the Graves, see LIDC 18.75.

13. *Nudd:* one of the Three Generous Ones, see TYP 476-77.

19. The term *eithefig* is used in the laws of the best oxen which were yoked nearest to the plough (Jenkins, 303). The metaphor is sustained by *cydwedd* in the following line.

25. *canghellor:* the king's chief official in a commote.

31-32. See note to 4.35-36.

38. This may be a reference to the triad 'Tri Aur Dorllwyth Ynys Brydein', see TYP 186.

48. *Pen Môn:* the headland at the north-eastern tip of Anglesey known as Penmon.

52. *ail drigiant:* lit. 'second dwelling'. Rheged was the kingdom of Urien in the Old North.

61. *Erddreiniog:* near Tregaean.
Clorach: between Llannerch-y-medd and Llanfihangel Tre'r-beirdd.

6

Gronwy died by drowning in Kent on 22nd March 1382, probably whilst on official business, since he had been appointed constable of Beaumaris castle only four days before his death. He was only the second Welshman to have held that important office. His body was brought back to Anglesey to be buried in the Fransiscan friary at Llan-faes. The magnificent alabaster altar tomb in Penmynydd church is generally believed to be that of Gronwy and his wife Myfanwy, removed from Llan-faes at the dissolution of the monastries. Gronwy's brother Ednyfed seems to have died a short while before him. The greater part of this powerful elegy consists of a series of conceits expressing the prevalence of black clothes in mourning for the brothers.

3. Easter was one of the three principal festivals when the poets would visit the houses of the nobility.

19. *brisg:* This has been taken to be the native word meaning 'path', referring to the travels of the musicians, rather than a borrowing from the English *brisk*, 'lively', which does occur in Iolo's period (see GPC 326).

21. *haul Iddewon:* referring to the darkening of the sun when Christ was on the cross.

25. Rhys and Gwilym were brothers of Gronwy and Ednyfed. Again no mention is made of the fifth brother, Maredudd.

30. Escheat involved the reversion of land to the feudal lord on the death of a tenant without heirs.

40. *ellyll:* this seems to mean a body without a soul, cp. GDG 89.39-40, 'Yna y mae f'enaid glân, / A'm *ellyll* yma allan.' (DGSP 146).

50. The long night of Mawddwy, caused by the depth of the valley, seems to have been proverbial.

60. Llan-faes was in the commote of Dindaethwy.

64. At that time the year began on 25th March, three days after Gronwy's death.

67. *Cellan:* Gronwy had inherited land in Ceredigion by his descent from Ednyfed Fychan.

68. *Celliwig:* Arthur's court in Cornwall.

73-76. The three fates of Greek mythology are referred to in the account of the Lord Rhys's death in the 'Red Book' *Brut y Tywysogion* (ed. Thomas Jones, p. 178).

97. *pwynt:* from the English *point* in the sense of 'condition, plight'. Iolo is here pleading for the release of the brothers from Purgatory.

7

Sir Rhys ap Gruffudd of Llansadwrn in Carmarthenshire was another of the descendants of Ednyfed Fychan, and is perhaps the best example of a successful *uchelwr* in fourteenth-century Wales. He was loyal to King Edward II, and suffered exile on his downfall, but was restored to royal favour early in the reign of Edward III. He was a distinguished soldier who fought in the battle of Crécy in 1346, and was active in recruiting troops for the wars in France and Scotland. He held many important offices in the service of the Crown in south Wales during his long administrative career, see PWLMA, I, 99-102. He died in May 1356, and Iolo here gives an eyewitness account of his funeral in Carmarthen, showing the practice of displaying the dead warrior's military apparel around his tomb in the church.

4. *llyfr y ganon:* this has been taken to refer to the Bardic Grammar of Einion Offeiriad, to whom Rhys is thought to have given patronage, see LlC vii, 234. But since *canon* meant originally ecclesiastical law, and then

law in general, it seems more likely that this refers to Rhys's work as a judge in Carmarthenshire.

9. The Arthurian hero Cai is presented in a much more favourable light in the bardic tradition than in the romances, see TYP 303-7.

12. *Beli:* see note 3.64.

16. *oeri traed:* this seems to correspond to the English expression 'to get cold feet', see D. J. Bowen's note in YB x, 201.

18. *engyl:* lit. 'angel(s)', this came to mean 'fire' because fire is supposed to have come to earth from heaven according to the Prometheus myth. But *engyl* could be taken literally here, referring to the trumpets of the angels on the Day of Judgement.

26. *Brynaich:* see note 1.30.

27. *Philip of Valois:* Philip VI of France (1328-50).

29. *Uthr Bendragon:* father of Arthur.

42. This line could also mean 'who was not thus on a day of booty', contrasting his present state with his former glory. But I prefer to take *dydd anrhaith* as referring to the day of the funeral.

44. This refers to the spurious derivation of *Caerfyrddin* from Myrddin (Merlin), the poet of Emrys Wledig according to Geoffrey of Monmouth.

8

Owain Glyndŵr was descended in direct line from the princes of Powys, see J. E. Lloyd, *Owen Glendower* (Oxford, 1931), and Bartrum under *Bleddyn ap Cynfyn* 5. That line is recited in ll.16-27, missing out four generations between Madog Fychan and Gruffudd Maelor. Maig Mygrfras, and y Gwinau Dau Freuddwyd son of Pywer Lew, were legendary ancestors of the princes of Powys. On his mother's side Owain was descended from the princes of Deheubarth, see Bartrum under *Rhys ap Tewdwr* 6 and 7, and ll.26 and 35 here. Owain was more indirectly connected to the royal house of Gwynedd through his great-grandmother Gwenllian, wife of Madog Fychan, who was descended from Gruffudd ap Cynan, see Bartrum under *Gruffudd ap Cynan* 2, and ll.40, 46 and 96 here. Owain therefore had a very special status in the eyes of informed observers such as Iolo, because he combined in his person the three royal lines of the Age of the Princes. For that reason Iolo here proclaims him 'sole head of Wales', appearing to anticipate his role in the rebellion of 1400. However, it seems to me that Iolo is not urging Owain to rebel against English rule, but rather to demand his legal rights under that rule. Two claims are referred to: a very ambitious, and perhaps largely theoretical claim to the old kingdom of Powys (ll.9-16), and a smaller, more immediate claim to lands in Pembrokeshire (ll.59-64) which belonged to Owain's mother's sister. It seems clear that this second claim was the immediate occasion for the poem. Iolo stresses Owain's status as rightful heir to these lands, using the old terms *gwrthrych* and *gwrthrychiad* from the Welsh laws, which is in fact somewhat ironic since Owain's family had the privilege of being subject to English law. Welsh law would not have permitted the inheritance of land through a female line. It seems that Owain's claim failed, since in the 15th century Trefgarn belonged to Sir John Burrough, Lord of Mawddwy (see GGGl XLV. 56), who was also connected to Owain's mother's family through a female line.

6. *y Sirwern:* a hundred in south-west Ceredigion, where Owain had inherited land from his mother, of which Is Coed (l.77) was a part.

9. *byd:* here and elsewhere in the poetry of the period this seems to have a more positive force than simply 'world'.

11. *y ddwy Faelawr:* Maelor Gymraeg and Maelor Saesneg.

12. *Mathrafal:* the principal court of the princes of Powys near Llanfair Caereinion.

16. *Nudd:* see note 5.13.

19. *medeingl:* this compound adjective is composed of the stem of the verb *medi*, 'to reap', and the noun *Eingl*, 'Angles'.

28. On the legendary Aedd Mawr, father of Prydain (from whom Ynys Prydain was supposed to have derived its name), see TYP 263-64.

30. *Carneddau Teon:* Stiperstones in Shropshire, see B vii, 368-69. According to tradition Teon was the son of y Gwinau Dau Freuddwyd.

33. The reference here may be to Ednyfed Fychan, whose descendants were legion in 14th-century Wales, but it has not been possible to trace Owain's connection to him.

34. *Uchdryd:* Owain's great-grandmother belonged to this prominent family of Englefield, as did Ithel ap Robert (see 13.73).

37. *Maig Mygrfras:* brother of Brochfael Ysgithrog, king of Powys in the 6th century according to tradition, see TYP 455-56.

47. *y ddwy Wynedd:* see note 4.58.

54. *Beli:* see note 3.64.

55. *Prydain:* normally 'Britain', but this and *Prydyn*, 'Scotland', were often confused. The reference is to Owain's part in the Scottish wars (on which see the following poem).

Peredur: hero of the Arthurian romance, *Peredur Son of Efrawg.*

60. *Tref-y-traeth:* Trefdraeth (Newport).

62. *Tref-y-garn:* Trefgarn Owain in the parish of Brawdy.

64. *Acharn:* this may have been the old name of the commote, which gave the name *Talacharn* (Laugharne).

77. *Is Coed:* see note 6 above.

79. *Brynaich:* see note 1.30.

87. *da daint rhag tafod:* a proverb, see B iii, 27.

90. *Is Aeron:* see note 6 above.

93. This line maps out the extent of Owain's territory in Powys, referring to three rivers. The northern boundary is the river Dee, and to the South the river Cain near Llanfyllin, which gave its name to the cantref of Mechain. The river Conwy marks the western boundary. Corwen was in the commote of Edeirnion in the valley of the Dee, where Owain held ancestral lands on the other side of the Berwyn range from his estate at Sycharth.

96. *Aberffraw:* principal court of the princes of Gwynedd. The lord referred to is Gruffudd ap Cynan.

100. Owain's court at Sycharth was situated in the commote of Cynllaith.

9

Owain and his brother Tudur are named amongst the garrison of Berwick under Sir Gregory Sais in March 1384, and Owain went on an expedition to Scotland in 1385. His feats there were also celebrated by

Gruffudd Llwyd, IGE² 122-24. Both poets refer to the shattering of his spear. The contrast between the two sections of this poem reflects the contrasting aspects of the ideal nobleman, gentle and civilised in his court, and fierce on the field of battle.

6. *Pywer Lew:* see 8.32.

10. *mab Llŷr:* Bendigeidfran.

11-12. The same couplet occurs at 8.43-44.

17. *Hiriell:* a traditional hero of Gwynedd, see B iii, 50-52.

42. The bird of Egypt was probably the flamingo.

44. Sir Gregory Sais was a soldier from Flintshire who fought with the Black Prince in France, see THSC (1977), 50-51.

58. *Deifr:* originally the inhabitants of the old kingdom of Deira in north-east England. Like *Brynaich* (see l.30), it is used by Iolo to mean the Scots.

64. *Maesbury:* near Oswestry.

10.

This poem was probably composed about 1390, at a time when Owain was a loyal and well-respected member of the lesser nobility of Richard II's kingdom, living peacefully on his estate at Sycharth in the parish of Llansilin. He was married to Margaret, daughter of the eminent judge Sir David Hanmer. There is no suggestion here of the discontent which led to the rebellion of 1400. On the contrary, this poem displays a profound sense of order and stability, and is one of the most satisfying expressions of the paternalistic social ideals held by the Welsh gentry and their poets. The building itself is absolutely central, and its symmetrical, tightly linked construction is a resonant symbol of the ideal social order. On the architecture of the house see the article by Enid Roberts, 'Tŷ pren glân mewn top bryn glas', TDHS xxii, 12-47. After reading Iolo's description of the fine wooden house it is painful to realize that it was burnt to the ground by Prince Henry during the rebellion.

21. On Maig Mygrfras see note 8.37.

27. *Couple* is an architectural term: 'One of a pair of beams, that meet at the top and are fixed at the bottom by a tie, and form the principal support of a roof' (OED).

29-30. St Patrick's Cathedral in Dublin and the new cloister of Westminster Abbey were two fine examples of contemporary ecclesiastical architecture. *Ffrengig* is very often used by the poets as a term of praise.

37. *Plate* is another English architectural term: 'A horizontal timber at the top or bottom of a framing; often supporting other portions of a structure' (OED). Nine is probably an ideal number with no real significance, since nine was the number of 'houses' in the royal court according to old Welsh law (see Jenkins 41), as in ll.49-50 below. The plural *tai* is an archaic usage, referring to the buildings of the court, which would by this time have been under one roof.

48. *lle magai'r mwg:* this reading, supported by the best manuscripts, is the complete opposite of that given by Henry Lewis, *ni fagai fwg*, which would seem to refer to the possibility of smoke billowing back into the hall. This couplet is in fact describing the roof of the house, and of course

smoke coming from the chimney was a sign of a warm hearth inside. Cp. DGG² XXXIX.22, 'Mwg y byd yn magu o bell.'

51-52. Of course there were no shops at Sycharth. This is an image describing the richly stocked wardrobes, which were small rooms adjoining the sleeping chambers.

53-54. This is also to be understood figuratively. The cross-shaped structure of the house resembled a church, and the small rooms adjoining the hall were like chapels attached to the main body of a church.

63. *tir bwrdd:* this is a semi-translation of the English term *bord-land*, which was in fact land held under *bordage* tenure, that is by serfs under the feudal system.

94. *Pywer Lew:* see 8.32. It is difficult to be sure of the precise extent of reference of the term *gwlad* here. See note 8.93.

11

Nothing is known of the Llywelyn who gave Iolo a knife, since not even his father's name is given. Guto'r Glyn has a poem requesting a knife very similar to this one, with small blades on its scabbard (see ll.17-18 here), GGGl LXXX.

10. *Ffrainc:* cp. 10.29.

11. On the similar oath 'mefl ar fy marf' see PKM 223.

20. *treinsiwr:* from Middle English *trencheour*, a kind of knife.

36. *ysbard bol:* I take this to refer to the small blade on the scabbard—cp. *cefn* in 18 above.

38-47. Five legendary swords are named here: Durendardd belonged to Roland, Hawd y Clŷr to Oliver, Angau Coch ('Crocea Mors' in Latin) to Julius Caesar, Caledfwlch to Arthur, and Cwrseus to Otfel, another hero of the Charlemagne cycle.

53. *Elian Ceimiad:* patron saint of Llaneilian in Anglesey and Llanelian in Denbighshire, see LBS, ii, 435-44.

76. *dail:* a thin layer of brass to decorate the sheath.

77. The purpose of the fillet was to strap the sheath to the leg.

94. *Cuhelyn:* the identification with the Irish hero Cú Chulainn proposed by Dr Bromwich in YB xii, 65-66 and followed in GIG is probably incorrect. Judging from references by the poets, Cuhelyn was a character in native Welsh legend famous especially for his shield.

12

This poem begins by offering to exchange a praise poem for a horse, stressing that a poem does not decay, as Iolo's old horse has done. After deciding to ask Ithel ap Robert of Coedymynydd for a horse from his herd, Iolo states precisely what sort of horse will suit him, showing his expert knowledge of the subject, and also making fun of his own decrepit condition. Ithel ap Robert was Iolo's third cousin, since his great-grandfather and Iolo's great-great-grandmother were both children of the Gronwy ab Einion mentioned in 1.51 here. This poem was composed sometime between 1375 and 1382, when Ithel was Archdeacon of St Asaph.

3. *morc:* from English *mark*, which is defined thus in OED: 'A denomination of weight formerly employed (chiefly for gold and silver) throughout western Europe; its actual weight varied considerably, but it was usually regarded as equivalent to 8 ounces'.

19. *llyngoes:* spavin or scratches, a disease of the horse's leg.

21. *ffarsi:* from English *farcin*, see OED s.v. *glanders:* 'A contagious disease in horses, the chief symptoms of which are swellings beneath the jaw and discharge of mucous matter from the nostrils'.

34. *Coedymynydd:* Ithel's home near Caerwys.

41. *tabl:* I take this to refer to Ithel's genealogy, which is threefold in the sense that it contains two other Ithels.

42. *personaidd:* The parson was a very low-ranking churchman, so this is intended to suggest that Ithel was humble despite his high rank.

47. *clo:* 'lock', used figuratively here to mean the peak of excellence.

49. I have not been able to locate Gronwy Llwyd in the genealogies of either Ithel or Iolo.

50. *y Drefrudd:* a placename in Shropshire, see GGGl 336.

53. *Eingl:* this seems to refer to the inhabitants of *Tegeingl*, rather than to the English. Cp. 13.78, 15.19, and perhaps 34.15.

63. The English *rouncy* is normally a neutral term for a riding-horse, but it seems to be used contemptuously here, in the sense of 'nag'.

83. The term *hackney* is defined thus in OED: 'A horse of middle size and quality, used for ordinary riding, as distinguished from a war-horse, a hunter or a draught-horse; in early times often an ambling horse'.

13

Here Iolo thanks Ithel ap Robert, presumably for the horse requested in the previous poem. This poem is given a dramatic opening by the conversation between the poet and his old horse, which advises him to ask Ithel for a new one. Like the previous poem, this contains much self-mocking humour, as Iolo envisages the dangers of the journey on horseback along the road from Denbigh to his home in Llechryd.

1. *rho Duw:* lit. 'between me and God'.

18. Ithel was both Archdeacon of St Asaph and a canon in the diocese of Bangor.

20. This refers to the poets' practice of journeying from one noble house to another on extensive circuits.

36. *buanrhwydd:* the emendation suggested in GIG, reading *rhwydd* instead of *rhudd* has been adopted in order to give a more meaningful compound, and to avoid the contradiction with *blawr*, 'grey', below.

40. *olwyngarn:* in *GIG* I tentatively accepted Ifor Williams's explanation of this word as containing *olwyn*, 'wheel', referring to the shape of the hoof (B viii, 236-37). But since the word *olwyn*, composed of *ôl* + *gwyn*, is used on its own as an adjective describing horses (e.g. LGCD 4.5, rhyming with -*yn*), it is more likely that that is the first element of this compound, referring to the tufts of white hair hanging down over the hooves.

58. *Henllan:* a village on the road between Denbigh and Llechryd. The river Meirchion runs between Henllan and Llechryd, and the ruins of a watermill are still to be seen there.

73. Ithel was descended from Uchdryd of Englefield on his mother's side, cp. 8.34.

76. *y Berfeddwlad:* composed of the hundreds of Rhos, Rhufoniog, Dyffryn Clwyd, and Englefield, see *HW* 239.

78. *Eingl:* the people of *Tegeingl,* see note 12.53.

82. *Nudd:* see note 5.13.

85. This line is thought to be a metaphorical description of Ithel's white hair, which is compared to the plumage of a bird the colour of white wine and foam.

102. Ithel's mother was descended from Ricart grandson of Gruffudd ap Cynan, cp. 8.40.

14

The dialogue between the body and the soul was a common form in medieval religious literature, of which several examples have survived in Welsh. It had a clear moral purpose, castigating the sins of the flesh and warning man of the danger to his soul. The form is here used purely as a dramatic device to give an account of one of Iolo's bardic circuits around Wales, making good use of the convention that the soul is free to wander whilst the body lies in the grave—or rather lies in a drunken stupor. The circuit takes Iolo from his home in Denbighshire southwards through the Marches as far as Elfael, then across to the southwest through Buellt and Ystrad Tywi to Kidwelly and Whitland, before turning northwards through Ceredigion and then homewards via Owain Glyndŵr's court at Sycharth, finishing the journey with Ithel ap Robert at Coedymynydd. The whole poem is of course an elaborate compliment to Ithel, since once he has reached his house Iolo need journey no more. It probably belongs like the previous two to the period 1375-82 when Ithel was Archdeacon of St Asaph. It is clear from ll.15-18 that Iolo visited the houses of Gwynedd on a separate circuit. No mention is made of Glamorgan, apart from in the copy made by Iolo Morganwg, which contains an additional passage extending the journey to 'Morgannwg wen'! Other than Ithel and Owain Glyndŵr, no poems have survived by Iolo to the lords mentioned in this poem, which gives some idea how much of his work has been lost. This is particularly vexing in the case of Rhydderch ab Ieuan Llwyd, the great literary patron from Glyn Aeron, since some later references suggest a close connection between him and Iolo. For instance, Lewys Glyn Cothi has this to say of them (LGCD 11, 12-24):

> Iolo'n wir, yng Nglyn Aeron,
> A wnaeth wers yn y iaith hon.
> Eithr y mab oedd athro mawr,
> Ac i Rydderch yn gerddawr.
> (Iolo indeed, in Glyn Aeron,
> made a verse in this language.
> But the lad was a great teacher,
> and minstrel to Rhydderch.)

16. *y ddwy Wynedd:* see note 4.58.

32. *Ceri:* a small commote in Montgomeryshire.

33. The borough of Newtown was established in the late 13th century, see TMW 209-11.

35. *Maelienydd:* one of the cantrefs of southern Powys.

37. Lleon Gawr was traditionally believed to have founded Caerlleon (Chester).

38. *Phylib Dorddu* (lit. 'black-bellied'): ancestor of a powerful kindred in Radnorshire who were prominent patrons of the poets in the 15th century.

41. Some lines may be missing here, since the sons of Phylib Dorddu of Maelienydd can hardly be referred to as men of Elfael, a cantref to the south of Maelienydd.

43. *Buellt:* a cantref to the north of the Epynt mountain.

49. Dafydd ap Gwilym and Gruffudd ab Adda also refer to the ground trodden by Adam after leaving Paradise, see GDG 83.47-50, DGG² LXV.39-42, and Dr Bromwich's note in DGSP 155.

55. The three cantrefs of Ystrad Tywi were y Cantref Mawr, y Cantref Bychan, and Cantref Eginog. Caeo was a commote of y Cantref Mawr.

57. Kidwelly was a thriving trading port in this period, see TMW 152-54. The 'men of Kidwelly' may well refer to the Don family. Henry Don is known to have supported Owain Glyndŵr's rebellion in 1401, see G H Hughes, 'Y Dwniaid', THSC 1941, 116.

64. The Cistercian monastery at Whitland was founded in 1151.

72. On *morc* see note 12.3

76-77. Rhydderch ab Ieuan Llwyd, owner of the White Book of Rhydderch and a prominent patron of poets, was an authority on Welsh law. His home was Parcrhydderch in the parish of Llangeitho. On Iolo's connection with him see the introductory notes above.

78. The *provost* was 'an officer who had the management of a royal or feudal establishment and the collection of dues' (OED). The Welsh term *probost* seems to be a direct borrowing from the Latin *propositus*.

82. Probably Llywelyn Fychan, abbot of Strata Florida 1344-81.

83. This may refer to Wiliam Clement, lord of Tregaron, whose daughter Mawd was the second wife of Rhydderch ab Ieuan Llwyd.

85-87. The descendants of Gruffudd ab Einion Fychan of Tywyn near Cardigan are well-known in the 15th century as patrons of Dafydd Nanmor.

89. Dafydd of Rhos in the commote of Caerwedros cannot be identified.

93-94. Gruffudd ab Ednyfed Fychan was the ancestor of a family living at Aberllolwyn near Aberystwyth.

100. The noble was a gold coin worth 6*s* 8*d*.

110. *y Berfeddwlad:* see note 13.76.

117-18. The difficulties discussed in the note in GIG are in fact illusory. The subject of the verb *cyfyd* (emended from *gyfyd*) is Ithel, who shows his humility by paying respect to even low-ranking visitors.

119. *Culfardd:* a legendary poet of whom little is now known. Cp. 22.36.

15

It is likely that Ithel died in 1382, since someone else was appointed archdeacon of St Asaph that year. The opening lines of this poem suggest that he died of the pneumonic plague, which was just as common as the better known bubonic variety at that time. The symptoms were fever and sweating (here attributed to the earth, because of the prodigious weather at the time), and the victim would usually die within three or four days. The first line must refer to the earthquake which is known to have taken place in Britain in 1382 (cf. also ll.123-24). The structure of this poem was first elucidated by Saunders Lewis in YB iii, 11-27, drawing attention to the value of the copy by John Jones of Gellilyfdy, who was descended from Ithel's brother Cynrig ap Robert. In fact the best copies of all four poems to Ithel ap Robert are those of John Jones, who was certainly drawing on manuscripts handed down in his family. Only in his version is the structure of this elaborate poem clear. As the previous poem to Ithel is based on the dichotomy between the body and the soul, so this elegy describes the fate of each as they are separated on Ithel's death, his soul being received by a host of angels and his body lamented by a human host. The centre piece is the vivid description of the impressive funeral, which according to Glanmor Williams was, 'the most remarkable funeral in fourteenth- or fifteenth-century Wales of which we have any account. Even allowing for poetic exaggeration it seems certain that it was, both in size and demonstrativeness, quite exceptional' (WCCR 127, n.4). But although the description of the funeral reaches a striking climax with the image of the church trembling like a ship on the sea, followed by despair as the body is interred, the elegy ends on a note of Christian comfort by extending the temporal perspective as far as the Judgement Day, when Ithel will be seen again in all his glory.

6. *acses:* from the English *access* in the sense of a fever.

19. *Eingl:* see note 12.53.

22. *Croes Naid:* a relic supposed to be a piece of the true Cross, in the possession of the princes of Gwynedd until the Edwardian conquest, see NLWJ vii, 102-10.

23. In view of 13.86, 'A phryd archangel a'i ffriw', it is likely that *bryd* here is a mutated form of *pryd*, 'appearance', rather than *bryd*, 'mind'. The editor has inserted a comma after *angel*, taking the rest of the line as a *sangiad* in order to explain the mutation, as suggested in GIG. Angels were commonly depicted with youthful faces in medieval art.

24. The subject of the verb in this line is the event of Ithel's death, that is *marw o Ithael* in l.13 above.

80. *clêr:* normally minstrels, but here and in 107 below this seems to mean 'clergy', possibly influenced by the Latin *clerus* (cp. Irish *cléir*, which also has both meanings). See also 29.92, 36.92.

110. *cyfanheddu:* The principal meaning of this verb is 'to dwell', but more appropriate in the context of singing is the secondary sense, 'to entertain'. Cp. GDG 137.65-66: 'Ac amser i bregethu, / Ac amser i gyfanheddu' (DGSP 152).

135-36. Elijah and Enoch were assumed directly to heaven, see Genesis 5.22, II Kings 2.1-11, and Hebrews 11.5.

143-44. It was believed in the Middle Ages that the Last Judgement would take place on the Mount of Olives, cp. 27.110.

16

There were two bishops of St Asaph named Ieuan Trefor in Iolo's period, the first from 1346 until his death in 1357, and the second from 1394 until he joined Glyndŵr's rebellion in 1404. Ieuan Trefor II is certainly the subject of the next poem, which refers to his diplomatic expedition to Scotland in 1397, and it is reasonable to assume that this poem is addressed to the same man. The reference to Llywarch Hen in l.21 here suggests that Iolo was an old man at that time, and that is the impression conveyed by the respect payed to him in the bishop's court (cp. no. 10 from about the same period). However, we know that Iolo had close connections with St Asaph early in his career, since he sang to Ieuan Trefor I's predecessor, Dafydd ap Bleddyn (no. 18), so it is perfectly possible that Ieuan Trefor I is the subject of this poem, as Enid Roberts has argued in TDHS xxiii, 70-103 (an article which gives much valuable information about the life of the court here depicted). But in the absence of definite evidence to the contrary I assume that this poem, like the next, is addressed to Ieuan Trefor II. In view of the heraldic knowledge displayed in Iolo's work it is interesting to note that Ieuan Trefor II was an authority on heraldry. E. J. Jones has argued that Ieuan was the author and translator into Welsh of a Latin tract on the subject, see *Medieval Heraldry* (Cardiff, 1943), xxx-xlix.

1. The Trefor (= Tref Awr) kindred of Powys Fadog traced their ancestry back to Awr.

4. The expression *mab llên* means 'cleric, scholar'. *Lleodron* is the plural of *lleawdr*, 'reader'.

7. The chamberlain attended on a lord in his bedchamber.

9. The word *darpan* (= darpar?) is not otherwise attested. The line may be corrupt, and should perhaps read *A'r pêr gog, darpar a gad*, 'and the sweet cook, provision was had'.

11. The pantler supplied the bread and had charge of the pantry. The butler had charge of the wine-cellar and dispensed the liquor.

14. The cater was a buyer of provisions or 'cates'.

21-22. Llywarch Hen was one of the 'Three Unrestricted Guests of Arthur's Court', and this is evidently a citation of the triad, see TYP 172-73. The term *trwydded* is used in the laws in the sense of 'permission to stay at a court at its lord's expense.'

41. The line as it stands in the manuscripts and in GIG is a syllable short. I have added *mên*, from English *mean*, the first of the four voices in plainsong. The quatreble was a note higher than the treble, an octave above the mean, whilst the bourdon was a low accompaniment to the leading voice. Osian Ellis kindly advised on this point.

71. *grawn de Paris*: the term *greyn de Parys* is used by Chaucer as a name for cardamom seeds in his translation of *Le Roman de la Rose*, see OED s.v. *grain* 4.

82. *pwrffil*: from English *purfil*, the embroidered border of a garment.

83. The cymar was a loose upper robe worn by a bishop. The sense is most appropriate here, but there is a problem with the phonetics of the borrowing, since the English word was pronounced with initial *s*. Could this be a learned borrowing based on the written form of the English word?

17

This is the latest of Iolo's poems that can be dated with certainty. Bishop Ieuan Trefor went to Scotland as ambassador of King Richard II in 1397. This poem seems to have been intended both to reassure him at the prospect of such a dangerous journey, and to act as a charm against evil, like the protective prayers attributed to St Patrick and St Curig (on which see Brynley Roberts, 'Rhai swynion Cymraeg', B xxi, 197-213). Iolo refers to the legend about St Patrick ridding Ireland of all vermin, suggesting that Ieuan will rid Britain of the Scots in the same way.

3. On the legal term *priodor*, 'proprietor', see Jenkins 374-75.

4. *prydlyfr:* see note 31.18.

35. *Deifr a Brynaich:* both these terms are used elsewhere by Iolo to refer to the Scots, see notes 1.30 and 9.58. But the context here demands that they refer to opposing sides in a dispute. Deira was the more southerly of the two old kingdoms, but it is likely that both names simply meant the people of northern Britain to Iolo.

36. *adfer:* the sense is rather obscure here, and this should perhaps be emended to *adfyd*, 'affliction'.

41. The lorica was a prayer for protection against evil (lit. 'breastplate').

44. *rhwyddynt Padrig:* the precise meaning of this term is uncertain, but it was probably a prayer attributed to St Patrick, perhaps to protect travellers.

57. The Isle of Wight was one of the 'Three Chief Adjacent Islands' of Britain, see TYP 228-32.

83. *y gŵr:* probably 'y gŵr drwg', i.e. the Devil.

96. *cire:* the sense suggests that this is a borrowing from the French *curé*, 'priest'. The Welsh form should perhaps be emended to *cure*.

18

Dafydd ap Bleddyn was bishop of St Asaph from 1314 to 1345, so this is Iolo's earliest dateable poem. Dafydd was second cousin to Ithel ap Robert, both being descended from Uchdryd of Englefield, see Bartrum under *Edwin* 12. This poem follows the traditional pattern of the *awdl*, using only one metre, *gwawdodyn*, rather than a combination of several metres as was common from the 14th century onwards (compare nos 19 and 38, and contrast no 31). It is a rhetorical tour-de-force consisting of two extended sequences, the first being a list of legendary heroes on the pattern 'da fu . . .', culminating with the naming of Dafydd ap Bleddyn, better than all, and the second describing Dafydd on the pattern 'gŵr . . .', with the variant 'gwrda' signalling the end of the poem.

1-4. Mordaf, Nudd and Rhydderch were the 'Three Generous Men of the Island of Britain', see TYP 5-6.

3. On the tradition that Rhun son of Maelgwn Gwynedd was an illegitimate child see TYP 502.

5. On Rhuawn Befr ('the radiant') son of Dewrarth Wledig see TYP 500.

6. *Meiriawn:* grandson of Cunedda, after whom Meirionnydd is supposed to have been named.

Mwrawg: patron saint of Llanfwrog, see LBS iii, 505-6.

7. *Mynyddawg Eiddin:* lord of the Gododdin tribe, see Jarman, *Y Gododdin*, xviii.

8. *Cynin:* patron saint of Llangynin, see LBS ii, 261-62.

9. *Morien:* one of Arthur's knights.

10. *Edwin:* king of Northumbria in the 7th century. An account of his conflict with Cadwallon is given in Geoffrey of Monmouth's *Historia Regum Britanniae*. The epithet *dewin* here may be a confused reminiscence of that story, in which Edwin's magician plays a crucial role until murdered by Cadwallon's nephew.

11. Eudaf ap Caradog was the father of Elen, wife of Maxen Wledig. He

is known as *Eudaf Hen* in the genealogies (see TYP 357), and Iolo seems to have substituted a synonym for the sake of *cynghanedd*.

12. *Coel Godebawg:* forefather of Urien and Llywarch Hen, see PT lvii-viii.

13. *Geirioel:* Pope Gregory the Great (590-604), who was famous in the later Middle Ages for his eloquence. The adjective *oriawg* seems to be derived from *oriau* in the sense of canonical hours.

22-23 Dafydd ap Bleddyn is known to have made efforts to secure qualified musicians to sing mass in the cathedral, see TDHS xxiii, 92.

31. On Cynog Sant son of Brychan see LBS ii, 264-71.

32. *anllyfodawg:* I have assumed that this word contains the root *llw*, 'oath', but its morphology is curious, and since its form is not determined by the *cynghanedd*, and the line is a syllable too long, the reading may be corrupt.

19

Hywel ap Madog Cyffin was dean of St Asaph from 1380 to 1397. It is very likely that he was the Hywel ap Madog on whose behalf Iolo composed nos 34 and 35 attacking the Grey Friar. His court is here named as *Gwernyglastir*, which is perhaps to be associated with the place-name *Glastir* in the parish of Llanasa, see Ellis Davies, *Flintshire Place-names* p. 73. This simple *awdl* consists of nine-syllable lines with assonantal rhym (*proest*) instead of the full rhyme normally used in this measure.

6. *tefig:* the only other example of this word is in Pughe's dictionary, which gives the meanings 'over-spreading; sovereign'. But cp. *taf gwr* in the obscure Gorchan of Maelderw, *Canu Aneirin* ll. 1473, which may mean 'giver' according to Ifor Williams.

9. *cardinal:* a hyperbolical expression of Hywel's high status in the church.

12, 15. The second element of the compounds *llyseufag* and *beirddfag* is the stem of the verb *magu*, 'to grow, rear'.

23. To cry havoc originally meant to give soldiers the signal to seize spoil. Here it suggests that everyone in Hywel's court is free to drink as much ale as he likes.

20

Sir Roger Mortimer, Earl of March, held the lordship of Denbigh, and was therefore Iolo's feudal lord. He was born at Usk in 1374, and was recognized as heir apparent to Richard II in 1385 by virtue of his descent from Lionel, Duke of Clarence, second son of Edward III. He was also of Welsh royal blood, his ancestor Sir Ralph Mortimer having married Gwladus Du of the royal house of Gwynedd, so that Iolo can here anticipate the fulfilment of the prophecy that a Welshman would gain the throne. Sir Roger's immense estates included hereditary lands in England, France, Wales (the Mortimer family seat was at Wigmore in the March) and Ireland, and Iolo here makes a spurious connection between the four countries and the four heraldic colours in Roger's coat of arms. In 1394 Roger embarked on a campaign to suppress Irish uprisings led by MacMurrough of Leinster and Niall of Ulster, and he was killed in battle there in 1398, apparently following Iolo's bloodthirsty advice. Roger seems to have been in England when this poem was composed (see ll. 17-18 and 115), perhaps before embarking for Ireland in August 1394, but equally possibly on one of his visits during the long Irish campaign. The political background to this poem is discussed by Eurys Rowlands in J. Carney and D. Greene (eds), *Celtic Studies: Essays in Memory of Angus Matheson 1912-62* (London, 1968), 124-46.

5. *Rhos:* a cantref within the lordship of Denbigh.

11. *edling:* from Old English *aetheling*, here with its original meaning 'king's successor'.

14. The lord of Aberffraw in Anglesey was Llywelyn Fawr, father of Gwladus Du who married Sir Ralph Mortimer.

15. The vague phrase *yny soedd yr eigiawn* occurs elsewhere, but here it perhaps refers particularly to Roger's campaign in Ireland. In this and the following line Iolo uses two different loan-words meaning 'dragon'. *Draig,* the standard Modern Welsh word, is an early borrowing from the Latin *draco,* whilst *dragwn* is an ad hoc borrowing from the English *dragon* (which also derives ultimately from the Latin). The two borrowings naturally form *cymeriad cynganeddol* linking the two lines of the couplet.

22. The term *balc* from English *balk* is here used in the sense of a fault or lack, which developed from one of its original meanings, 'a ridge left in ploughing'. The original meaning is perhaps played upon in the image *bual corniog* here, and is certainly apparent when the word recurs towards the end of the poem, l.129 below.

35. *hengsmon:* from Middle English *henxmon,* 'a squire or page of honour to a prince or great man, who walked or rode beside him in processions, marches, etc' (OED).

48. Roger inherited the title Earl of Ulster through his mother, Philippa daughter of Lionel, who was a great-granddaughter of Richard de Burgh, Earl of Ulster.

50-52. Roger's grandfather Lionel, Duke of Clarence, was lord of Guienne in south-west France.

53-68. This passage is in the style of the *brudiau,* Welsh prophetic poems which predicted vengeance on the Saxons, using obscure animal symbolism. The lion here refers to King Richard II, who had proclaimed Roger as his heir, and the bear to the Earl of Warwick, who was hostile to the king.

60. *Brynaich:* see note 1.30.

63. Roger's parents died when he was a child, and he was a royal ward until he came of age in 1393.

69-78. An illustration of Roger's coat of arms is given in A. C. Fox-Davies, *A Complete Guide to Heraldry* (1909), p. 137. The term *amrosgoyw,* 'diagonal', probably refers to the divisions of the shield, of which section 1 corresponded to 4, and 2 to 3. The correspondence between the colours and the countries is of Iolo's own invention. Red, here linked to the red dragon of Wales, in fact represented Ulster.

82. *mam cynfyl:* this seems to have been a proverbial expression, since 'Bychan yu mam y kynuyl' occurs in the list of proverbs in Peniarth 17 (see B iv, 4). *Mam,* 'mother', is used figuratively in the sense of cause.

89. *Maeloegr:* this place-name is not otherwise attested. It may be a compound of *mael* + *Lloegr,* 'princely England'.

98. One of the meanings of *cinnabar* was 'dragon's blood', a red resin used in colouring.

105. The Mortimer estates in the March included Caerllion (Caerleon), site of Arthur's court, according to Geoffrey of Monmouth. Iolo was also familiar with the older tradition that Arthur's court was at Celliwig in Cornwall, see 3.44, 6.68. It is interesting to note the existence of a manuscript written at Wigmore in the 14th century (now in Chicago) which contains Arthurian material, see *Speculum* xvi, 109-20.

106. The manuscript reading, *uwch*, has been taken as 'higher', but it may represent *ywch*, 2nd person plural form of the preposition *i*, 'to', indicating possession. The plural form is used to address Roger in l.98 above for the sake of rhyme, but there is no good reason for its use here.

111. The Arthurian knight Galahad was the hero of the Grail story, translated into Welsh as *Y Seint Greal*.

117. Trim was a lordship in County Meath, some 30 miles north-west of Dublin, with a very fine castle. The term *tref tad*, 'patrimony', is significant here, since Roger inherited Trim from his father Edmund, unlike the rest of his lands in Ireland which came from his mother.

119. *Matholwch:* King of Ireland in the second branch of the Mabinogi.

123. *bwysmant:* a borrowing from the English *bushment*, 'ambush'.

126. Roger was in fact killed in battle at Kellistown in County Carlow in 1398.

128. Elystan Glodrydd was lord of Rhwng Gwy a Hafren in the 11th century.

129. On the term *balc* see note 22 above. The image here is of Ulster as arable land which has not been properly ploughed. A balk could be left deliberately in ploughing, but the balk is here said to be false because it should not have been left unploughed.

131. *Gred:* from English *Great*, which corresponds to the Irish name *Niall Mór*.

21

On Dafydd ap Gwilym and his pioneering contribution to the development of the *cywydd* measure see Dr Bromwich's introduction to DGSP. Iolo here pays tribute to that contribution by the dramatic device of personification, making the *cywydd* itself lament Dafydd's death, and then telling it that it is without honour now that its chief practitioner is dead. This short elegy has none of the personal warmth of Iolo's elegy to his companion Llywelyn Goch, no. 22, but it does express the respect of a young poet for a great master. The date of Dafydd ap Gwilym's death is still a matter for debate. He is traditionally thought to have died about 1370, but Professor Geraint Gruffydd has recently argued in his monograph in the 'Llên y Llenor' series for a date as early as 1350. Such an early date is supported by the suggestion in the opening lines of this elegy that Dafydd died young. It would therefore seem prudent to place his death in the period 1350-60. It is possible that this elegy was composed while Dafydd was still alive, as Dr Bromwich has suggested in *A Guide to Welsh Literature*, vol 2, 154-56, but there are no firm grounds for assuming that to be the case.

1. The combination *hudol / hoedl* occurs very often in elegies of this period, expressing the deceptive brevity of life. For instance, from Dafydd's own work, 'Hudol yw hoedl i lawer' (GDG 16.12).

3. *diungor:* lit. 'not of one strand', referring to the complex interwoven patterns of sound and syntax in the traditional odes.

5. *wrth y llinyn:* this image refers to the line or cord used by builders to ensure that their work was straight or plumb.

13. There are at least three possible interpretations of this often-quoted image. The most obvious, perhaps, is that Dafydd preys on girls like a hawk. The hawk is also often used as an image of sovereignty. The trained hawk would perch on the hawker's wrist, an image which suggests that Dafydd was the girls' docile pet (cp. *tegan* above). The second and third possibilities together seem to me to give the most satisfactory interpretation.

25. *pensel:* from the French *pennoncel*, a small banner, here to be imagined flying from the tower of a castle (cp. 2.49), expressing Dafydd's excellence.

22

The poet Llywelyn Goch ap Meurig Hen, a nobleman of the Nannau family of Meirionnydd, is thought to have died about 1390. Like Iolo, he was a pioneer in the use of the *cywydd* metre, and he also composed a number of very fine *awdlau* which have been preserved in the Red Book of Hergest. On his work, and especially his famous elegy to Lleucu Llwyd, see Dr Bromwich's essay on the earlier *Cywyddwyr* in *A Guide to Welsh Literature vol 2.* Dr Bromwich suggests there that this elegy was composed as a compliment to Llywelyn before his death, it may be taken to take it as a genuine elegy. It opens in dramatic fashion with a conversation between Llywelyn's devotees, the young people of Meirionnydd, and Iolo himself, who informs them of his death.

4. The point of this line is that Llywelyn was brother to the legendary poet Tydai Father of the Muse, see l.35 below.

9. *teuluwas:* this seems to correspond to the terms *bardd teulu* of the laws (Jenkins 20) and *teuluwr* of Einion's Grammar (see GWL, vol 2, 64, and cp. 36.6), a type of poet who entertained audiences with the kind of love poetry for which Llywelyn was famous. Iolo here claims that despite the popularity of Llywelyn's love poetry, he was of a higher grade, being an authority on the art of poetry, and has gone to heaven in that capacity.

11-12. This can be taken literally to mean that Llywelyn went on a pilgrimage to Rome at the end of his life, but going to Rome may be meant figuratively in the sense of dying (cp. the practice of going to a monastery to die). The shire is Merionethshire.

17. The translation of this line replaces the possibilities discussed in a note in GIG. *Rhif* may refer to the metre of poetry (cp. English 'numbers').

29. *difys:* lit. 'without finger', this seems to refer to 'cerdd dafod' as opposed to 'cerdd dant', which is referred to in the following line.

35-36. Tydai Dad Awen and Culfardd were two legendary poets often referred to as standards of excellence.

43. Ovid was regarded in the Middle Ages as the paragon of love poets, because of the popularity of his *Ars Amatoria* , see R. Bromwich, APDG, 70-73.

44. *prifai:* from Middle English *privei* in the sense of 'possessing esoteric knowledge *of,* versed or skilled (in some subject)' (OED).

47-50. This is reminiscent of the story of the Anglo-Saxon poet Caedmon who was supposed to have been taught religious poetry by an angel in his sleep.

55. The poets visited the houses of their patrons mainly in the winter months.

60-61. The story of the two companions Amicus and Amelius was extremely popular in the Middle Ages, and was translated into Welsh as *Kedymdeithyas Amlyn ac Amic* (ed. Patricia Williams, Cardiff, 1982).

65. According to the laws there was room for eight oxen in the long yoke. Iolo, the last of the old generation of poets in Gwynedd, must now bear it alone.

84. *cerdd Lleucu Llwyd:* this may refer to the whole body of poetry to Lleucu that Llywelyn can be assumed to have composed, rather than just the famous elegy. The only other poem by him to Lleucu which has survived is 'Y Penloyn', OBWV no 50, sending a titmouse as a love-messenger to her.

85. The example of King David was commonly cited in defence of poetry against moral criticism, for instance by Dafydd ap Gwilym in his debate with the Grey Friar (DGSP 152). Cp. 32.11-16.

23

It has been assumed on the basis of the first line of this poem that Ithel Ddu was a native of Trefeilir in Anglesey, but l.20 here and 36.6 suggest that he was from Llŷn. Meilyr Brydydd was court poet to Gruffudd ap Cynan, and it is likely that his 'bro' means the whole of Gwynedd. The irreverent tone of this elegy indicates that it was composed in jest whilst its subject was still alive. Compare no 36, a travesty of an elegy which Iolo claims to have composed at the instigation of Ithel. Only one poem by Ithel Ddu has survived, and appropriately enough it is a self-mocking account of a farcical incident, no 69 in *Blodeugerdd Barddas o'r Bedwaredd Ganrif ar Ddeg* (ed. Dafydd Johnston, 1989).

8. A reference by Dafydd ab Edmwnd to 'cae Ithael' (GDE p.10) suggests the existence of a poem by Ithel about a brooch or garland given to him by a girl, one of the conventions of love poetry of this period.

9. *Gwyddelig:* synonymous with 'wild, barbaric', the direct opposite of *Ffrengig* (see 10.29). Cp. l.15 below.

20. *yr Eifl:* a mountain at the base of the Llŷn peninsula.

21. *awgrym:* from Middle English *awgrim* (= algorism), a corruption of the name of the Arabian mathematician, Al-Khowarazmi, through whose work the Arabic system of numerals became known in Europe. It is used here in the sense of system or rule. *Troed* is taken to be the past impersonal form of the verb *troi*.

27-28. Y Brem and Gwyddelyn seem to have been stock figures of fun used in bardic flytings of the period, see no 37.

34. I take *march cregyn* to be the same as *cragen march*, an excrescence on the skin (= 'lichen').

35. The shout referred to here is Ithel's lampoon.

41. The expression *mynd â'r bêl* meant 'to excel', referring to some ball-game.

51. *Ynys Bir:* = Ynys Bŷr off the Pembrokeshire coast?

56. According to tradition Lleudad (more commonly *Lleuddad*) was the first abbot of the monastery on Bardsey Island, see LBS, iii, 369-74.

57. Saint Cynon is supposed to have accompanied Cadfan to Bardsey Island, see LBS, ii, 272-73.

67-68. Talbod Talba and Iolyn Ddu may have been legendary poets, as suggested in GIG, or alternatively these may have been the names of two of Ithel's hunting dogs.

24

This poem has the honour of being the only *cywydd* in the extensive collection of 14th-century poetry in the Red Book of Hergest, probably on account of its highly ornate and intricate style in the manner of the traditional court poets. The ordered structure of the description follows an established rhetorical pattern, as shown by Ann Matonis in *Y Traethodydd* (1978), 155-67, but since the structure is perfectly logical, working downwards from the head, it is not necessary to assume that Iolo was familiar with any rhetorical treatise. The same structure is used by Iolo's contemporary Gruffudd Gryg, DGG² LXXII. It has been argued by Gilbet Ruddock in LlC xii, 117-20, that the subject of this poem was a nun (consider in particular ll.59-60).

2. *cwrel:* from English coral, of which *OED* notes, 'historically, and in earlier literature and folklore, the name belongs to the beautiful Red Coral, an arborescent species, found in the Red Sea and Mediterranean, prized from times of antiquity for ornamental purposes, and often classed among precious stones.'

4. On the girl's name *Tegfedd* see B v, 136.

14. *Llywy:* a girl's name meaning 'beautiful', she is often referred to as a standard of beauty.

18. *dewisiad:* Taken to be a compound of *dewis* + *iad*.

On the fragmentary remains of the Tristan and Isolde story in Welsh see R. Bromwich, 'The "Tristan" poem in the Black Book of Carmarthen', SC xiv/xv, 54-65.

23. *Eigr:* mother of Arthur (Igraine in the French tradition).

26. According to John Davies's *Dictionarium Duplex* Tiboeth was the name of the book of St Beuno in the church of Clynnog, which had a black stone on it. *Caead* is translated as 'clasp', but it can also mean 'cover', since jewels were sometimes inlaid into the bindings of manuscripts.

40. *ystudfwm:* A borrowing perhaps from the Middle English *stude,* 'one of the upright timbers in the wall of a building', in its Latin form *studum* (which does not actually occur, but the variant *stodum* does, see Latham, *Medieval Latin Word-List*, 456). The *f* in the Welsh form is probably corrupt. The comparison expresses the straightness of the girl's body.

58. *pwynt:* from English *point* in the sense of 'condition'.

63. *paham:* a noun here, 'reason' (cp. 14.21). The point seems to be that Iolo cannot hope to win the girl's love because of her high social standing (cp. GDG no 37, 'Caru Merch Fonheddig').

25

Llywelyn Goch, Llywelyn ab y Moel, and Rhys Goch Eryri all have poems complaining about their beards (DGG² LXXXIII, IGE² LXIX, CX). These belong to the common type of humorous poem dealing with the hindrances which prevent the amorous poet from fulfilling his desires. The device is also used in praise poetry by Lewys Glyn Cothi, LGCD 47.

5. *Gwyddelig:* see note 23.9.

24. *penwar:* a leather muzzle with sharp nails sticking out of it, used to wean calves.

26

Accounts of this game are also found in poems by Dafydd ap Gwilym and Ieuan ap Rhydderch (GDG 50, IGE² LXXVI). It seems to have been a folk-custom designed to ascertain whether a lover was faithful to one of the two players. If the number of nuts held in the hand of one of the players turned out to be an odd number, then the lover was faithful. Here the girl's husband instigates the game in order to find out whether she has committed adultery with Iolo. The whole poem is of course an elaborate device to boast Iolo's sexual prowess, as well as a complaint against the stock figure of the jealous husband.

1. *sientli:* from English *gently*, as in *gentleman*, etc.

29. This is probably Candlemas, the festival of the purification of the Virgin Mary, on 2nd February.

42. *syre:* from English *sirrah*, a term of address expressing contempt. OED has no example earlier than the 16th century.

27

The people of medieval Wales were constantly reminded of the terrors of the Last Judgement, from both pulpit and stage and by wall-paintings and stained-glass windows in churches, see Glanmor Williams, *Welsh Church*, 468-70. Although devotion to the Apostles is recommended here as a means to salvation, the account of the horrors of the Day of Judgement leads Iolo to conclude by putting his faith in Mary's intercession. Compare his ode in praise of Mary, no 31, and the emphasis upon her protection in the conclusion to no 28.

7. St John was traditionally symbolized by an eagle.

8. The Apostle John is here confused with John the Baptist, whose mother Elizabeth was related to Mary.

31-32. Jesus is said in Mark vi.3 to be the brother of Simon and Jude.

34. Thomas is traditionally believed to have brought Christianity to India.

35-42. The tradition that Mary threw down her girdle to Thomas as she ascended into heaven comes from a version of the text *Esgyniad Mair i'r Nef* (Mary's Ascent into Heaven), see B xviii, 131-57, xxv, 73-74. The incident was a popular theme in medieval art, see B xxxiii, 95-100. Several cities claimed to possess the girdle, the best-known being Prato in Tuscany.

35. The 'beneficial word' is Mary's name, cp. l.121 below.

47-50. Although Iolo actually says here that the Apostles will judge the world, he is probably referring to the belief that they would surround Christ at the Last Judgement.

52. *tawdd:* the meaning is uncertain, since the root of the verb *toddi*, 'to melt', seems inappropriate here. See CA 259 on *tot*.

61-70. It was believed that the five ages of the ancient world would be led by Adam, Noah, Abraham, Moses, and David.

77. The seven planets were the Sun, the Moon, Mercury, Venus, Mars, Jupiter, and Saturn.

90. *aedsios:* from the Greek *hagios*, 'holy'.

28

The deeply conservative social philosophy expressed in this poem is probably a response to the disturbances of the Peasants' Revolt of 1381, see p xv above. The portrayal of the humble ploughman receiving his reward on the Day of Judgement is clearly influenced by contemporary sermons. The learned reference to the *Elucidarium* in l.37 suggests that this poem was intended for an ecclesiastical audience. It should be borne in mind that the Church held substantial lands and therefore had a vested interest in the humility of the labouring classes. This poem divides neatly into three quite distinct sections, the central one being a fine example of the technique of *dyfalu* used to describe the plough, giving variety and visual interest to what would otherwise be a rather sombre piece of sermonizing.

2. *peibl:* plural form of *pabl*, 'lively'.

3. In the translation it is assumed that *eiddun* is a noun, 'desire', referring to God's will (cp. 27.11), but it can also be an adjective, 'desirable', perhaps referring to the ploughman's ultimate reward.

5-6. *Mynydd Olifer:* cp. 15.143-44.

7. *diledlaes:* lit. 'not at all loose'.

30. Arthur was one of the 'Three Red Ravagers of the Island of Britain' (see TYP 35-36), and this disparaging reference may be a reminiscence of that triad.

37. *Lusudarus:* the title of the 12th-century religious work *Elucidarium* by Honorius of Augustodunum is here taken as the name of an author. There is a Welsh translation of the work in LlA 3-76. See pp. 40-41 for the passage referred to by Iolo: 'Beth am lauurwyr y dayar. rann vawr onadunt a iacheir. kannys buchedoccav a wnant yn vul. A phorthi pobyl duw oc eu chwys megys y dywedir. gwynn y vyt a vwytao o lauur y dwylaw.'

41-62. For details of the type of plough described in this passage of *dyfalu* see Ffransis Payne, *Yr Aradr Gymreig*, (Caerdydd, 1975) pp. 73-77.

53-54. The 'knife' is the plough-share cutting the earth, and the 'table' is the piece of wood which turned the earth from the furrow. These are all under the 'thigh', that is the plough-beam.

61. This image refers to the chain linking the plough to the team of oxen.

62. The three words in this line are taken as adjectives describing *gwas*. The compound *esgeirbren*, 'wooden-legged', refers to the part of the plough known as the 'plough-foot' (see l.52 above).

63. *Hu Gadarn:* Hugon le Fort of the Charlemagne cycle, the legendary ploughman-king of Constantinople, see A. C. Rejhon, 'Hu Gadarn:

Folklore and Fabrication', in P. K. Ford (ed.), *Celtic Folklore and Christianity* (Santa Barbara, 1983), 201-12.

71. In order to correct the *cynghanedd* the editor has emended the reading of GIG from *dieithr* to *oddieithr*, which must be stressed on the final syllable, the *i* of *oddi* being elided.

77. *goryw:* pres. form of the verb *gorfod*, which has been taken in the sense 'prevail'.

<hr>

29

It was very common for Welsh poets of the Middle Ages to compose poems in praise of the saints because of the widespread belief in the efficacy of their intervention on behalf of their devotees. The cult of St David was of course the most widespread of all the Welsh saints. Other poems to him have survived by Gwynfardd Brycheiniog, Ieuan ap Rhydderch, Lewys Glyn Cothi, Dafydd Llwyd, and Rhisiart ap Rhys (HGC XVIII, IGE² pp. 242-45, LGCD 44, GDLl 13, GRB 9). Iolo's poem draws heavily on the Welsh Life of St David (edited by D Simon Evans, Cardiff, 1988), but also adds some incidents which seem to derive from folk traditions about the saint.

4. Note emended reading of the manuscripts followed in GIG, *ddidrist*, which does not give good sense. The word *dudrist* also occurs in 1.55.

8-10. Two pilgrimages to St David's were normally considered as equivalent to one to Rome, and three as equivalent to one to Jerusalem.

30. This may refer to Eisteddfa Badrig in Glyn Rhosyn, from which an angel is supposed to have shown Patrick Ireland according to the Life of St David.

42. On the use of *pan* in the sense of 'that' see GMW 79-80.

61-62. The number of the saints is not given in the Life, but this number also occurs in the ode of Gwynfardd Brycheiniog, HGC XVIII.28.

69-72. In the early Christian period neither meat nor fish were eaten during Lent. This harsh rule (referred to as *y Garawys du* here) was relaxed around the 9th century, allowing fish to be eaten. It seems that there was a tradition in Wales that St David was responsible for allowing the eating of the herring in Lent (cp. IGE² 243.21-22, GRB 9.18).

71. *brut:* the chronicle of the history of Britain, deriving from *Brutus* of Troy, first king of Britain according to Geoffrey of Monmouth.

73-82. This story is not attested elsewhere, but the punishment of being turned into wolves is similar to that inflicted on Gwydion and Gilfaethwy in the fourth branch of the Mabinogi. It is suggested in LBS ii, 312, that Gwydre Astrus and Odrud are the same as Gwydrut and Gwydneu Astrus, 'the two cubs of Gast Rymhi', in the story 'Culhwch ac Olwen', CO ll. 315-16.

75. *tir hud:* this may mean Dyfed, referring to its magical devastation in the second branch of the Mabinogi.

83-88. The only other reference to this miracle is in the poem by Rhisiart ap Rhys, GRB 9.9-10.

92. *clêr:* 'clergy', see note 15.80.

103. *noter pyblig:* from the English *notary public*.

30

Apart from the Greek and Latin terms in the opening lines, which are further evidence of Iolo's ecclesiastical education, this poem is interesting chiefly for the riddling description of Christ, containing echoes of 'Canu y Gwynt' in the Book of Taliesin.

1. The phrase 'Christe audi nos', occurs in the Mass.
craton cyrios: these are Greek words, both meaning 'lord'.

7-9. Compare BT 37.7-8: 'Ac ef ny anet. Ac ef ny welet. Ef ar vor ef ar tir ny wyl ny welir.'

14. *asau:* a variant form of *aswy* in the sense of 'clumsy'.

19-20. Compare BT 36.24-25: 'ny byd hyn ny byd ieu.'

30. *oerglau:* the second element has several meanings, see GPC 491. In l.26 above 'swift' is most appropriate, but here I prefer 'prominent' (cp. 20.55).

55-65. This list seems to deliberately include saints from all parts of Wales, but the saints of the diocese of St Asaph, including Sanan, would have been of particular importance to Iolo.

60, 62. On Nudd see note 5.13.

31

The cult of the Virgin Mary was extremely popular in late medieval Wales, see Glanmor Williams, *Welsh Church,* 479-85. The *Officium Parvum Beatae Mariae Virginis* was translated into Welsh, probably during Iolo's lifetime, as *Gwassanaeth Meir* (ed. Brynley F Roberts, Caerdydd, 1961). It is clear that Mary occupied a special place in Iolo's religious beliefs, as the conclusions of poems 27 and 28 indicate. This poem is noteworthy for the emphasis on the paradoxes of Mary's relationship to Christ. This *awdl* consists of three *englynion* of differing types (the technical terms are *proest, gwastad,* and *unodl union*), followed by an extended mono-rhyme passage of nine-syllable lines (*cyhydedd nawban*).

9. *eirial:* this word is not otherwise attested, and taken to be a variant of *arial* as an adjective, 'lively, enlivening', referring to Christ's conception.

10. *trendal:* possibly a borrowing from the Middle English *trendal,* 'coronet', but it could be a native compound composed of *tren,* 'strong' and *tâl,* 'front'.

17. *moes eryres:* this may refer to Mary's ascension into heaven.

18. *prydlyfr:* 'songbook', here used figuratively in the sense of 'exemplum, pattern', cp. 17.4.

25. *nid eres:* this is rather feeble, and should perhaps be emended to *neud eres,* 'it is a wonder'.

29. *chwegair:* the first element is *chweg,* 'sweet'. The word referred to is the 'ave' pronounced by Gabriel.

31. This was a common comparison explaining the Immaculate Conception, cp. IGE² 96.9-10, 145.23-24.

33. The idea that the Virgin contained the Trinity in her womb was widespread in medieval literature and art, see Andrew Breeze's note in *Celtica* 22, 1-13.

36. The prophecy is Gabriel's message to Mary.

61. *geirlles:* cp. 27.35, 111.

62. *meiriones:* a female form of *maer*, 'steward', this probably means 'mistress of a household' here (cp. *maeronesferch medd*, GDG 88.6), but note that in the other early examples given in GPC the meaning is clearly 'concubine'. In view of the context the sexual meaning can hardly be ignored.

32

On the two types of harp described here see A O H Jarman, 'Telyn a chrwth', LlC vi, 154-75. The traditional harp favoured by Iolo had a wooden sounding-board and strings of horsehair, whilst the new type had a leather sounding-board and a mixture, apparently, of metal and gut strings. In addition to its sound, the curved shape of the leather harp seems to have been repugnant to Iolo.

1. *rho Duw:* cp. 13.1.

9. *gwangledr:* because of the leather used in place of wood.

31. *ewingorn:* this refers to the style of plucking the strings with the fingernail rather than with the tip of the finger, a style appropriate only to metal strings.

39. *Coludd* has been taken as describing *sain*, but it may be a noun meaning the inside of the instrument where the sound is produced, see LlC vi, 162.

41. *cwr:* the normal term for the comb holding the strings on the neck of the harp is *crib*. Jarman (167-8) suggests that the Irish term *corr* may have influenced the Welsh here.

46. *gwilff:* apart from dictionaries, this word occurs only in Iolo's work. It seems to be a borrowing from English *gill*, 'mare'. The form *gwil* occurs in the compound *gwilers*, 'mare's arse', in 36.71.

48. The reference is to the plague which is supposed to have killed Maelgwn Gwynedd in the church of Rhos, see TYP 438-39.

50. *Gwyddeles:* this may show that Iolo was aware of the Irish origin of the leather harp, but *Gwyddel* etc is a very common term of abuse in the period, see 23.9.

70. *dydd brentisiaid:* this seems to mean inexperienced apprentices. Cp. English 'day-labourer'.

33

Rhys ap Robert of y Cilmael (Cinmel) near Abergele is the subject of an article by A D Carr in TDHS xxv, 155-70. He was a descendant of Ednyfed Fychan, and held the office of sheriff of Flintshire in the 1350s. His son Ieuan was one of Owain Lawgoch's principal lieutenants in France, and Carr suggests that this poem may refer to a voyage to France as Rhys's emissary to Owain. There is, however, no evidence in the poem itself to support that suggestion, and the present editor does not consider the poem to Owain Lawgoch printed in IGE[2] 91-92 to be Iolo's work. Rhys's mother, Lleucu ferch Robert, was sister to Ithel ap Robert of Coedymynydd, so he was a distant relation of Iolo's (see 1.60). Rhys is known to have died in 1377. This poem is unusual in being a combination of praise and satire. The elaborate recital of the discomforts of the ship is intended to heighten by contrast the desirability of Rhys's court.

29, 32. *gwilff:* see note 32.46.

32. This could be hyperbole, and does not necessarily prove that the ship was on its way to France, but nevertheless it is quite possible that it was taking a cargo of ale and cider (ll.4-6), perhaps for the English army in France, to return with a cargo of wine.

34. *a'i brath dan ei bron:* referring to the ship's bowsprit. The same expression is used by Gruffudd Gryg of Christ on the cross, DGG² LXXXVII.2.

36. The first element of the compound *ymwasgargorc* is the root of the verb *ymwasgaru*, 'to scatter, disperse', referring to the unstable motion of cork in water.

37-38. One of the 'Wonders of the Island of Britain' was the hollow stone on top of a mountain which filled up with water and emptied as the sea-tide ebbed and flowed, see B v, 22.

cyffes Arthur: this seems to play on *serthedd* as 'wantonness', referring to the Arthurian court of the romances.

43. On Sir Fulk fitz Waryn see note 3.41. His horse seems to have been particularly spirited.

52. *blowmones:* feminine of *blowmon* from Middle English *bleoman*, 'negro'.

59. *Lasar:* Lazarus the beggar (Luke xvi. 19-31), the patron saint of lepers, after whom hospices for the sick were named in the Middle Ages. The point of the reference is that Rhys's court is also open to all, cp. LGCD 4.29.

63. *dyhuddglo:* This translation follows the meaning given to this compound in GPC, taking *clo* in a figurative sense. But 'comforting conclusion' is also possible, taking *clo* to refer to the end of the poem.

34

The occasion of this and the following poem was a sermon preached by a Fransiscan friar condemning women who had sexual relations with clerics, apparently at a gathering of high-ranking churchmen and their concubines. Iolo sprang to the defence of his clerical patron, Hywel ap Madog (perhaps the same man as the subject of no. 19, dean of St Asaph 1380-97), composing two satires which are a virulent expression of popular prejudice against the friars. There was considerable ill-feeling and rivalry between secular clerics and the friars, see Glanmor Williams, *Welsh Church*, 187-92. Professor Williams sees in these two poems 'much of the intense hatred and jealousy felt by the laxly disciplined seculars for what they regarded as meddlesome interlopers who condemned their morals, poached their fees, and undermined their parishoners' confidence.' Dafydd ap Gwilym also clashed with the friars over his licentious way of life, but rather than resort to satire he defended himself by dismissing the whole basis of their moral criticism, see DGSP no 43.

34 The term *dychan* (*cân*, 'song', preceded by the pejorative prefix *dy-*) is generally translated as 'satire', but it is quite different in character to the neo-classical literary genre normally associated with that term in English. *Dychan* was an elaborate form of invective practised by the poets of Wales and Ireland, which was believed to have the power to cause physical harm to its target. It was traditionally a weapon to be employed

in deadly earnest, as in these two poems and no 38, but it could also be used with humorous effect in mock flytings such as nos 36 and 37.

4. *o addau Taliesin:* cp. 35.1-4. It seems that Taliesin's prestige extended to the field of love poetry, cp. DGSP 22.24. As it stands this line contains nine syllables, but *o* and *a* can be elided with the following vowels.

15. *engl:* This is assumed to be a borrowing from the English *angel*, as suggested in GPC, but it may be worth considering the possibility that this is a singular form of *Eingl* in the sense of the people of *Tegeingl* (Englefield), see note. 12.53.

27-30. Should clerics not be allowed to take a wife or concubine openly then Iolo suggests that they resort to the secrecy of the woodland tryst, one of the conventions of contemporary love poetry. The reference to the jealous husband in 34 below is another such convention.

32. *brwysg:* G and GPC list this example under the meaning 'drunken', but 'impetuous' preferred (an extension of the meanings 'lively, fierce') because of the emphasis on the haste of the friar's condemnation.

43. The point of the references to the friar's physical strength is to suggest that he has no right to beg for alms.

53. *cri:* this is synonymous with *crai*, 'coarse, rough', and is here used as a noun meaning a kind of coarse cloth.

57. *ysgrin:* from Middle English *scrine* (= shrine), a box for keeping valuables, especially saints' relics. It is used as a metaphor for the ship in 33.28.

58. *belgod:* this is a compound of two borrowings from English: *bel* from *ball*, 'testicle' (on *a > e* i loanwords see EEW 54-58), and *cod*, 'bag'. The expression *ball-cod* is not attested, but *ballok-cod* does occur in Middle English in the sense of 'scrotum'.

61. *Sirioel:* a variant form of *Geirioel* (see 18.13), the Welsh name for Pope Gregory the Great.

70. *wnder:* this borrowing from English *wonder* is otherwise unattested in Welsh, and it is based on the reading of only one of the four MSS which contain this couplet, but it seems here to give excellent sense.

73. It is worth quoting Glanmor Williams's comment on this line, *Welsh Church*, 189: 'The anger aroused by his claims to bury parishioners is concentrated with memorable force in the barbed metaphor *barcud bedd*.'

35

This satire differs from the previous one only in the use of pseudo-learned arguments, such as the references to saints whose fathers were priests, see Glanmor Williams, *Welsh Church*, 187-88.

1-4. See note 34.4.

1. *hygyrch:* lit. 'much-frequented'.

12. *dragwas:* the first element of this compound is a borrowing from the English *drag*, 'piece, fragment', here functioning as an adjective in the sense of 'ragged';

35. *meinir fudd:* it is to a girl's advantage, according to Iolo, that it is no sin to bear the child of a priest. The compound *meinir* is composed of *main* + *hir*, lit. 'long and slender'.

37-38. *Ieuan Fendigaid:* = Prester John (otherwise known as 'Preutur

Siôn' in Welsh), fabled king of a legendary empire in the East. The twelfth-century Latin text, *Epistola Presbyteri Johannis*, was translated into Welsh as *Ystorya Gwlat Ieuan Vendigeit*, LlA 164-71.

43. Gwynnog and Noethan were believed to be sons of Gildas, see LBS iii, 116, 242-47. Gwynnog is commemorated at Llanwnnog in Montgomeryshire, but the two brothers were generally coupled together, and shared the same festival, October 22nd.

46. On Elian Ceimiad see note 11.53.

52. The *cynghanedd* of this line is faulty, and the verb *gofreinio* (from *breinio* 'to honour') is not attested elsewhere, but nevertheless the sense of the line is perfectly satisfactory, referring to the honour which pertains to the priest's office.

36

This and the following poem seem to have been part of a humorous bardic contention, in which the participants were set tasks by Ithel Ddu (see no 23), probably during Christmas festivities, judging from the reference to 'before the snow of February' in l.8. Iolo was given the task of composing an elegy to the old woman Hersdin Hogl, a stock figure of fun. Another poet must then have played the role of Hersdin's son Gwyddelyn, composing a satire on Iolo for his disrespect to her—a poem which has unfortunately not survived. Iolo then replied to that satire with poem no 37 attacking Gwyddelyn. This elegy to Hersdin Hogl can be seen as a parody on the conventional elegy, giving a repugnant portrait of her in place of praise, describing a farcical funeral (cp. nos 7 and 15), and concluding by complaining that she did not die soon enough!

6. *teuluwr:* see note 22.9.

11. *Hersdin* seems to be composed of two synonyms, the first element being a borrowing from Middle English *ers*, 'arse', and the second the native word *tin*. *Hogl* means literally 'hovel', and is used figuratively of an ungainly person.

15. *Meheldyn:* diminutive of *Mahald* (= Mallt), another stock figure of fun, see GDG 554-55.

17. *merch Rwsel:* I know of no other reference to this character. Russel is a common enough English surname, but it is worth noting that *russel* could mean 'a reddish thing or animal' in 15th-century English (see OED). This could well be a satirical nickname.

26. *ystrethbis:* both the elements of this compound are borrowings from English. The first is from the Middle English verb *strayth*, a variant form of *strait*, 'to shut up or force into a narrow space', and the second is a noun from *piss*.

30, 41. The preparation of the shoe to fit the foot seems to be used as a metaphor for the composing of suitable praise.

37. It was customary for a day to be appointed for poets to recite their elegies to the departed.

44. *ar awr dda:* lit. 'at a propitious hour'.

46. *Ceridfen:* the witch of the folk-tale *Hanes Taliesin*, see TYP 308-9.

49. *deugrest:* crest here is probably a borrowing from the English *crust*, 'scab'.

64. *plwyw:* this does occur as a variant form of *plwyf*, 'parish, parishioners', a sense clearly not appropriate here. Taken to be a

borrowing from one of the numerous Middle English forms of the noun *plough* (such as *plouw*) in the sense of 'arable land', here extended to mean the soil itself. The word also occurs in an *englyn* of uncertain authorship, attributed to Iolo in one manuscript, where the sense 'arable land' seems most appropriate, see GIG 172-73 and CMCS 12, 77-78.

71. *gwilers:* another compound of two loanwords, *gwil* from *gill* (see note 32.46) and *ers* from *arse*.

73. *cateirch:* the first element is a borrowing from English *cate*, 'food', and the second is the 3rd sing. pres. form of *erchi*, 'to beg', used in place of the verbal root *arch* (see my discussion in B xxxv, 22).

79. *hudffat:* the second element is a borrowing from Middle English *fat*, a variant form of *vat*, 'cauldron' (cp. Mod. Welsh *twmffat* from *tun*, 'vessel', and *fat*).

86. Lepers used an instrument known as a 'clapper' to warn people of their approach.

92. The term *clêr* seems to mean 'clergy' here (see note 15.80), who are to be paid to pray for her soul, but it could be part of the satire that Hersdin deserves only common minstrels to pray for her.

piner: from English *pinner*. OED has no example of the English word earlier than the 17th century, at which time it meant 'a coit with two long flaps, one on each side, pinned on and hanging down and sometimes fastened at the breast'. The word is still used in Welsh in the sense of 'apron'.

37

On the circumstances of this satire see the introductory notes to the preceding poem. It can be assumed that Iolo is in fact satirising the poet who played the part of Gwyddelyn in the mock contention.

1. *Gwyddelyn:* cp. 23.28 and see note 23.9.

2. *gwifrwn:* from English *wyvern*, a winged two-legged dragon with barbed tail, a common heraldic device.

4. *haul y meirw:* judging by the other references to Gwyddelyn's red hair and complexion, this must mean a red sun, perhaps because it is the colour of blood.

6. *gwiws:* the first element of this compound is a borrowing from the Northern English dialect word *whie*, 'heifer' (see OED s.v. *quey*), and the second is from *house* (cp. *betws*).

gisa: from French (perhaps through English) *guise*, 'appearance, manner'.

15. *car:* a variant form of *cer*, 'by'. The river Soch runs into the sea at Abersoch. Like Ithel Ddu, the poet here satirised was clearly a native of Llŷn.

17. *coc:* this is probably English *cock* in its primary sense, but the slang meaning 'penis' should not be discounted. *Rhonallt* (from English *Ronald*) is probably another of the fictitious characters referred to in these poems.

27. The legal term *gwlad* can mean an oath of compurgators (see GPC 1676), which may seem appropriate in connection with a dumb man. But the expression 'ni roir gwlad i fud' occurs in *Llyfr Blegywryd* 112.15-16, where the dumb man is said to be one of the three sons who cannot inherit

land. Compare also R 1326.39-40, where the same expression is referred to as a proverb.

40. Dinllaen was one of the three commotes of Llŷn.

42. The poet Ithel Ddu seems to have been the instigator of this mock contention, see the opening lines of no. 36.

47-48. Some of the work of Madog Dwygraig (*fl.* 1370-80) has been preserved in the Red Book of Hergest, including a number of scurrilous satires.

52. The term *clêr* is generally used by Iolo in the neutral sense of 'poets' (e.g. 3.48, 10.44), but here and in l.12 above it is used in a pejorative sense referring to an inferior class of rhymesters, clearly distinguished from trained poets such as Iolo and his colleagues.

83. *wtir:* an impersonal form of the verb *wtio,* 'to drive out', which derives from English *out.*

85. The words *twncl* and *tancern* are not otherwise attested. I take the first to be a borrowing from English *toncuer,* given in EDD as a Norfolk dialect name for the fish commonly known as 'sole'. The second is probably connected with the English *tang* in the sense of 'a projecting pointed part or instrument', used of a snake's tongue amongst other things.

38

Unlike the two previous poems, this is a serious satire cursing a nobleman who had refused to welcome the poet in his house. It seems from the reference to St Asaph in l.4 and the disparaging comment about the standard of his learning in l.10 that Madog ap Hywel was an ecclesiastic in the diocese of St Asaph.

The verb *costio* seems to be used in different senses in lines 1 and 3. In l.1 it means 'to provide', in the ironic sense of gaining revenge by satirising. In l.3 the most appropriate meaning is 'to be obligatory', of which the earliest example in GPC is from the letters of Goronwy Owen in the 18th century.

8. *nid* has been emended to the affirmative particle *neud,* as suggested in GIG.

10. *paraff:* from Middle English *paraf,* 'paragraph'.

11. *fflocs:* a borrowing from the plural form of the English *flock* in the sense of 'a tuft of wool'.

12. *cawldrwm:* from English *cauldron,* with *m* substituted for *n* (cp. *patrwm* from *pattern*).

13. The Red Book of Hergest reads *colwyd,* a word not otherwise attested. It has been emended to *colwydd,* 'neck', as suggested in GIG. The expression *bugail Pedr* seems to refer to Madog's office as a priest, Peter representing the papacy.

39

This sequence of *englynion* may well have been part of some mock contention between poets, like nos 36 and 37. This and the previous poem are part of a substantial corpus of 14th-century satirical verse preserved in the Red Book of Hergest.

2. *bici:* taken to be a borrowing from Middle English *beeke,* 'beak',

which makes good sense in the context, but the final vowel is a problem, since English *-e* is not known to have given *-i* in Welsh (see EEW 93-95). This may be a scribal error influenced by *bawci* in the preceding line, and should perhaps be emended to *bica*.

cannwyr: this is quoted in GPC as the only early example of the meaning 'sheep ear-mark shaped like a V'. If so it presumably refers to the shape of a bird's beak. However, it is preferable to take it as a compound adjective composed of *cant*, 'rim', and *gŵyr*, 'crooked'. On the mutation of medial *nt* to *nn* see J Morris Jones, *Welsh Grammar*, 169-70.

17. *lleibr:* in translation the editor has followed GPC in taking this as a variant form of *lleipr*, 'flabby' (and emended the punctuation of GIG accordingly), but it may be worth considering the suggestion made in GIG that this is a plural form of a borrowing from Latin *labrum* 'lip'.

INDEX